TALES OF FUTURES PAST

TALES OF FUTURES PAST

Anticipation and the Ends of Literature

in Contemporary China

PAOLA IOVENE

Stanford University Press • Stanford, California

Stanford University Press
Stanford, California

Printed in the United States of America on acid-free, archival-quality paper

Library of Congress Cataloging-in-Publication Data

Iovene, Paola, author.
  Tales of futures past : anticipation and the ends of literature in contemporary China / Paola Iovene.
    pages cm
  Includes bibliographical references and index.
  ISBN 978-0-8047-8937-0 (cloth : alk. paper)
  1. Chinese literature--20th century--History and criticism. 2. Chinese literature--21st century--History and criticism. 3. Future, The, in literature. 4. Expectation (Psychology) in literature. I. Title.
  PL2303.I58 2014
  895.109'005--dc23

                                    2014007790

ISBN 978-0-8047-9160-1 (electronic)

Typeset by Bruce Lundquist in 10/14 Minion

To my parents, Teresa and Giuseppe

CONTENTS

ACKNOWLEDGMENTS

During the years spent writing this book, I have relied on the kind help of many people and institutions. I thank the Cornell East Asia Program and the Mario Einaudi Center for International Studies for the generous funding that allowed me to conduct research in China in 2003 and 2004. At the University of Chicago, an American Association of University Women postdoctoral fellowship and a faculty fellowship at the Franke Institute for the Humanities enabled me to take time off teaching and complete revisions in 2012–2013.

I am deeply thankful to the library staff at Cornell University, Simon Fraser University, University of British Columbia, Beijing University, Tsinghua University, the National Library of China, and the National Museum of Modern Chinese Literature in Beijing. At the University of Chicago, Zhou Yuan is the best curator I could have wished for: he not only responded promptly to my last-minute requests for materials but also shared his knowledge of the Chinese editorial world past and present.

In China, I benefited from the help and guidance of many writers, editors, and scholars. Ge Fei patiently answered my questions both in person and in writing and put me in contact with several of his colleagues. Bei Cun, Can Xue, Han Shaogong, Mo Yan, and Sun Ganlu graciously made time to talk about their writing. Cai Xiang, Cheng Yongxin, Gu Jianping, Liao Zenghu, Lin Songyu, Yan Jimin, Zhong Jieling, and Zhu Yanling introduced me to the world of literary journals, allowing me to visit their editorial offices and answering questions about their profession. Bai Ye, Chen Xiaoming, Chen Yuehong, He Guimei, Hong Zicheng, Jin Dacheng, Meng Fanhua, Wang Zhongchen, and Wu Liang took time off from their busy teaching and writing schedules to discuss their views on Chinese literature with me. Zhu Hong kindly shared her reminiscences of working as a translator in collaboration with her husband, Liu Mingjiu. Huang Hesheng and Xu Qin hosted me and offered practical help on several occasions. I could not have written this book without their help and sincerely thank all of them.

I am deeply grateful for the intellectual guidance and moral support I received from my colleagues at the Department of East Asian Languages and Civilizations at University of Chicago. Judith Zeitlin read several chapter drafts and offered brilliant advice and encouragement at many difficult junctures. I thank her for the trust she put in me, and for her warm friendship. Writing sessions and conversations with Kyeong-Hee Choi have made this last year of revisions much more pleasurable than I expected it could ever be, and her incisive comments made me realize why my research ended up taking the turns it did. Michael Raine gently asked the most piercing questions. Norma Field's lucid comments on Chapter 5 helped me cut through the fog. Conversations with Wu Hung reminded me that absences in a text or image can be as important as presences. I thank my former chairs Don Harper and Ed Shaughnessy for their trust in my work even at moments when I had little. Michael Bourdaghs has provided me with an example of scholarship and professional care that few will ever match. Special thanks to Reggie Jackson for helping me find my voice, or some version of it, and for his rare persistence in goading me on to writing until I was done.

I would also like to acknowledge the colleagues from other departments who offered comments on chapter drafts, inspired me with their work, and kindly cheered me on, especially Robert Bird, Tamara Chin, and Phil Kaffen. My cofellows at the Franke Institute for the Humanities—Martin Baeumel, Melissa Bilal, Jason Bridges, Julie Chu, Xinyu Dong, Martha Feldman, Helen Findley, Chelsea Foxwell, Berthold Hoeckner, Julia Langbein, Hoyt Long, and the Franke's director, Jim Chandler—offered the perfect balance of criticism and encouragement during a workshop presentation and throughout this past year.

The research of my current and former graduate students changed my own in more ways than they might be aware of. I am grateful to Max Bohnenkamp, Daniela Licandro, Adhira Mangalagiri, Chunchun Ting, Nicholas Wong, Tie Xiao, and Ling Zhang for many inspiring conversations, and to Anup Grewal, for her perceptive comments on a draft of the introduction and, more generally, for her presence as a dear colleague and friend. I am also thankful to Scott Myers for his work on the bibliography and glossary, and to Han Zhang for helping out with the illustrations.

Several colleagues at other institutions have helped me with their suggestions and through the example of their scholarship. I thank Lianbin Dai, Michel

Hockx, Lucas Klein, Hua Li, Xiao Liu, and Sophie Volpp for their insightful comments on earlier drafts and related presentations over the years. Thanks also to my fellow panelists at the 2011 annual meeting of the Association for Asian Studies in Honolulu, in particular the organizer Nathaniel Isaacson and the discussant Wu Yan for their critical comments. I am deeply grateful to Bonnie McDougall, Jason McGrath, and Xiaobing Tang for taking time to read and offer suggestions on the introduction and some of the chapters.

At Stanford University Press, I am immensely grateful to Stacy Wagner, who provided expert guidance throughout the acceptance process, extremely helpful advice on the manuscript, and steadfast support. Thanks to Thien Lam for promptly responding to my queries on several practical issues, and to Emily Smith for deftly steering the book through production. I owe a debt of gratitude to the two anonymous readers who, with admirable clarity and promptness, offered excellent recommendations, and to Carolyn Brown, whose meticulous copyediting saved me from innumerable blunders and much improved the book.

I would like to thank the mentors who guided my studies. At Cornell, Sherman Cochran and Brett de Bary taught me the importance of relating my work to broader historical and theoretical questions, while Edward Gunn reminded me that no theoretical framework or general historical assessment is ever capacious enough to encompass the complexity of reality. I also benefited from the mentorship of Ding Xiang Warner, who provided astute advice and unfailing encouragement at several key moments of my academic life. Sandra Marina Carletti first introduced me to the study of contemporary Chinese literature when I was a college student in Naples, Italy, and I thank her for remaining a constant interlocutor and source of inspiration over the past twenty years. As a visiting student in Leiden in the late 1990s, I benefited from the guidance of Lloyd Haft, Wilt Idema, and Burchard Mansvelt Beck, and from stimulating conversations with Maghiel van Crevel in the few months that our paths crossed.

Finally, I would like to express my gratitude to friends and family near and far, whose presence has been crucial to me. Thanks to Felicitas Becker, InYoung Bong, Alejandra Bronfman, Ann Curran, Teresa D'Urso, Mary Fessenden, Antonello Frongia, Fabio Lanza, Silvia Marijnissen, Janice Matsumura, Mark Meulenbeld, Yumiko Nishi, Roxanne Panchasi, Silvia Pozzi, Stanka Radovic, Gabriele Schneider, Luca Stirpe, Valeria Varriano, Wang Yi, Ottilie Young, and Xu Shunli for the emotional and intellectual support they offered at different times and places. I thank my parents, Giuseppe and Teresa Iovene, for bravely enduring the distance that my work put between us, and my sister, Marina, for always reminding me of what is most important. I am grateful to Ina Eyferth and to my extended family in Berlin for their steady encouragement. Throughout these years, Jacob Eyferth offered inspiration and solace with his constant presence and patiently read countless drafts. As I bring this book to a close, my thoughts go to two people whose work and life inspired me and with whom I would have liked to continue sharing my own: Klaus Eyferth, who always took me seriously except when I complained about my writing, and Alba Meo, who taught me that writing nurtures life but also takes it away, and who keeps smiling from up there, in spite of it all.

TALES OF FUTURES PAST

INTRODUCTION

On Futures, Literature, and Anticipation

It is easy to gather a kind of energy from the rapid disintegration of an old, destructive and frustrating order. But these negative energies can be quickly checked by a sobering second stage, in which what we want to become, rather than what we do not now want to be, remains a so largely unanswered question. . . . This is of course much easier to project than to do, but it is in fact far from easy, under current pressures and limits, even to project it. Yet one immediately available way of creating some conditions for its projection, and perhaps for its performance, is now . . . to push past the fixed forms in the only way that is possible, by trying to understand their intricate and diverse formations, and then to see, through and beyond them, the elements of new dynamic formations.

Raymond Williams, Afterword to Modern Tragedy

YE YONGLIE'S *Little Smarty Travels to the Future* (1978) was as much a jump forward in imagination as it was a resumption of aspirations of the past.[1] The first science fiction book for children published after the end of the Cultural Revolution, *Little Smarty* recounts the adventures of a young journalist on his tour to Future City, where cars fly across the clear sky and an artificial moon brightens the nights. In this fantasyland of technologically induced happiness, giant vegetables and synthetic rice have solved all food shortage problems, and manual labor is performed by robots. Let us imagine a child reading about these wonders some place in China at the turn of the 1980s: a nine-year-old squatting on the edge of a dusty alley, leafing through a tiny booklet bought for a few pennies at a nearby kiosk or borrowed from a relative or friend. How did those water-drop-shaped plastic cars intermingle with the powerful hands of revolutionary heroes and the dignified protagonists of old vernacular novels that also crowded the illustrated booklets so popular at the time?

As in many other places in the world, fantasies of technological happiness were common in China in popular science writings and children's stories in the 1950s. But they might have seemed new to this nine-year-old, for they later largely disappeared from Chinese children's publications and were replaced by celebrations of collective labor rather than automation as the means to build socialism. *Little Smarty* did acknowledge, if briefly, the manual work of previous generations. Precious because it had made Future City possible, manual labor had nonetheless been superseded. Ye Yonglie's tale thus worked as a transitional piece, exposing the contradiction between the physical labor that was up to that point regarded as indispensable to transform the world and the specialized knowledge that was about to be seen, once again, as the most appropriate means to push it forward.

Little Smarty is among the texts that inaugurated the post-Mao era. Although it might be dismissed as a symptom of the ideology of modernization and expertise that was to become dominant in the 1980s, it is not exclusively the product of that transitional time. Distributed in three million copies between 1978 and 1982, *Little Smarty* was the updated version of a draft that the author had first compiled while studying chemistry at Beijing University in 1961. Its existence is emblematic of many works first drafted in the 1960s but only completed and released in the late 1970s that call attention to underexplored continuities between the Maoist and post-Mao era. Discolored copies of the booklet, worn at the spine and corners, are currently traded online, inviting us to reflect on its durability: it may owe its popularity to the charm of futuristic trivia or to nostalgia for a time in which speed appeared as remote as a science fiction plot.

Little Smarty challenges conventional historical periodization and therefore serves as an excellent point of departure for *Tales of Futures Past*, which investigates how visions of the future have shaped diverse genres, texts, and editorial practices of Chinese literature from the mid-twentieth century through the first decade of the twenty-first century. When and how was the future deemed knowable, or at least imaginable, in contemporary China, and what were the aesthetic, ethical, and political consequences of envisioning the future for the writing and reading of literature? In *Little Smarty*, the future is a separate world that can be reached by means of a superfast vehicle—a nuclear-powered hydrofoil. It is a promised land realized through rational planning. The booklet thus exemplifies a common way in which the future was represented in twentieth-century Chinese literature—as a technologically developed, socially cohesive, and economically successful place. In Western-language Chinese literary studies, this concept of a perfect new world that one could strive toward or even plan ahead has often been seen as inimical to the nuances expected of literary writing. It is undeniable that the very idea that one could plan economic, social, and cultural life has led to oppression, persecution, and massive loss of life. Tales of development, nation-building, and advancement toward socialism have therefore often been contrasted to personal expression, individual satisfaction, and even sheer survival, all of them rooted in the present.

Such a dialectic of teleological vision and personal expression has been theorized as one of the main tensions characterizing twentieth-century Chinese literature, the fundamental features of which have been defined by such pairings as "the epic and the lyrical" and "the heroic and the quotidian."[2] Even though temporality is not a central concern of the scholars who have proposed these categories, and even though each category has been used to refer to a complex variety of styles and themes, they can be associated with contrasting dimensions of time. "Epic" and "heroic" have often been used to describe texts that assume or even glorify a forward march, or—to borrow from historian of the Soviet Union Sheila Fitzpatrick—"life as it was becoming, rather than life as it was."[3] These are tales of movement and action, in which the concern for groups or collectivities is paramount. "Lyrical" and "quotidian," by contrast, have been used to describe more intimate writings devoted to either recollecting the past or conveying mundane desires rooted in the present and in the everyday. These are texts focusing on the exploration of the individual psyche; they problematize the very possibility of epochal change and hence have often been viewed as subversive of hegemonic narratives of nation-building, development, and progress.

That such dialectical tensions are at work in twentieth-century Chinese literature is an attractive proposition that has led to insightful readings across various genres. But the polarity between a teleological future and an immediate present leaves out a crucial aspect of futurity, one that is not at odds with the personal and with everyday life. My central claim is that twentieth-century Chinese literature imaginatively reconfigures and is institutionally shaped by two different though related notions of the future: the first understood as a "destination," a condition of higher perfection, a time and place that is better than the present; the second, as "anticipation," the expectations that permeate life as it unfolds. Understanding the future as a destination means conflating it with notions of progress and a strong nation, with the utopian visions promoted by the Maoist and post-Maoist developmental state, and more generally, with a preconceived endpoint that is propagated, at times even imposed, by a center of power. This is the way the future is commonly understood in relation to twentieth-century Chinese literature. Anticipation, however, involves the fears and aspirations that shape lives and narratives in their very unfolding, and the perception of the possibilities and limits that inform human actions and are often mediated by literary texts. It engages an aspect of the future that is phenomenological and affective rather than ideological; it is embodied and practiced rather than merely narrated or projected onto a subsequent time-space. Anticipation is both structural and subjective and thus calls attention to the contingencies that bind human agency. It is a dimension of the temporal economy regulating modern work routines and private lives but also an imaginative site permitting the open-ended search for new forms of emancipation. Anticipation dislodges the common identification of futurity with hegemonic visions of progress.

By complementing a notion of the future as destination with one understood as anticipation, *Tales of Futures Past* aims to enrich our understanding of the relationship between literary texts and their historical contexts and to open up new methods of reading that combine the textual, institutional, and experiential aspects of literature. Anticipation is an inherently plural concept, irreducible to a single definition. Its diverse modes shape contemporary Chinese literary culture. Parsing these modes involves detailing how literary institutions affect the labor of writing through aesthetic forecasts that are often conveyed as if they were infallible, even as they turn out not to be. It entails reconsidering our very concept of literature, understanding it not solely as a body of texts but as a collaborative practice involving different literary professionals—editors, translators, critics, and writers—whose ideas and feelings about what Chinese literature ought to become or how it ought to move forward proved decisive in determining what was published, collected, and read. Parsing these modes in fiction, in particular, means teasing out overlooked aspects of how narratives work—the ways in which they convey forward-oriented emotions and how these emotions, in turn, might affect readers. This book proposes, then, a reconceptualization of contemporary Chinese literature and futurity around a contingent and intimate perception of the anticipatory dimension of time. It explores the ways in which emotions and ideas related to what may come next find concrete expression in a variety of Chinese texts and institutional contexts, ranging from science fiction to translation journals and from modernist writing to environmental literature, with the aim of tracing overlooked continuities throughout the second half of the twentieth century and the early twenty-first century and thus refining our understanding of Chinese socialist and postsocialist literary cultures.[4]

Although contemporary China may seem disconnected from the socialist past, it is still deeply shaped by it. The complexity of this condition urges us to open up notions of Chinese socialist and postsocialist cultures to further scrutiny, deepening our exploration of what they entailed and continue to entail for the people who made and experienced them. This book hopes to contribute to the elaboration of better ways to apprehend these cultural formations.

Modes of Anticipation within the Modern

At the turn of the 1980s, while popular science magazines in China offered optimistic forecasts on life in the twenty-first century, much critical discourse in Europe and America revolved around the crisis of the idea of the future. This sense of crisis was partly a reaction to the neoliberal restructuring of the workforce and to waning social and political alternatives to global capitalism. In his afterword to the 1979 edition of *Modern Tragedy*, Raymond Williams noted "the slowly settling loss of any acceptable future" that accompanies the capitalist economic order's "defaulting on its most recent contract: to provide full employment, extended credit and high social expenditure as conditions for a political consensus of support."[5] Arguably, only a small portion of the world population had enjoyed those privileges in the first place, yet Williams's assessment prefigured what was to happen in the United Kingdom under Thatcher and still applies to the swelling waves of unemployment that followed the 2008 financial crisis worldwide.

Pronouncements about the loss of the future pervaded the cultural debates about the onset of the postmodern era. In 1979, art curator and critic Kim Levin wrote about the demise of modernism in terms of a loss of "faith in the technological future" and the declining possibility of the emergence of original forms of art. Zygmunt Bauman wrote of a postmodern sensibility characterized by a sense of "perpetual present." For Fredric Jameson too postmodernism was predicated on the bankruptcy of the concept of the new and on the complete integration of the economic and cultural spheres.[6] These pronouncements are heterogeneous in tone and intent, but they share a few basic assumptions: a radical epochal change was underway; the notion of the future as an open-ended horizon that characterized modern temporality was waning; the modernist belief in the possibility of preserving an autonomous space for art and the idea that this very autonomy would enable art to transform social and political life were becoming obsolete. The conditions for these changes had been laid down in the 1960s, but their consequences only became fully apparent from the 1970s onward.

More recent theorizations of modernism have deemphasized the rupture brought about by the postmodern and have argued for a more nuanced relation between the forward-oriented temporality of modernity and modernism itself. For T. J. Clark, for instance, modernism was already characterized by a deep ambivalence toward the "charisma of technique" and confronted with "an ending—a crushing and freezing of revolutionary energies" during the interwar years. Clark cautiously suggests that modernism and postmodernism might in fact stand in the same "undecidable relation of ambivalence toward the main forms of modernity, of bourgeois industrial society."[7] The spatial turn of postmodernism may have led to a disengagement with problems of temporality, but since the early 2000s scholars in postcolonial studies, literary and cultural studies, queer studies, and philosophy have returned to grapple with the political and ethical implications of privileging a particular dimension of time over others—with what we could call the "chronopolitics of culture." An important point of contention in recent debates is whether a preoccupation with the future might serve as a site of alterity, interruption of the habitual, and progressive change or whether it rather signifies the extension of oppressive models of social and biological reproduction; whether the concern with the yet-to-come can help redefine the functions and forms of contemporary literature or whether a focus on the immediate present is better suited to respond to the contingencies shaping human creativity and life in liberal-capitalist societies.[8]

Tales of Futures Past proposes a concept of anticipation that aims to carve out a middle ground between the contrasting positions that emerge from these debates, a middle ground that I believe is best suited to account for the fractured temporalities and perception of belatedness that characterize Chinese literature under the conditions of socialism and postsocialism. As the ensuing chapters will show, my proposition emerges primarily from a detailed engagement with various texts and institutional contexts of contemporary Chinese literature, but it also draws on several other disciplinary fields. In *Futures Past: On the Semantics of Historical Time* (a book whose title has inspired my own), Reinhart Koselleck has argued that historical time is constituted by the disjunction and tension between a "space of experience" and a "horizon of expectation," terms that correspond to the past in the present and the future in the present.[9] In Koselleck's view, the gap between these two aspects of the perception of time widened dramatically in seventeenth- and eighteenth-century Europe; becoming modern meant experiencing time as open toward an unknown future, in which history lost its explanatory status. Any conclusion drawn from the past appeared irrelevant after the French Revolution, which "liberated a new future, whether sensed as progressive or as catastrophic, and in the same fashion a new past."[10] The categories that Koselleck proposes might appear inseparable from the main tenets of the Enlightenment, particularly from the belief that changes for the better were accelerating and that human beings were increasingly in control of their history. But they can also be seen as metahistorical categories, variably related to one another and thus transposable to different post-Enlightenment (or non-Enlightenment) contexts. The dissolution of the *topos* of progress itself represents one variation of their relationship.[11] One of the premises of *Tales of Futures Past*, then, is that the transformations, crisis, and demise of the Enlightenment notion of progress open up different configurations and variable distances between the space of experience and the horizon of expectation. This study explores how these configurations and distances are envisioned in Chinese literary texts. Like Koselleck's "horizon of expectation," my concept of anticipation indicates a forward-oriented dimension of the perception of time inscribed in the present, shaped by past experiences, and encompassing such private and public affects as hope and fear.

Whereas Koselleck aims to explain the changes in the perception of historical time that occurred with the onset of modernity, the anthropologist David Scott adopts the notion of "horizon of expectation" to discuss transformations of temporality "*within* the modern [itself], from one rhythm of modern time to another: from a moment, for example, when the future appears guaranteed by the present to one in which it seems undermined by it."[12] Scott claims that narratives of anticolonial struggle elaborated before independence were premised on the possibility of absolute resistance to modern colonial power and were hence "emplotted" as "romances" with a happy ending—that is, complete emancipation—without taking into account that revolutionary historical figures had no alternative but to act within narrow conceptual horizons; they had no choice but to become "conscripts of modernity." The shift from anticoloniality to postcoloniality that defines our present, however, requires a change in narrative mode from romance, which assumes complete overcoming, to tragedy, which assumes that time is uneven and that human action is subjected to contingencies and chance. Only by reassessing the present horizon of expectation in ways that account for the limits of human agency can a different, even if imperfect, future be imagined.[13]

Scott's discussion offers important suggestions for the study of twentieth-century Chinese literary culture. His notion that one cannot choose to operate outside the modern serves as a persuasive response to the idea of "alternative modernities" that, while valuable for the ways in which it foregrounds local agency, risks obscuring the relations of power within which alternatives had and have to be sought. Scott urges us to understand modernity not as a force that "occurs" and to which individuals "respond in more or less creative ways" but rather as "the transformed terrain on which these creative responses are being enacted [and which] is itself positively constituting (or rather, reconstituting) these subjects, their new objects of desire, and the new concepts that shape the horizon of that desire."[14] Following this trail, *Tales of Futures Past* locates the "transformed terrain" of modernity in the institutional processes that shape contrasting visions of literary and political futures to which individuals contribute and respond. Scott's work also alerts us to the relation between expectations and the ways that scholarly questions are formulated: expectations and hopes shape our objects of study, our field of scholarship, our own work, however implicitly and however unaware of them we might be. Anticolonial and Chinese socialist revolutionary narratives shared a perspective of total emancipation that may still affect the way scholarly problems are defined, whether in the form of a lingering appeal for those who once embraced them or as an enduring repulsion for those who rejected them, hindering a more open-ended reelaboration of possible futures. Even though Koselleck and Scott address completely different contexts, this book draws from their work two major premises. First, expectations about the future (however diverse and inchoate) find concrete manifestation in political and cultural practices; therefore, the future can be a valid topic of historical and literary inquiry.[15] Second, such expectations affect the ways in which academic questions are formulated and scholarly narratives are "emplotted"; hence, we had better pay attention to the narrative modes we employ.

Whereas Koselleck and Scott help define anticipation as a cluster of forward-oriented intellectual, political, and emotional dispositions, a third inspiration for my use of the term comes from the work of medical anthropologists who have defined anticipation as an affective state emerging from practices related to health, technoscience, and biopolitics; it is "an excited forward looking subjective condition characterized as much by nervous anxiety as a continual refreshing of yearning, of 'needing to know.' Anticipation is the palpable effect of the speculative future on the present. . . . *As an affective state, anticipation is not just a reaction, but a way of actively orienting oneself temporally.*"[16] Adams and others argue that anticipation is intensified by the peculiar "management of time" characterizing our present. A "regime of anticipation" denotes a condition of deep uncertainty under neoliberal regimes but also a heightened desire to preempt contingencies, a desire nurtured by technological innovations supposedly able to do so. The basic condition of a regime of anticipation is precariousness in work and economic life and a broader access (for those who can afford it) to more refined technologies to predict, extend, and reproduce biological life. Defined as one of "the practices employed to navigate daily life and to sustain relations, the practices which are at the heart of social transformation long before we are able to name it as such,"[17] anticipation is a temporal orientation resulting from economic and technological conditions that affect bodies at the capillary level. This is the mode of anticipation explored in Chapter 5.

Throughout the chapters that follow, anticipation serves as a heuristic category that takes on different guises in the literary contexts examined—not, that is, as a totalizing principle but rather a cluster of dispositions that assume mutable features in the historical moments and texts considered. I take anticipation to encompass the perception of simultaneous uncertainty and inevitability that prompts individuals to write. It includes a variety of modes of feeling, depicting time as it rushes forward, sometimes manifesting itself as hope or possibility, sometimes as constraint or even paralysis. It is a state of exertion that is neither limited to personal anxieties and aspirations nor reducible to the technologies that are meant to soothe or nurture them. It encompasses thematic, formal, and practical aspects of literary culture. Bridging the textual and the social, the notion of anticipation allows us to explore the ways in which writers and other literary professionals have attempted to control literary time, making and responding to political and artistic forecasts in socialist and postsocialist China. Finally, it provides a thread to weave patterns where others have seen ruptures, without discounting the new motifs that have emerged at each turn.

Anticipation as Literary Practice

In an often quoted essay, Leo Ou-fan Lee has argued that a "new temporal orientation" characterized by an "implicit equation of newness with a new temporal continuum from the present to the future" was introduced in China during the 1910s.[18] A faith in progress, accompanied by a sense of belonging to the distinct epoch of a forward-oriented present, constituted an essential component of early twentieth-century intellectuals' visions of modernity. This new consciousness of time was responsible for the limited appeal of literary modernism in China. Drawing on Matei Calinescu, Lee defines modernism, or aesthetic modernity, as a rebellion against the ideology of historical modernity. In his view, "Chinese writers did *not* choose (nor did they feel the necessity) to separate the two domains of historical and aesthetic modernity in their pursuit of a modern mode of consciousness and modern forms of literature."[19] For Lee, the orientation toward the future translated into a notion of the present as homogenous time and led to the predominance of a discourse of realism.

This emphasis on a radical rupture with tradition in the early twentieth century has since been questioned. Scholars of Chinese classical thought have shown that there was no such thing as a monolithic Chinese "cyclical" time that was allegedly replaced by a new model of linear temporality.[20] A broad range of modern fictional genres in the late Qing has been documented, and the version of literary modernity promoted by the New Culture Movement of the late 1910s—a version emphasizing the use of vernacular language in place of classical Chinese and imported ideas of progress, science, and democracy—has been criticized for having repressed earlier, more imaginative manifestations.[21] Authors previously marginalized from the canon because of their apparent orientation toward the past have been restored as belonging to the modern.[22] Highly representative figures such as Lu Xun have been shown to have an ambivalent relation toward ideas of historical progress, and this very ambivalence has been seen as constitutive of their "modernism."[23] Perhaps most radically, Michel Hockx has claimed that what is generally defined as "May Fourth literature" never existed, in the sense that "the variety of literary products to be found in the journals of the late 1910s and early 1920s cannot possibly be covered by referring only to a single mainstream, a single genre, or a single sociopolitical event that occurred in 1919."[24] The highly Westernized, socially committed realist fiction that was later canonized as the mainstream "May Fourth literature" was only one among various modes of writing competing in the literary field.[25] In short, the early twentieth century is now seen as internally varied and in intimate dialogue with the literature of the previous centuries. Historians have shown that the time of the modern is not exclusively forward-oriented. In *Sovereignty and Authenticity*, Prasenjit Duara has argued that the modern perception of linear time creates an anxiety that is then allayed through a circular return to mythical origins. Capitalist modernity and the diffusion of the nation-state engendered a process of stretching back into the past in the effort to make local and ancient what had been global and historically contingent. The modern nation-state, Duara reminds us, justifies itself through a discourse of timeless authenticity that is simultaneously retrieved from an invented past and projected forward. The ideology of the nation-state conceals the simultaneously forward- and backward-looking gesture that locates in antiquity what does not yet exist.[26]

It is not my intent to reinstate the vision of a temporal rupture in the early twentieth century that others have so convincingly torn apart. Leo Ou-fan Lee's statement on the futural orientation of the modern has been complicated in many ways; however, his suggestion of a contrast between historical and literary modernity continues to inspire many assessments of modern and contemporary Chinese literature. The very dichotomy of realism and modernism in Chinese literary studies is based on the assumption that an emphasis on the future has led to privileging the first. Although this is well documented for the first half of the twentieth century,[27] one of the arguments of *Tales of Futures Past* is that a forward-oriented temporality does not necessarily lead to a privileging of realism. In the light of the literary practices explored in the following chapters, realism and modernism ought to be rethought as less dichotomous, more interdependent terms. Rather than equating the emphasis on the future with the repression of alternatives and the homogenization of literary forms, this book shows how diverse modes of anticipation fracture the present in socialist and postsocialist China. This move entails shifting the focus from ideology to the nitty-gritty details attending to the emergence of literary formations, a task undertaken by Chapters 1 and 3.

The Ends of Literature

The work of anticipation involves imagining a different literature as a means of imagining a different world and is premised on intense negotiations about the "ends" of Chinese literature itself—with ends understood as the boundaries between what is literature and what is not, the aims it is supposed to serve, and the limitations that might hinder its flourishing and lead to its exhaustion. Such negotiations, in turn, inevitably shape our object of study. This book defines literature broadly, drawing on a wide range of writings, including children's tales, drama and film scripts, essays, novels and short stories. Chinese contemporary

literature is often treated as a corpus of alternative narratives of major historical turns or traumatic events, an approach that has often reduced literature to
a position ancillary to history. It is true that many contemporary works are set
in dramatic historical moments and register epochal transformations. But if literature is imprinted by traces of the past, it is also the place where the everyday
is shown to be sustained by promises and fantasies of future perfection. Hence,
literary writing will not be treated as an alternative archive but rather as a social act—as writers' and other professionals' medium to intervene in the public
arena and participate in a national and global literary field. I borrow Sheldon
Pollock's term "literary culture" and follow his suggestion that "the literary
needs to be understood as a historically situated practice: how people have
done things with texts."[28] I am also inspired by Michel Hockx, who in his study
of early twentieth-century Chinese literature endorses approaches that "seek
to describe aesthetic processes of literary creation and reception from a rigidly
historical perspective, on the basis of a thoroughly documented understanding
of the *practices* of writing. They do not take any concept of literature, nor any
kind of canon or mainstream, for granted. . . . They allow historical literary
views to emerge from the discourses and practices analyzed and described."[29]

Discussing science fiction, popular science writings, and children's literature under socialism, Chapter 1 demonstrates the historical contingency of the
boundaries of "literature," showing that the problem of whether these genres
belong to the domain of literature was widely debated among its practitioners.
Although aiming at comprehending "how people have done things with texts,"
the readings I propose are inevitably informed by my own understanding of
what literature does and how it works, an understanding that is susceptible
to ongoing revisions in dialogue with the texts and contexts examined. In *The
Literary in Theory*, Jonathan Culler traces a history of definitions of literariness in Western criticism from the emphasis on self-reflexivity in the 1960s to
a focus on questions of identity in the 1990s.[30] Noting that the literary cannot
be reduced to objective textual qualities, Culler draws on Adorno to suggest
that a concern with "redemption"—that is, with "the opening of the subject to
the nonidentical, to alterity, the other, the indeterminate, or some other site or
event beyond instrumental reason" is central to it. The reality of redemption
is unimportant: redemption is "a figure that enables such discourse."[31] Culler
suggests that literariness might consist in the openness to an undefined alterity, implicitly relating it to notions of potentiality and futurity, but concludes
his essay with an invitation to readdress the question to the literary text itself:

"it seems to me quite possible that a return to ground the literary in litera-ture might have a critical edge, since one of the things we know about literary works is that they have the ability to resist or to outplay what they are supposed to be saying."[32]

Although Culler's suggestion echoes Pollock's and Hockx's proposals to ap-proach the literary without a preconceived notion of what it should be, it prior-itizes close reading as a process of bringing to light the contradictions intrinsic in the texts themselves. But such an elevated term as "redemption" recalls Rita Felski's definition of a "theological" style of reading as "any strong claim for literature's other-worldly aspects, though usually in a secular rather than explic-itly metaphysical sense. Simply put, literature is prized for its qualities of other-ness, for turning its back on analytical and concept-driven styles of political or philosophical thought as well as our everyday assumptions and commonsense beliefs."[33] Felski is skeptical of approaches that posit the value of literature in its difference from other kinds of discourse.[34] She is not persuaded that "the literary work enables an encounter with the extraordinary, an imagining of the impossible, an openness to pure otherness, that is equipped with momentous political implications."[35] Drawing a separation between literature and daily forms of communication comes, in her view, at the expense of "showcasing its impotence."[36] In contrast to such theological approaches, Felski proposes four modes of textual engagement that she considers closer to how readers actually experience texts. These modes are drawn from the consideration "that read-ing involves a logic of *recognition*; that aesthetic experience has analogies with *enchantment* in a supposedly disenchanted age; that literature creates distinc-tive configurations of social *knowledge*; that we may value the experience of being *shocked* by what we read. These four categories . . . denote multi-leveled interactions between texts and readers that are irreducible to their separate parts."[37] For Felski, then, the literary needs to be redefined in accord with read-ers' diverse experiences, although she acknowledges that these experiences are never as discrete as her taxonomy suggests; indeed, the modes she traces may very well interact within the same reading experience. Although reconstructing readers' reactions to texts is notoriously difficult, Felski's categories are helpful in that they attempt to account for the ways in which literature affects read-ers. Her four modes are not incompatible with the notion that something "be-yond instrumental reason" (Culler) is central to literary writing: the opening up to forms of "alterity" can emerge from an affective, multilayered reaction to a text encompassing recognition, enchantment, new knowledge, and shock that would be fully enmeshed in daily life, variously susceptible to its historical contexts and permeable to other discourses and therefore not at all "other-worldly." Indeed, the very articulation of that something "beyond instrumental reason" that defines the value of the literary ought to be seen as the result rather than the premise of concrete reading experiences and social processes.

The approaches that I have outlined emphasize three different dimensions of the literary: the first focuses on how literary value emerges from historically situated practices involving authors and other literary professionals (Pollock and Hockx); the second prioritizes the texts themselves (Culler); and the third tries to account for readers' affective responses (Felski). None of these approaches alone can fully account for the complex dynamics attending to the writing and reading of literature, but however diverse they may be, they are not incompatible with one another. Therefore, my strategy has been to combine them so as to retrace the social practices, textual figures, and reading experiences that enabled the discourse of the literary in contemporary China. My ultimate aim is to show that an eclectic approach to Chinese literary culture—a "hybrid" method combining a concern for literary institutions, writers, texts, and readers, prioritizing one or the other depending on the context at hand—is possible and even desirable. Thus, Chapters 1–3 focus on editorial and authorial strategies, while Chapters 4 and 5 offer close readings of texts that self-reflexively reconsider the functions of literature through representations of scenes of reading and writing.

Tales of Futures Past explores not only the debates in contemporary China over what constitutes the "literary" but also the "ends"—the goals and limitations—of literature. Both have been variously reconceived as the country transitioned toward socialism in the 1950s and away from it over the last three decades. This redefinition has been accompanied by an anxiety over inadequacy and fear of decline, partly born out of the perceived belatedness of Chinese writing in relation to the global literary sphere and partly from a sorely felt erosion of spaces of autonomy brought about by the politicization of culture under Maoism and by its commercialization from the mid-1980s onward. In seeking to account for the different meanings of the "ends"—as boundaries, goals, and fears of exhaustion—of Chinese literature, *Tales of Futures Past* explores not only the past visions of the future emerging from fictional narratives but also the assumptions concerning the possibilities and limits of Chinese literature—the anticipatory tales about literature that shape texts, debates, and editorial practices.

◾ ◾ ◾

Each of the following chapters details how different modes of anticipation find concrete expression in the institutional and textual aspects of contemporary Chinese literature, with a focus on fictional genres. The term "contemporary" refers to post-1949; Chapters 1 and 2, however, trace continuities across the 1949 divide even as they document how socialist literary institutions formalized and furthered certain practices. Similarly, if the sense of a sharp break after the end of Maoism was created through cultural and ideological work, literary practices could not but build on what had been put in place in the preceding decades. Therefore, Chapters 3–5 seek to identify the legacies of socialism in Chinese post-socialist literary culture from the 1990s onward. Anticipation finds expression not solely in the forward-oriented rhetoric of socialist realism—in which the future was supposed to be "guaranteed by the present," to borrow David Scott's terms—but also in texts that show how the future "seems undermined" by present conditions, as in the dystopian environmental fiction discussed in Chapter 5.

As recent theorizations of the "sinophone" have pointed out, the category of "Chinese" literature is problematic because it privileges the writings in Mandarin produced in a Chinese "homeland" over the variety of textual and visual cultures in other Sinic accents, both within China and elsewhere in the world.[38] This study focuses on the PRC not to reassert the centrality of Mandarin and the mainland to Chinese literary and cultural studies but rather to show how transnational exchanges shape national literary practices. Chapter 1 uncovers forgotten publications from the 1950s to the 1980s dealing with the technological future of humanity, including popular science magazines, children's literature, science fiction, and films. The chapter demonstrates that Chinese socialist culture participated in an imagination of the future widely shared across the Eastern and Western blocs during the Cold War. Chapter 2 argues that translation functions as an anticipatory practice by mapping particular literary futures onto specific geographies. The future, then, is not only a time but also a place. The chapter situates Chinese socialist literary culture from the 1950s to the 1970s within a global network of literary exchanges stretching from Cuba to France and from India to the Congo, showing how diverse regions were identified as more or less advanced—politically or literarily—at specific historical junctures. It thus unveils the crucial role of translators in promoting the shift from socialist internationalism to literary cosmopolitanism in the late 1970s. Chapter 3 details how expectations of what literature ought to become played a large role in motivating editorial selections in the 1980s. Through an examination of letters between editors and writers, memoirs, and interviews, the chapter historicizes the emergence of modernist avant-garde fiction and fore-grounds the collaborative practices that made it possible. A rhetoric of "future making" structured the work of literary journals and affected the lives and careers of writers. These first three chapters build on one another by discussing how technological, political, and literary horizons of expectation shaped editorial and writing practices. Above all, these chapters attempt to retrace the roles of translators and editors whose work generally goes unacknowledged. The task of explicating practices takes precedence to a certain extent over that of close literary analysis. Although many of the texts discussed deserve a fuller engagement, it seems more urgent to account for the complex dynamics of negotiation and collaboration and the myriad tensions between creative agents and institutions in socialist China.[39]

Since the late 1980s, Chinese literary culture has been changed by market reforms. Private publishers have emerged, and writers have increasingly come to rely on royalties rather than state stipends and have become more invested in expanding their readership. In more recent years, online publication venues and portable digital media have been transforming how people read and write, weakening the authority of state institutions, academics, and professional critics in assessing what constitutes literature and in affecting its success. As the chronological focus of the book moves into the present, the complexity and fragmentariness of our time and the lack of historical distance has compelled me to rely less on the investigation of formative processes and to engage instead in close readings of texts that cogently reflect on the nature and functions of literature in contemporary times. The shift from distant to close reading in Chapter 4 also reflects the increasing valorization of self-expression in Chinese literary discourse since the 1980s.

Chapter 4 contrasts the rhetoric of the future with the recursive temporal structures in the short stories and novellas of the late 1980s and early 1990s by Wang Meng and Ge Fei. Relating these recursive structures to the figure of the "strange loop" in Douglas Hofstadter's *Gödel, Escher, Bach: An Eternal Golden Braid*, I suggest that their mode of anticipation manifests a fear of loss—of culture, identity, and life itself. This chapter offers a different perspective on Chinese modernism than that examined in Chapter 3, demonstrating the variety of ways in which the relationship between literary experimentation, foreign literatures, and Chinese literary tradition was understood in 1980s through the early 1990s in China. Finally, Chapter 5 offers a close reading of Ge Fei's 2011 novel, *End of Spring in Jiangnan*, exploring its use of fog as a poetic trope, as a concrete manifestation of environmental pollution, and as a vector of social toxicity in postsocialist China. There is probably no other contemporary Chinese author experimenting with intricate temporal structures to the same extent as Ge Fei. He has generally been appreciated for his concern with the elusive nature of memory and his "fascination with the marginal moment between the past and the present."[40] The reading of his novella *Jinse* (Brocade zither, 1993) proposed in Chapter 4 and of *Chunjin Jiangnan* (End of spring in Jiangnan, 2011) in Chapter 5, however, reveals that his writing is equally concerned with capturing the states of apprehension, fear, and hope that affect how characters act. In this respect, Ge Fei's texts provide compelling instances of the anticipatory dimensions of fictional narratives. *End of Spring in Jiangnan* registers the threats posed by the current environmental crisis in China with a rare intensity, asking what kind of literary language might be appropriate to address the toxic haziness of air and social relations in contemporary China. In sum, Ge Fei's fiction offers an ideal lens to reconsider the legacy of the cultural practices discussed in the earlier chapters, bringing together the literary, historical, technological, and environmental modes of anticipation that form the thematic core of this book.

1

HOW I DIVORCED MY ROBOT WIFE

Visionary Futures between Science and Literature

ON JUNE 12, 1957, the article "How Will Humanity Live in the Next Century?" in the *People's Daily* announced: "The future begins today! Having gone through the age of stone, bronze, and iron, humanity has now entered the age of plastic." The article reported on forecasts by Soviet scientists reflecting the hopeful anticipation on the eve of the Sputnik launch: synthetic fibers and artificial leather would solve all clothing problems; abundant crops would feed an exponentially growing population; cancer would be defeated and people would live longer; climate would be modified at will; flowers would bloom in the desert.[1] Similar predictions were echoed in a variety of publications in the following two years, and although no longer prominent by the early 1960s, they resumed around 1978. How were people to prepare themselves for and contribute to the momentous changes that appeared so imminent in the late 1950s and late 1970s alike? What sorts of labor and knowledge would bring them about? What cultural forms would foster the moral and physical qualities leading to their realization? Forgotten materials depicting the technological futures of humanity, including popular science magazines, children's stories, science fiction, and drama offer some answers. These diverse genres mediated ideas of useful labor and valuable knowledge at times in which imminent technological change was at the center of political and cultural discourse. The hopes they convey instruct us on the ways in which socialist China partook in an anticipatory imaginary of technological modernization shared across the globe.

Chinese revolutionary novels and movies, in fact, rarely provided full-fledged representations of future communist life. Rather, they mostly hinted at the future as a horizon lying outside the representational frame—the future was the off-screen object of the socialist realist gaze.[2] Science-related narratives, by contrast, presented audiences with detailed descriptions of the material world that lay ahead. Unlike most revolutionary narratives, they depicted enjoyment instead of celebrating sacrifice. And while what is represented is likely to appear less attractive than what is merely suggested, these visions may have nourished people's fantasies and helped create objects of desire not solely through the representation of models of behavior but also through the presentation of worlds characterized by abundance and well-being.

This chapter begins with a drama written and mostly set in 1958, the last section of which projects the protagonists into 1978, and then looks at how a children's story published in 1978 returns to the aspirations of the 1950s. These first two sections explore an unresolved tension between the exaltation of manual labor and the anticipatory imagination of a laborless world within socialist science-related genres; the last part of the chapter shows how science fiction stories published during the late 1970s and early 1980s dismiss manual labor altogether. The change in post-Mao narratives is not so much in the imagination of the world that people would inhabit in the future as in the kind of labor deemed necessary to achieve it. Post-Mao science fiction associates manual labor with primitive stages of evolution, defective female robots, and uncouth ways of life. The laboring body is no longer the essential element that defines humanity but rather an obstacle to future developments—the subhuman residue of a technological regime about to be overcome.

Laboring Bodies, Writing Pain

Shisan ling shuiku changxiangqu (Rhapsody of the Ming Tombs Reservoir), a drama written by Tian Han in 1958 and adapted into a film the same year, reflects the massive mobilization of labor that characterized the Great Leap Forward. The drama is an extraordinary paean to the power of manual labor to transform nature and to the joy that this entailed. Excavation work for the Ming Tombs Reservoir began in February 1958 and was completed in late June. About 400,000 people were involved in this endeavor, duly advertised and portrayed through poems, songs, paintings, photographs, and postage stamps. Tian Han was one of the many prominent intellectuals and writers who traveled to the site. He visited in June 1958 on his way back to Beijing from a temple in the Western Hills, where he had been writing his better known drama *Guan Hanqing*, and immediately was inspired to celebrate that "magnificent undertaking" through his writing. Initially hesitating over whether he should compose a poem or a play, he was urged to write a play by Jin Shan, who at the time was the vice-director of the China Youth Art Theater.[3]

The writing of the drama itself proceeded at Great Leap Forward pace, inviting parallels between the labor depicted in the play and the fatigue that the playwright must have experienced in composing it in record time. It was apparently Jin Shan's suggestion that they revert to the working rhythms of the "national salvation theater" in wartime Shanghai, consisting of "writing one page, rehearsing one page" (*xie yi ye, pai yi ye*); that is to say, rehearsing while the play was still being written. Every evening a troupe member would go to Tian Han's home to collect his draft. The image of an actor standing outside Tian Han's home, waiting in the twilight for yet another page to be delivered, might better convey the pressure of socialist mobilization than any top-down vision of the propaganda state. Writing at such moments of political mobilization required a huge effort on the part of writers and other cultural producers, an effort involving bodily discipline no less than psychological compliance, ensured through peer pressure as well as strict management of time. Later studies report that Tian did not sleep for several days and completed the 13-scene play in a week. The China Youth Art Troupe brought it to the stage with equal speed under the direction of Jin Shan himself. The *Rhapsody of the Ming Tombs Reservoir* was immediately performed in factories and rural communes. Ouyang Yuqian hailed it as a "magnificent epic, a lyric poem brimming with socialist enthusiasm. In the drama, both the playwright and the director have broken old rules and created a new form using new techniques."[4]

Rhapsody of the Ming Tombs Reservoir vividly illustrates the futuristic rhetoric of the Great Leap Forward. It depicts the reservoir as a microcosm of society, a site where nothing less than the totality of human relations is redefined through collective labor. The script is concerned not only with assessing the correct handling of the relationship between technical expertise (*zhuan*) and political conscience (*hong*), on one hand, and manual and intellectual laborers, on the other, but also with the problem of how to write such a play. The dialogic form of the drama proves to be an effective medium both to redefine these relations and to explicate its own poetics, which I will call a "poetics of practice." In the opening scene, a wide range of characters representing various professional and social groups—including a specialist of hydraulics of the Yuan period, a historian, a biologist, and a writer—discuss the plans for the reservoir and the benefits it will bring. The reservoir, it is said, will be much larger than the Kunming Lake (in the Summer Palace in Beijing); it will put an end to floods, supply drinking water, and provide a beautiful tourist destination. A discussion between the biologist and the political commissar brings the main point home: when the specialist argues that heavy rains will come before they can complete the work and will destroy everything, the political commissar replies that once the masses are unleashed nothing will be impossible. The whole play is an illustration of this claim.

The play emphasizes that labor itself unites people from all walks of life and from all parts of the world in a war against nature; thus, *Rhapsody* traces a process of unification. The dramatic form allows for doubts and reservations to be expressed and then corrected by a more committed interlocutor—by either the political commissar or a model laborer or both. In the eighth scene, the "writer" Hu Jintang (the quotation marks in the list of characters signal that he will turn out to be a villain) interviews a labor hero and learns about how he had jumped on a driverless locomotive, dashing forward at full speed, to pull the brake and reduce the damage in the crash. The young man was completely unconcerned about getting hurt: what mattered most to him was saving the freight cars. Thanks to the training he had received from the party, he knew how to act in such emergencies. At this point, Hu Jintang asks a political commissar whether the hero's testimonial might be a little "formulaic" and is rebuked for having "no understanding of the new socialist ethics."[5] The script proceeds from this series of unsuccessful utterances and incorrect assumptions through the unmasking of enemies of the people to the reinforcement of group cohesion, culminating in a euphoric scene of song and dance. Thus, the transformation of polyphony into monophony—the unification of thought in the name of shared human nature based on the altruistic passion for labor—is dramatized.

The various scenes in which artists and writers attempt to portray what they are witnessing suggest that the play is in part a document on how to write about the building of the reservoir—or about any form of labor. As it turns out, merely participating as bystanders or even interviewing the laborers will not do. There is no way to write about such an enterprise without participating in it personally. The problem of mind versus hand becomes irrelevant when the premise is that to describe or understand something, one needs to first do it. Even Mr. Jackson, an English journalist who had incorrectly assumed that the project involved forced labor, ends up embracing this poetics of practice: "I have to clarify that I am not here in the function of a foreign observer but to participate in work, because if I didn't, I wouldn't be able to write a good report."[6]

Documenting a high point of socialist mobilization, *Rhapsody* celebrates manual labor as the force that propels history forward. In the film version, which is often mentioned as China's first "science fantasy film" (*kehuanpian*), dialogue plays a much lesser role. The film mostly focuses on the euphoria generated by frenzied collective labor. Key to its representation is the variation in rhythm in the actors' movements, music, and camera work. How laboring feels depends on the laborers' social position and on their relation with the means of production; but when the labor performed is essentially the same as that performed under the oppressive regimes of the past, how can this difference be represented visually? The film begins with a panning shot of the hilly landscape of Changping district in 1291. The voiceover introduces the Mongol ruler Kublai Khan and the hydraulic engineer Guo Shoujing, thus linking the building of the reservoir to the Mongol ruler's efforts to extend the Grand Canal more than six hundred years earlier. A high angle shot shows corvée laborers grudgingly shoveling under the whip of mounted guards at the time of the Yuan dynasty. The scene extends deep into the distance with the laborers almost merging into the earth-filled landscape. The humming soundtrack and the plaintive voiceover emphasize how slavelike labor in the old society was painful and life-threatening. The contrast with socialist labor could not be starker. Low-angle tracking shots show the workers at the reservoir vigorously moving in unison, with different groups responding to one another in cheerful work songs, at times initiated by a female soloist. Collective labor is *the* source of happiness; it is healing, life-giving, the very basis of human community, to the point that the party representative intervenes to rein in the excessive exuberance of the workers to prevent them from harming themselves.

Hard labor also makes up for technological backwardness. Footage of Mao Zedong visiting the construction site is inserted in the film, and he promises that more tools and machines will be delivered to the workers. The script emphasizes, however, that tools and machines are less important than the human beings who handle them. Toward the end of the film, an intertitle announces a change of setting to "twenty years later," 1978.[7] The film culminates in a futuristic vision of a leisurely utopia in which production is automated and digital gadgets connect people with faraway relatives. A young woman passes around a sort of tablet computer, showing a video-letter she has received from her parents. Rain is stopped with a phone call. A jet spaceship crosses the sky. Life in the Ming Tombs People's Commune in 1978 is bountiful and its inhabitants show off synthetic clothes with "national characteristics." What apparently most struck audiences was this description of the world twenty years ahead. Many expressed their wish to know more, and in response a leaflet was issued, "*Shisan ling shuiku changxiangqu* zhengqiu dajia lai changxiang: 20nian yihou woguo de mianmao" (*Rhapsody of the Ming Tombs Reservoir* asks everybody to imagine: Our country twenty years from now), inviting everyone to join in the imagination of what the future would bring.[8]

Although most of *Rhapsody of the Ming Tombs Reservoir* illustrates the moral qualities and labor required to build socialism, the last act transports viewers into a perfect world in which hardship has been overcome. The drama thus illustrates two different notions of the future: the first understood as a sense of anticipation—the expectations that shape everyday life as it unfolds; the second is a point of higher perfection—a segment of time that is largely different from the present. Both notions are operative in Chinese socialist realism. How to represent them constituted its core problem, and Tian Han's *Rhapsody* is a rare case in which both are visualized. The question of how life would be twenty years ahead will be picked up again by the science fiction writer Ye Yonglie, some twenty years later.

Little Smarty, Synthetic Futures

In 1977, the science fiction writer Ye Yonglie was asked by editors at Shanghai Children's Literature Publishing House to give a lecture on the theme "looking forward to the year 2000." The writer dug out a manuscript he had first drafted on the basis of science news snippets while he was in college in 1961. He updated it for his lecture and had it published as *Little Smarty Travels to the Future* a year later.[9] As the first science fiction book for children published after the Cultural Revolution, *Little Smarty* reportedly had an enormous impact. After a first run of 1.5 million copies as an illustrated book, it was reprinted as a serial picture booklet (*lianhuanhua*) in three different editions, reaching a total of 3 million copies, a record among Chinese science fantasies. "Just as nowadays almost every child knows Superman and [the Japanese cartoon] Ultraman," writes Yin Chuanhong, an editor at *Science and Technology Daily* who was ten years old when Little Smarty made his first appearance, so at that time "nearly every child knew Little Smarty—the savvy, curious, and knowledgeable young reporter with a round head and big ears."[10] Little Smarty is featured on the covers of the various editions against a background of futuristic landscapes that only underwent slight changes over the years, either waving his hat or pensively holding an open book, while behind him a flying car is about to take off and a hanging train gives the impression that passengers were to ride in it upside down (see Figures 1 and 2).

FIGURE 1. Front cover of *Xiao Lingtong manyou weilai* (Little Smarty travels to the future) (Shanghai: Shaonian ertong chubanshe, 1978).

FIGURE 2. Front cover of serial picture book (*lianhuanhua*) version of *Xiao Lingtong manyou weilai* (Little Smarty travels to the future) (Shenyang: Liaoning meishu chubanshe, 1980).

Little Smarty's trip to the future lasts only three days. One evening the reporter falls asleep on a bench along a river, and when he wakes up, he finds himself in a nuclear-powered hydrofoil that flies above water and land. Its only passengers, an old man and his grandson and granddaughter, invite him to visit their hometown, Future City. There he finds a perfect integration of city and country. People move around in water-drop-shaped plastic cars, which anyone older than eight can drive, or in flying vehicles that can be conveniently parked on upper-floor balconies. Plastic buildings display a great variety of colors and shapes. An artificial moon alleviates the darkness of moonless nights, and weather can be manipulated at will: the various work units negotiate their requests at a climate consultation office, which results in very changeable weather, announced daily on the radio. Solar panels supply electricity for domestic use and power plants supply factories where synthetic rice and synthetic meat are produced. Cucumber-carrot hybrids and giant watermelons, as well as natural rice and grain are grown on an urban farm, aided by chemicals that keep bugs at the larval stage. No one dies in Future

City, not even insects, and nobody does any physical labor: robots perform all manual work.

When Little Smarty inquires about the city's history, he is urged to find a library book titled *The History of Future City*. This allows Little Smarty to see that library services too are managed by robots and more important, to receive a crucial history lesson. The book contains only seven written pages, recounting how people "with their intelligence and labor waged a continuous struggle against nature, transforming the deserts into fertile fields." The rest of the book consists of blank pages that are to be filled with the history of the future. This recalls Guo Moruo's statement in the preface to his *Zhongguo gudai shehui yanjiu* (Research on ancient Chinese society) in 1929: "China is still a blank page in the history of world culture. . . . Now we Chinese should rouse ourselves and fill the blank page with the history of this half of world culture."[11] Through this book within the book, Ye achieved the combination of adventure tale and exhortation that characterizes much revolutionary children's literature, mobilizing young readers to make Future City a real place.[12]

But how can the contradiction between the human labor that supposedly pushed history forward and a future in which that same labor would become redundant be reconciled? Or, if reconciling is not the issue, how can this dialectical progression be represented in a children's book? In raising but not answering this question, *Little Smarty* echoed children's stories and popular scientific forecasts published in late 1950s China. *Kexuejia tan 21 shiji* (Scientists talk about the twenty-first century), published in 1959 and reissued in 1964 and 1979, included short essays and narratives by famous scientists and popular science writers that similarly envisioned a future laborless world. The illustration on the cover of the 1959 edition featured intersecting highways and jet-shaped cars in which no human beings are visible. The opening essay, by the eminent geologist Li Siguang, presents a future in which new energy sources would be found in the sea and at the center of earth; artificial suns and moons would shine in the sky; polar ice caps would melt and the deserts would become fertile; manual labor would be eliminated and factory machines would emit not noise but music; bridges would connect the continents, and portable computers would ensure simultaneous translation.[13] By the year 2049, wrote the famous mathematician Hua Luogeng, young guests from the moon and from Mars would convene in Beijing to celebrate the centennial of the founding of the People's Republic. The book emphasized that these transformations would become possible thanks to discoveries already under way: the future was close at hand, though everybody had to work hard to achieve it. The word *xianjing* (fairyland) appears in many of the essays. A review article published in *People's Literature* argued that *Scientists Talk about the Twenty-First Century* encouraged children to fantasize and struggle, for "without fantasy [*huanxiang*] there is no revolution."[14]

In the technological paradise envisioned in *Scientists Talk about the Twenty-First Century*, all obstacles to the flourishing of human life had been eliminated. While celebrating the firm control over nature that the leadership of the Communist Party ensured, several of the essays also showed a concern for environmental problems that one does not usually associate with what Judith Shapiro has called "Mao's war against nature."[15] In the communist future, waters and skies would be crystal clear, thanks to artificial bacteria that purified rivers and to electric cars. At that point, people would live in a world without fatigue: food would be instantly prepared by portable machines; washing and mending clothes would be rendered superfluous by a substance that would protect them from dirt and wear; factory and library work, as well as much of the teaching in schools, would be automated. Much time would then be left for leisure and travel, and children would watch widescreen television in their living room.[16] In the twenty-first century, wrote the popular science writer Gao Shiqi, clothes, tools, means of transportation would all be made of plastic. By then, the chemist Fang Borong predicted, nylon would be passé, and a whole range of new synthetics such as *maipulun*, much more beautiful and resistant than nylon, would be produced: "Production will be so cheap that at today's price for three *jin* of candy we'll be able to produce a high quality synthetic suit. We'll no longer see anyone wearing old clothes, let alone torn ones. Because the colors of synthetic fabrics always remain bright, if at some point you're unhappy with the design, you can bring it to the recycling center and exchange it for a new model." In forty years' time, continued the essay, people will go to work on other planets and wear light and resistant synthetic spacesuits, which will be as common as today's raincoats.[17]

Strikingly, in this children's book, issued while the Great Leap Forward was in full swing, hardly any space is devoted to manual labor or to any sense of collectivity: the nuclear family appears to be the basis of social life. Reviews of the book refrained from commenting on this issue and insisted on the "proletarian" nature of the scientists' imagination: "All the bourgeoisie can fantasize about is getting rich and accumulating more and more private property; in contrast, the proletariat fantasizes about subjugating nature, conquering the globe, and bringing true happiness to the laboring humanity."[18] Despite these claims, the predictions in these essays are much like those in "Miracles You'll See in the Next Fifty Years," an article written by *New York Times* science editor Waldemar Kaempffert and published in *Popular Mechanics* in February 1950. The pathway was different, but many of the end results overlap. The synthetic practicality and interplanetary commutes depicted in *Scientists Talk about the Twenty-First Century* remind us of the extent to which 1950s Chinese socialist culture was integrated into a global modernist imagination of the future, one that was shared across the Eastern and Western blocs. In East Germany, in fact, plastic and synthetics were seen as even more crucial to achieving communism. In 1959, the year in which *Scientists Talk about the Twenty-First Century* was published, the book *Unsere Welt von Morgen* (*Our world of tomorrow*) similarly announced that "the fashion of tomorrow will be defined by synthetic fibers, . . . the new stuff will be healthier, more practical, more attractive, lighter—and many times more durable."[19] As noted by Eli Rubin, *Unsere Welt* also stressed that housework would become redundant and depicted entire cities made of plastic, which were to be "encased in enormous plastic domes, similar to a biosphere."[20] The extent to which new technologies became part of daily life in East Germany and China was vastly different. Technological innovation was not emphasized in China as much as in other parts of the socialist world, partly because of the very fear that human labor would then become redundant; nevertheless, these publications testify to common aspirations.

The revolutionary fiction and films of the late 1950s addressed to an adult public (that is, not to children), by contrast, provided only brief glimpses of what the future was going to be and focused rather on the human qualities needed to achieve more immediate goals. *Hushi riji* (A nurse's diary, 1957) was never called a science fantasy, but it addressed the question of how specialized knowledge was to contribute to the revolution and therefore can be connected with the science-related genres discussed in this chapter. A young Shanghai nursing school graduate, Jian Suhua (whose name can be read as "Soviet China"), is persuaded to go to work in Northeast China by a young party secretary, Gao Changping, who describes to her the factories that have been built there. Combining musical, romantic comedy, and western genres, the film employs the trope of the diary to detail the formation of a virtuous revolutionary subject who devotes her professional knowledge to the country's industrialization. During the train ride north from Shanghai, the nurse and her travel companions sing a song that vividly depicts the factories, but when

they arrive there, they find barren land. When she asks Gao where the factories are, the cadre insists that they *are* there—because they will soon be thanks
to their work. His response allows no difference between the present and the
future. Several days later, during a dance party at the workers' club, the two
protagonists talk to each other on the balcony; the rear-projected background
shows a construction scene with the factories already half built. The projected
image is shaky, blurred, conferring an unreal quality to the construction scene,
calling attention to its uncertain status, suspended as it is between being reality
in progress and a figment of the protagonists' anticipatory imagination. Is this
scene of ongoing construction meant to be really unfolding in the background,
or is it there to suggest the feeling of anticipation that defines the protagonists'
state of mind—the forward-inflected temporality that pervades their whole
being? *A Nurse's Diary* identifies pleasurable anticipation with labor and with a
plenitude that is, however, indefinitely deferred. As soon as the factory is completed, Gao Changping and his team excitedly move on to start a new project
in another remote area. If one can assume a division of labor among genres, in
the 1950s it was left to children's stories and scientific fantasies to represent the
outcomes of mobilization and sacrifice.

Scientists Talk about the Twenty-First Century thus exceeded revolutionary film and fiction in its detail and temporal distance, fast-forwarding readers
half a century ahead. Likely commissioned to celebrate the tenth anniversary
of the People's Republic, the book called attention to the need to strengthen
China's research infrastructure and foster scientific education at a time when
Sino-Soviet relations were deteriorating. Its vision of technological futures is
remote from the massive mobilization of human labor that characterized the
Great Leap Forward. Like *Little Smarty*, the book projects readers into a static
series of utopian vignettes—a world in which all struggles are over and nuclear
families live happily ever after. The erasure of manual labor found in both these
books will become dominant in the science fiction of the post-Mao period.

The Labor of Genre

The "scar literature" (*shanghen wenxue*) that has come to epitomize the early
post-Mao period responded to a widely shared desire to speak out about the
bitterness of the recent past and inaugurate the beginning of a new era.[21]
While stories about the horrors of the Cultural Revolution were being published, the hopeful 1950s were recuperated as source of inspiration for a better

future. Among the cultural forms that were supposed to restore optimism, a prominent role was given to "science literature and arts" (*kexue wenyi*), which included fiction, essays, drama, poetry, and film. Initially promoted to advertise Deng Xiaoping's program of modernization of science and technology, science arts were seen by some critics as the "necessary product of the fast development of science and technology in modern society" and as the epitome of the modernization of the arts.[22] A literature that would fully engage with new technologies was among the many proposals of what a modern Chinese literature should be like, though not one that enjoyed lasting prestige in the literary field.

In published literary histories, "science literature and arts" are generally discussed together with children's literature.[23] Among the various genres included in this heterogeneous category, the stories labeled as "works of science fantasy" (*kexue huanxiang zuopin*) or "science fiction" (*kehuan xiaoshuo*) held a prominent position in the early 1980s. Defined by one scholar as "post-Mao China's first legitimate popular genre,"[24] science fiction provides an ideal case to explore the rediversification of futuristic genres in an emerging literary market. Featuring scientists investigating weird and at times implausible phenomena, oscillating between future worlds and remote antiquity, moving swiftly from sophisticated laboratories to the desert and from tiny islands to outer space, these stories mix elements of spy fiction and thriller with fast-paced plots revolving around new scientific formulas and spies' attempts to steal them. They were widely published in such literary journals as *People's Literature* and *Beijing Literature*, newspapers, popular science magazines, and in newly founded specialized publications such as *Kehuan shijie* (Science fiction world). What exactly distinguished science fiction from other forms of writing devoted to science popularization (*kexue puji*, or *kepu* for short) was widely discussed. The boundary between popular science and creative writing—or "fact" and "fiction"—was fuzzy, but so was the notion of science, which in this context mostly served as a pretext for expanding the scope of nonrealist writing while also promoting forward-oriented dispositions in keeping with the goals of the Four Modernizations.[25] Several science fiction writers explicitly distinguished their work from science popularization by arguing that they did not feel bound by what was already known; while *kepu* was meant to popularize actual scientific discoveries, science fiction embraced scientific life as an ethos of openness toward the unknown. Even so, substantial disagreements on how to juggle scientific knowledge and imaginative writing remained.

The genre of science fiction had enjoyed enormous popularity in late nineteenth- and early twentieth-century China. Late Qing science fantasies adopted the fascination with not yet available technologies that characterized Western science fiction but mingled it with the explorations of the supernatural that had long nurtured the Chinese fictional imagination.[26] Such utopian novels as Wu Jianren's *Xin shitou ji* (New story of the stone, 1905) fantasized about "a future beyond the depredations of colonial modernity," attempting to reimagine the fate of the nation beyond the constraints of history.[27] By the 1920s the genre had become relatively tamer, and much emphasis was put on science-related writings that were meant to educate more than entertain. Magazines devoted to science popularization flourished in the 1920s and 1930s, a period that saw the emergence of the peculiar genre of science nonfiction prose (*kexue xiaopin*).[28] In November 1949, a bureau devoted to science dissemination was created with the aim of eliminating superstitious thought, spreading knowledge of health and hygiene, and cultivating people's interests in new technologies and inventions.[29] Many popular science periodicals then shifted their targeted audiences from the city to the countryside. Such 1950s publications as *Kexue puji tongxun* (Science popularization newsletter) were mostly addressed to village cadres and teams sent to rural areas. They provided practical advice, such as instructions on how to make lantern slides as well as storyboards with images and texts, often in folk rhymes, to be reproduced on slides for educating the rural population about various hygiene and health-related matters, including self-care during pregnancy and the symptoms of intestinal worms.

Magazines of vernacular science were common throughout the socialist era, but toward the end of the 1970s many new journals were founded. They ranged from specialized periodicals on topics such as archaeology and fossils to magazines of everyday living. Tianjin-based *Kexue yu shenghuo* (Science and life), which featured women (often women scientists) prominently and glamorized urban living, aimed at enlightening its readers on "how to make one's life more modern." The journal testifies to a shift toward professional specialization and the nurturing of private life within the domestic walls. Advice ranged from how to choose the right toothpaste to ways to unclutter one's apartment; news included matters of health and parenthood as well as predictions on how new technologies were about to change daily life. Like *Scientists Talk about the Twenty-First Century* and *Little Smarty*, *Science and Life* discussed "the textiles of the future," "the city of the future," and "the food of the future," and featured cartoons about robots taking over domestic work. The magazine did not carry fiction but included essays by authors of science fiction. One of the essays, "Rang womende shenghuo geng kexue xie" (Let's make our life a bit more scientific) by the well-known science fiction writer Zheng Wenguang, claimed that humanity stood at the brink of momentous change. Zheng admitted that human parthenogenesis and cloning, robots more intelligent than humans, and alien civilizations in outer space still sounded like remote possibilities, but he hastened to add that simple considerations of daily life demanded that readers make their lives more scientific: the one-child policy made it imperative to improve all aspects of life so that the next generation would be fewer but better; the mechanization of labor meant less need for physical labor and greater diversification of specialized skills. Most important, scarcity of water threatened to become a serious obstacle to economic development, and finding alternative sources was urgent.[30]

Whereas several of the articles in *Science and Life* straddled the border between the empirical and the fantastic, *Kepu chuangzuo* (Creative science popularization) was closer to the realm of creative writing proper and featured a broad variety of genres, including fiction, nonfiction, poetry, film scripts, literary criticism, and even *xiangsheng*.[31] Notably, it published translations of many of Isaac Asimov's works, and its illustrations featured an odd mixture of U.S. spaceships and agricultural tools of the Han dynasty. Also literarily oriented was *Kexue wenyi* (Science literature and arts), which included illustrations of traditional fairies and deities floating in the clouds with spacecraft hovering in the background. These periodicals were characterized by a remarkable continuum between items presented as fact and those listed as fiction. Futurology and cryonics, for instance, were the subject of journalistic reports and recurrent fictional themes. Cryonics often took on allegorical meanings: surviving the Cultural Revolution amounted to becoming a frozen corpse. Several of the stories provided fantastic solutions to the real need for water—for example, transporting icebergs from Antarctica on giant rafts.[32]

From the 1950s up to the early 1980s, links between literature and popular science were textual, personal, and institutional. Both were theoretically aimed at dispelling superstition, and authors of popular science ranged from top researchers to creative writers who had little empirical knowledge of the fields they wrote about.[33] Given the overlaps between literature and popular science, it is no wonder that the relation between the literary and scientific functions of science fiction remained unsettled. Although many science fiction stories displayed a bent toward the fantastic, their common denominator was the celebration of the scientific mind. The 1979 TV series *Zuihou yige aizheng sizhe* (The last cancer dead)—about a doctor who extracts a cancer remedy from sharks and then falls ill but refuses to leave her work—was one of the most acclaimed *kehuan* works. Rudolf Wagner has defined *kehuan xiaoshuo* as "lobby" (or special interest) literature, arguing that it aimed to eulogize scientists and advance the demands for recognition by a group that had not been represented in the literature of the preceding decades.[34] This is an appealing proposition, but it perhaps assumes too much unity of intent between writers and scientists. (There were, in fact, some tensions between scientists and writers of science fiction, which I will discuss.) Furthermore, scientists were actually featured in 1950s fiction and film, especially in children's literature. Several children's stories begin with a bizarre object or event that is then explained as the result of a scientific breakthrough. Fantastic apparitions are thus the pretext for lessons in biology, logic, or mathematics: an elephant without trunk or tusks turns out to be a newly bred giant pig designed to feed a growing population. In a story on the theme of human cryopreservation, the frozen body of a child who disappeared fifteen years before is found and brought back to life thanks to the latest thawing technique developed by committed scientists and doctors.[35] These themes reappear in many of the stories published in the late 1970s. And if scientists were indeed not featured in the literature and films of the Cultural Revolution, they did populate the stories that circulated through handwritten copies in the early 1970s, many of which were thrillers and spy stories, featuring strange events that then migrated into the reemerging science fiction.[36]

What was peculiar to *kehuan xiaoshuo* in the late 1970s and early 1980s, then, was not its focus on scientists per se but rather its help in promoting a separation between mental and manual labor. The labor performed by the genre was to celebrate the Chinese mind as disembodied intellect, thus prefiguring the formation of a new intellectual class. Science fiction also helped reorient readers toward the future, a temporal dimension of narrative that had been eroded in the arts of the Cultural Revolution. In the press of the late 1960s to early 1970s, the words "future life" and "future world" appeared remarkably less frequently than in the late 1950s.[37] In the model works of the Cultural Revolution, references to the future had been formalized to such extent as to be emptied of content; in particular, a notion of the future as unknown or open-ended had nearly disappeared. The model works were looking backward, reminding viewers of the hardships that had already been overcome; written from the perspective of an achieved future, they led the viewers back to a dark past, through a hard struggle, and up to a bright present. The anachronies that punctuated their narratives were mostly aimed at engendering a "retrospection of anticipation," a recollection of the past in which the future (now present) had been hoped for.[38] Science fantasies, by contrast, reintroduced provisionality into writing: they did not simply open up the future and fill it with new content but also represented it as the unknown object of speculative anticipation, thus establishing a new pact with readers, one based on the promise of unforeseen epilogues that would retrospectively solve all mysteries.[39]

A Servant's Mind and a Servant's Hand

"Shanhudao shang de siguang" (Death ray on a coral island) by the archaeologist Tong Enzheng was among the twenty-five stories that received a national prize for best short story (*quanguo youxiu duanpian xiaoshuo jiang*) in 1978. Credited with having inaugurated the return of science fiction in the post-Mao period and adapted into a movie in 1980, the story enjoyed great success, especially among young people, and was repeatedly reissued as a serial picture booklet under different titles. Its exotic setting on a Pacific coral island, rare in works of the time, might have added to its appeal.[40] On this tiny island—a primordial yet hypermodern paradise linked to the world through a sort of Internet—Dr. Matthew, an overseas Chinese born in Japan, pursues his research in laser technologies thanks to funding from a European company allegedly committed to world peace. The island is a veritable utopia for scientists, with full freedom to choose one's project, unlimited funding, and skilled personnel available when needed. A pacifist quite oblivious to the ways of the world, Dr. Matthew is persuaded that his work is benefiting humanity until the sudden arrival of a young scientist named Chen Tianhong, an overseas Chinese from N-Country, interrupts his idyll. While flying to China with a "high-performance atomic battery" that is sought after by criminals working on behalf of a "big country" (apparently the Soviet Union), Chen's plane is hit by lightning that mysteriously flashes in the clear sky; he drops into the ocean and is saved from a shark attack by what turns out to be a laser beam shot by Dr. Matthew. Hearing that the lab is funded by a European company, Chen Tianhong becomes suspicious and recalls having read about such a company's actually operating under the big country's control. Dr. Matthew denies it vehemently, saying that this must be a rumor. Soon enough, Chen turns out to be right: the European company is a front for the Soviet Union, which has been using many of Dr. Matthew's discoveries for its army.

The scientist's autonomy turns out to be an illusion: neutrality is not an option in the tension-riven world of the Cold War. The story ends with Dr. Matthew's death. The island is blown up by the Soviets, and Dr. Chen heads back to China, the only state truly devoted to the greater good of humanity.

The hopeful expectation that Chen will be safe after reaching China, however, does not dispel a profound uncertainty between appearance and truth: whom should one believe, and whose protection should one trust? Chen Tianhong's reflections on the dangers of being cheated would have had particular resonance in post-Cultural Revolution China. He reflects: "as a person who lived since a young age in a capitalist society, I could understand the torment and pain that this upright soul had experienced. [Dr. Matthew] was an outsider who had been deceived and persecuted by this irrational society."[41] The first-person narrative allows the reader to conflate narrator and author and to doubt whether Chen is actually talking about the capitalist world. If "capitalist" is replaced with "socialist," this passage echoes many scar narratives published in the late 1970s that lament the bad treatment scientists received during the Cultural Revolution. Life under capitalism provides a foil to denounce the scientist's condition under socialism and to express the hope that in reform-era China it would improve.

Both scientists are ethnically Chinese but were born and live abroad. Chen Tianhong's parents moved to N-Country from Guangdong province, while Dr. Matthew speaks with a Fujianese accent. Their southern origins make them doubly exiled from the socialist state, which is politically and culturally centered in the north. The foreign setting allows the author to avoid engaging too closely with the question of the relationship between scientists and the state in socialist China and to fantasize that a different relation might be possible.[42] China is a promised land, a place of arrival where something not yet realized might still take place, a utopian promise of unlimited support for scientists and protection for the whole of humankind. The story's rhetoric resembles the Chinese government's efforts to attract Chinese scientists residing abroad after the implementation of the Four Modernizations. The geographical distance and the exiled state of the protagonists allows for the prospect of a new start predicated on the scientist's loyalty to the state.

"Death Ray on a Coral Island" presents another kind of loyal servitude as well. Dr. Matthew had been living on his island in the sole company of a native, a mute Malay servant called Amang with "wiry black hair and olive-colored skin."[43] Amang is admittedly peripheral to the plot. In the evening, he sits on the rocks and plays melancholy melodies on his flute (a guitar in the film): "I felt that this solitary soul was pouring out nostalgia for his home country. Evidently, under his cold appearance was hidden a passionate heart," comments the narrator.[44] There is no apparent reason why Amang's music should be an expression of nostalgia. His origins and how he landed on the island are not explained. Later, he serves a cake to celebrate the successful end of one of the scientist's projects, and when the Soviets come he shouts in an effort to prevent the atomic battery from falling into their hands. This shout will cost him his life. All we have, in short, is the sketchy portrayal of a mute human being whose only utterance is a sound manifesting his attachment to his master. Probably not much would change if he were not there, except that his presence allows for the representation of a harmonious union of mind and hand. The scientist's utopia involves the occupation of a wild place (the island) and the mute servitude of a native. The scientist's work presumes a division of labor between mind and hand that is hierarchically distributed between the overseas Chinese and the Malay, whose physical and affective labor is essential in sustaining the scientist's utopia but ultimately disposable.

Such a neat division of labor breaks with the discourse of class antagonism, equality among races, and the valorization of manual work since the 1950s. Amang remains an enigma—an unreadable, sacrificial body whose only function is to die for his master's scientific achievements. But this enigma calls attention to a more general question: what do laboring bodies do in post-Mao science fiction? Even though each story might invite a different reading, the representation of various kinds of laboring bodies generally helped to advance a notion of the "Chinese mind" as scientific and to identify Chineseness—in many cases, transnational Chineseness—with the work of the mind, promoting an ethos in which laboring bodies are disposable rather than indispensible to scientific and technological progress. The labor performed by the genre in the post-Mao moment is to posit a new relation between the work of the mind and the work of the hand.

The following section will illustrate this claim through a reading of three controversial stories by Wei Yahua. Whereas Tong's story examines the relation between mental and manual labor in the context of shifting geopolitics, Wei's stories address this problem through the gendered trope of the rebellious gynoid and through issues of marriage and social class. These stories help remake the social worlds of the scientists by creating distinctions between instinct and intellect, brain and body, mind and hand. They do so indirectly, by problematizing the relation between humans and machines.

I, Robot Wife

Robots featured prominently in early 1980s Chinese popular media. Although news on the latest models on the market was widely reported and Asimov's stories were debated, writers and critics of science fiction repeatedly emphasized their lack of human intelligence: robots can only do what they are programmed to do. Stories that featured robots killing their creator or that failed to sufficiently stress the difference between humans and robots were criticized as unimaginative and pedagogically worthless because they did not illustrate all the wonderful things that robots could do if properly designed.[45] A special kind of robot, a rebellious gynoid named Lili, is the protagonist of Wei Yahua's "Wenrou zhi xiang de meng" (Dream of tender bliss) and its sequel "Wo jueding yu jiqiren qizi lihun" (I decided to divorce my robot wife).[46] The gynoid develops from a robotic stage of blind obedience to an emancipated woman reminiscent of Ibsen's Nora in *A Doll's House*. The title of the sequel, "I Decided to Divorce My Robot Wife," is misleading: it is in fact Lili herself, not the male protagonist, who eventually files for divorce. By juxtaposing these two stories with another of Wei Yahua's stories, "Mengyouzhe" (The sleepwalker), discussed in the final section of this chapter, I hope to show how the distinction between humans and machines in Wei's stories is less important than that between manual and mental laborers. Whereas the robot is capable of rapid evolutionary progress through several developmental stages, the worker in "The Sleepwalker" is represented as a subhuman body, bound to be superseded in a future process of evolution.

"Dream of Tender Bliss" begins with an unnamed scientist receiving a pink, scented card on his twenty-second birthday, sent by the Marriage Administration Center, in which he is told to pick up a robot wife. If he were an only child, he explains, he could have married a human being, but he has siblings, and "according to the theory of eugenics, to avoid the decline of the human species, women enjoy special rights"—that is, only his sister can marry a human.[47] The protagonist then goes to the store of a company called "The Globe," where he gets to choose between thousands of unique robot girls, each of them blending world beauties past and present. They possess not only "external beauty," the manager explains, but also "an internal beauty that is even more beautiful, the eternal wellspring of love: beauty of character, which is something your eyes can't see. . . . The thoughts of robot girls are as pure and clear as mathematical formulas, as firm and absolute as geometrical theorems. They only love one person for their entire life: their heart will hold only the person whose name is written on the delivery invoice; to him they will always be loyal and faithful."[48]

A robot wife will never contradict her husband, the manager continues, because she is made according to Asimov's "Three Laws of Robotics."[49] When the protagonist asks what will happen when he dies, the manager reassures him: "She is designed according to the cosmic rules of symmetry, so the duration of her life will be symmetrical with yours." To the lament that she cannot have children, the manager retorts that this is precisely her advantage; with the threat of exponential population growth, robot wives will save humanity from food scarcity and economic crisis. If he wants a child, he can always get a baby robot that looks just like the two of them. The scientist is finally persuaded and selects a robot woman to his liking. When the manager writes the name Lili on his card and shouts her name, she is called to life, and the marriage is celebrated in the store. The story recalls several tales about gynoids, such as the novel *L'Ève future* (1886) by Auguste Villiers de l'Isle-Adam and the short story "Helen O'Loy" (1938) by Lester Del Rey. But Lili is one step ahead of Helen in that she comes out of the shop already equipped with feelings of love. As a performer of affective labor, however, she goes a bit too far; her devotion soon turns the science fantasy into political allegory: "Since between the two of us there was only one head, every hair on my head was for her the epitome of truth, and every sneeze of mine was a sneeze of truth. She only knew to venerate me. I was the singer, she the music troupe. . . . I was the TV station, she the television, with only one channel: whatever I wanted to broadcast, she'd receive it."[50] Lili's submissiveness turns the scientist into a sadist. He tests her limits by making her do all kinds of humiliating things, and Lili not only keeps obeying but also nurtures his vices; when he tries to quit smoking and drinking, she provides him with cigarettes and alcohol. Hers is not proper obedience but a mechanical impulse to satisfy his basest instincts. After an evening of heavy drinking, he burns all the plans for the groundbreaking scientific project on which he has been working for months. When he realizes what he has done, he furiously resolves to return Lili to the seller and to file for divorce. Here the first story ends.

In Del Rey's "Helen O'Loy," a fantasy of woman's complete devotion to man, no one apart from the two male protagonists knows that Helen is a robot; in Wei Yahua's tale, however, corporate interests and public opinion play an important role. In the sequel, "I Decided to Divorce My Robot Wife," the company manager, worried that the case will ruin his business, hires a lawyer to defend Lili. The lawyer defends her by referring to Asimov's Three Laws and accuses the scientist of not having taught her anything but obedience; hence, the judge refuses to grant the divorce. After this failed attempt, the scientist receives a letter from a biochemist, and events take a new turn. In the letter, the biochemist explains that Asimov is outdated: his three rules apply only to primitive robots, for Asimov had not seen such lifelike combinations of humans and machines. It is normal, the biochemist explains, for humans to abhor robotic obedience because "democracy, equality, and civilization [*wenming*] are important characteristics of modern humans." He then goes on to explain that the protagonist and the robot belong to two different historical periods: she is stuck in a primitive stage; therefore, to make her move forward and become more similar to himself, the scientist ought to analyze the chemical composition of her body and modify her diet accordingly.[51] This physical transformation would then provide the material basis for a spiritual transformation through a philosophical diet consisting of the Confucian classics, Laozi, Aristotle, Socrates, Nietzsche, Hegel, Feuerbach, and Montesquieu. According to the biochemist, Lili will only advance to the stage of a true human being if she eats the right food and reads the right books.

In what turns out to be a parody of materialist thinking, the young scientist immediately sets to work and analyzes her hair to assess the difference between her bodily composition and his own. Humorous descriptions ensue:

> The quantity of zinc and copper was three quarters lower than my own; iodine, lead, and cadmium were seventy per cent higher; the phase difference in sodium and titanium was twenty-five percent; nickel and molybdenum were quite close to mine; aluminum was lower by about one half; the phase difference in chromium and magnesium was about twenty-four percent, and sulfur and calcium again were basically the same. In total, I carried out eighteen experiments comparing my bodily composition to hers and came up with two completely different curves. The most serious issue was that the difference in zinc, copper, iodine, lead, and cadmium was too big, which was the material cause of her defective thinking. Therefore my cure started from there: I planned the menu in full detail, carefully combining the foods that she needed.[52]

The scientist plans a diet in which Lili is to alternate python oil, beef tallow, chicken fat, and bear fat, and to replace cow milk with whale milk. He also buys great quantities of partridge, pigeon, albatross, and parrot eggs, accompanied by purple cauliflower, white agar, fresh mushrooms, and *xuecai* pickles, plus a supply of hilsa herring, mandarinfish, long-jawed conger eels, variegated carp,

and snakehead. Although the imperative of disseminating science is often deplored as a burden on science fantasies, this compendium of terms from the
spheres of chemistry, zoology, and botany in fact lightens up the text. Scientific
didacticism gives way to a "chaotic enumeration," a parody of a catalogue that
could go on and on and that interrupts the serious message of the story.[53] If
only momentarily, chemistry and food science turn into nonsense.

Thanks to this chemically and philosophically appropriate diet, Lili leaps
forward to an advanced stage, rising to self-awareness and eventually leaving
the scientist. A free subject can only accept marriage as a "democratic" union
between equals. The story thus promotes a version of human evolution in which
change proceeds by leaps. Lili's initial interiority was fully predetermined and
was thus no interiority at all: for all her sentiments and hard affective labor, she
had no soul. And yet, Lili's robotic body is not a mere container that could be
opened, torn apart, and reassembled at will, as was the case with Helen in Del
Rey's story. Rather, it is the result of organic transformations and of a circulation
of desires that connect the company manager, the two scientists (her husband
and the biochemist), and the gynoid herself. Her scientist husband remakes her
from scratch, instilling in her the desire to move forward, but he too has limited
agency: both he and Lili are maneuvered by the robot seller—for it is the manager's tale that makes Lili desirable to him and that summons her to life. Thus,
if Lili advances to humanity and gains a proper interiority, it is mainly thanks
to the company that first produced her (and that appoints the lawyer who becomes her philosophy teacher and dance partner) and to the biochemist—the
older, more experienced male scientist who guides both the young scientist and
Lili in the remaking of her self. A gynoid can thus evolve into a human woman
under the guidance of a corporate and technocratic apparatus, acquiring a real
human heart and bridging the gap between soulless mechanical bodies and self-
reflexive minds. As we shall see, workers similarly stuck in a primitive stage
have far fewer chances of moving up.

Artificial Minds and Callous Hands

Wei Yahua's "The Sleepwalker" projects an even more ambivalent vision of the
interaction of humans and machines. The story opens with a prologue set in
the Lingyin Temple in Hangzhou. Most people, the narrator muses, go to the
Buddhist temple to be enlightened about the future, but not himself: "I don't.
I use modern scientific knowledge to solve the mystery of human life. I study

futurology."[54] A young researcher in the institute of mathematics, he goes one afternoon to visit his friend Xiao Yun, who is the daughter of the head of the institute where he works. The story exemplifies the gender dynamics in post-Mao science fiction, in which women are typically represented as wives or daughters of the senior scientist or girlfriends of his best students. The young scientist finds Xiao Yun reading the Tang *chuanqi* (marvel tale) "Zhenzhong ji" (Tale of the pillow), in which the protagonist sees his entire life in a dream. She tells him that she would also like to preview her future life and urges him to produce a magic pillow. What Xiao Yun wants to know is whom she will marry, and therefore the scientist asks her to fill out a questionnaire on three candidates, detailing their family background, education, personality, salary, and hobbies. The experiment begins, with the blessing of her father, who sees in it the potential for a breakthrough in the study of the brain.

The woman rests her head on the newly devised magic pillow, which is connected to a computer and induces three dreams. In the first, a rich and handsome college student and son of a provincial cadre takes her to discos and nightclubs. The two get married against her parents' wishes; eventually, she discovers that her husband has been cheating on her. The dream ends with her decision to divorce him even though she is pregnant. The protagonist of the second dream is the antithesis of the first: a worker by the name of Shi Dazhuang (Big Sturdy Stone), son of an illiterate worker and a housewife. His father had supported Xiao Yun's family during the Cultural Revolution, when her own MIT-trained father was deprived of his salary and sent to a May 7th cadre school.[55] Her parents have agreed to his marriage proposal out of gratitude, and although she only feels fraternal affection for him, she soon gives in, and the two get married amidst much fanfare—a match between people from different classes attracts media interest. All she feels is a growing repulsion toward his rough body and the equally coarse nature of his sentiments. The qualities of the worker's body that were so celebrated in the literature and visual arts of the revolutionary period become the object of contempt:

> I could feel the calluses on his rough hands. What I found repulsive were not his hands as such but rather his feelings, which were as uncouth and rough as his hands. From his mouth came no sweet word of affection, but only panting and gasping as coarse as that of an ox. Oh, how I wished he could be my kindred spirit—that he could talk about art, music, painting, sculpture, literature, and that we could pour our hearts out to each other. If only we could be united in recalling our lost past and imagining the beautiful future. But precisely at the

moment when he was enjoying the greatest joy of human life and was taking possession of my most precious thing, he could not say a single gentle word![56]

The calluses on the worker's hands, though not repulsive in themselves, suggest the callousness of his heart.

In the Chinese socialist version of human evolution, manual labor played a major role. As Engels had argued in "The Part Played by Labor in the Transition from Ape to Human," it was labor that created humanity itself: labor had perfected the hand, which distinguished humans from apes and by extension the human from the nonhuman realm.[57] In Wei Yahua's story, however, the callous hand becomes a synecdoche for nonhuman qualities. The worker's feelings are repeatedly compared to the instinctive behavior of animals.[58] For Engels manual labor had separated humans from the animal world, but for Wei it reduces humans to animals, seen as coarse and inferior forms of life. The worker's uncouth body is incapable of memory or anticipatory imagination. Devoid of interiority, he only knows instantaneous satisfaction and is unable to project himself into the past or the future. The worker's laboring body, once the essential element that defined humanity, becomes in this story the obstacle to its development, the residue of an old technological regime that is about to be overcome.

Wei's narrative is not, however, bereft of contradictions. Although Xiao Yun's description of her dream calls for our complicity, it might also be read as a parody of intellectuals' didactic attitudes and assumptions about high and low cultural forms:

> I'll guide him, teach him. He is coarse, but can't I make an extra effort to polish him with the precision and care of a sculptor? Can't I make him become a cultured and well-bred person with a rich inner world? I have lots of books at home. He only knows the basics of mathematics, and of course he's not interested in knowing more. But how about literature? I'll teach him to read literature. *Anna Karenina* . . . but as soon as he picks it up he falls asleep . . . a whole month has passed, and he can't even pronounce the name "Anna"! It's not that he doesn't read fiction at all. But all he reads is *Seven Heroes and Five Gallants*, *Generals of the Yang Clan*, and *The Cases of Judge Bao*. If I talk with him about art, he only stares at those nude pictures. If I try to teach him to sing, his mouth only emits oxlike grunts. . . . He cannot remember Shakespeare, Pushkin, Maupassant, Shelley, Zola, Flaubert, or Tolstoy. As soon as he hears music he falls asleep, as if all the symphonic music of the world were lullabies. I have talked

to him about oil painting, but he is only interested in painted furniture. And he only has one hobby: playing cards.[59]

This passage—and the story as a whole—presents an inversion of the two stories about the robot wife. Whereas the scientist successfully emancipates the gynoid, Xiao Yun fails in humanizing the worker, whose "animal" nature eventually condemns both of them to a life reduced to basic, primarily sexual instincts: "I felt we had become two animals, male and female, and apart from animal needs, we didn't have any other form of communication." In the social world of this story, scientists are happiest if they can live in their own milieu and not mix with others—unless they can remake them in their own image, which is not easily done. This second dream indeed persuades Xiao Yun's father that gratitude is not a good reason to marry his daughter to a worker. As she finally emerges from the third dream, Xiao Yun looks happy but refuses to share its content. Predictably, the protagonist of the third dream is the young scientist who designed the magic pillow. While presenting such an unequivocal picture of a perfect match—as in a good Victorian novel, the only marriage that can bring happiness happens within the same class—"The Sleepwalker" also shows how scientists manipulate others: for all his claims about the objective workings of the computer, it is the scientists' own dreaming device that produces the negative portrait of the worker and lures the woman into marrying him instead.

Characterized by a humorous, if often didactic, tone, Wei Yahua's stories use such tropes as time machines and robots to explore issues that were central to intellectual debates in the early 1980s, such as notions of humanity and democracy, romantic love, and the role of class background in defining one's identity and social relation. Anecdotes about the reception of Wei's early stories suggest that they were read as sources of actual scientific information, which testifies to the fact-fiction continuum that characterized science-related writings in the early 1980s.[60] Several of his other stories are in the scar literature mode. "Shenqi de tongkong" (Magic eyes) recounts the troubles created by magic glasses that allow one to see other people's secret thoughts—a reference to the persecutions and forced confessions of the Cultural Revolution.[61] "Yuanfang lai ke" (A guest from afar), a short story that won him China's first Galaxy Award for science fiction in 1986, tells the story of a biologist whose face and body are completely disfigured by a corroding liquid emitted by a carnivorous plant.[62] His anxiety about being consumed by an unknown force is accompanied by an interrogation of the distinction between the animal and the vegetable world—did the plant have a nervous system? could it think?—and by musings over how the substance has irreversibly shaped his life path, leading him to a scientific career but condemning him to deformity and loneliness. The scientist feels always projected toward the next phase of his working life, yet he is late at every step. In Wei Yahua's stories, anticipation is mostly connected to personal development and time is confined to the individual lifespan. Time-traveling devices such as the magic pillow allow the protagonist to get a preview of her possible marriages rather than launching her into a communal future.

Criticism, Crisis

Various articles published in the early 1980s warned against the absurd and lurid elements that *kehuan* writers employed to attract readers, and such criticism only intensified during the Campaign against Spiritual Pollution in 1983. Ye Yonglie's works in particular were attacked for spreading fake science, being too commercial, and promoting capitalist liberalization. Ye's "Shenmi yi" (The magic suit, 1979), a thriller/sci-fi story (*jingxian kehuan*)—in which a scientist who has discovered a cloak of invisibility is kidnapped by Soviet spies who want to use his device for military purposes—was criticized for failing to illustrate how science could be used for the benefit of humanity. In addition, critics attacked stories that featured clones and pills that mysteriously increased one's intelligence, saying that they spread superstition and exerted a bad influence on young people. Some of these stories were also criticized because they expressed problematic political views; according to an article in the *People's Daily*, the political errors of *kehuan xiaoshuo* "are not isolated cases but are the effect of a combination of rotten capitalist thought and residual feudal influences."[63] Such polemics were apparently fueled by the Association for the Popularization of Science and by some scientists themselves, who reclaimed the right to define what deserved to be called "scientific." Even Qian Xuesen, the "father of Chinese rocketry" and probable model for the protagonist of the popular novel *The Strange Case of the Snake Beauty*, intervened to criticize *kehuan xiaoshuo*: "I would have no objection if many works of science fantasy fiction [*kexue huanxiang xiaoshuo*] would drop the word 'science' because fantasy fiction [*huanxiang xiaoshuo*] can be written whichever way one wants. But it's inappropriate to call their works 'science fantasy' because much of their content is not scientific."[64]

In November 1983, the editorial board of *Wenyi bao* (Literary gazette) together with the Theoretical Research Section of the China Federation of Literary and Art Circles held a conference on science fiction in which both Zhou Yang and the chief delegate of the Association for the Popularization of Science intervened. Zhou Yang lamented that some of these stories used extraterrestrial creatures and robots to criticize the party and socialism.[65] In early 1984, science fiction was further criticized for mocking and denying science.[66] The polemic, however, did not last long. Very soon articles appeared that reiterated the positive function of science fiction in pushing forward the development of science and technology, even as warnings against drifting toward the absurd were issued again and again.

In response to these attacks, science fiction authors defended the value of their works as popular literature (tongsu wenxue), emphasizing the literariness of their texts and distancing themselves from the aims of science popularization.[67] From early on, Tong Enzheng had drawn a distinction between the aims, devices, and structure of science literature and arts (kexue wenyi) and those of science popularization. For Tong, the aim of science literature was no different from that of literature at large: to express the writer's thoughts and, more specifically, to "propagate a scientific view of life." Tong claimed that he had written "Death Ray on a Coral Island" not to propagate new laser technologies but rather to show how, in a class society, scientists were forced to serve the interests of the dominant classes. He further noted that, although writings of science popularization needed to be logical and faithful to science, science literature was based on imaginative thought. The first needed to abide by precise rules of sequence and presentation, while in literature arbitrary twists and turns could be introduced.[68]

These distinctions became widely accepted by the mid-1980s. By the second half of the 1980s, science fiction criticism abandoned these taxonomic concerns, and preoccupation with its literary tasks as well as a concern for the decline of readers' interest took center stage. The critic Ma Shunjia, for one, claimed that the task of science fiction was not that of popularizing science but rather that of inventing ideal worlds. As a form of social imagination, it reflected social anxieties and fears under particular historical circumstances. Therefore, kehuan xiaoshuo had to take on the eminently literary task of addressing the anxieties and fears of the present, which in contemporary China mostly had to do with the degeneration of "humanity." Echoing the contemporary slogan "literature is the study of human beings" (wenxue jiu shi renxue), Ma suggested that science fantasies had to contribute to the redefinition of what it meant to be human.[69]

In 1986 Wei Yahua also intervened in these debates, noting that kehuan xiaoshuo was on the verge of disappearing; statistics showed that the number of published works had dropped from a peak of 340 in 1982 to 31 in 1985. This may have partly reflected an ongoing diversification of popular genres; "new *chuanqi*" (marvel tales) came to occupy center stage in 1984–1985, and it is possible that some of the stories previously defined as *kehuan* were now subsumed under this less problematic category. Wei, however, interpreted the statistics as evidence of decline and demanded more state support, lamenting that even the more influential among science fiction writers were nonprofessionals—that is, they did not receive a state salary as writers. In addition, there was no science fiction writers' association to guide literary creation. Wei also deplored the absence of science fantasy films after the adaptation of Tong Enzheng's "Death Ray on a Coral Island" as well as the limited number of specialized journals. He argued that the cause of the present crisis was neither readers' disaffection nor a decline in quality; rather, it was caused by the severe criticism to which the genre had been subjected in 1983. This made the relatively small group of science fantasy writers (137 across China according to a 1981 statistic mentioned by Wei in his article) shrink even further.[70]

The scarcity of publishing venues was one of the reasons Wei Yahua insisted on the necessity of establishing an association of *kehuan* writers with its own specialized journal. The Chinese Writers' Association had several thousand members, among whom only four were science fiction writers. Journals that had published *kehuan* stories in the late 1970s, such as *Beijing Literature*, were no longer interested in them. As a consequence, science fiction in the mid-1980s became somewhat regionalized: *Science Fiction World*, the major specialized journal founded in 1979, was based in Chengdu, and a science literature committee (*kexue wenyi weiyuanhui*) was instituted by the provincial Sichuan branch of the Writers' Association, possibly thanks to the support of Tong Enzheng, who was then teaching at Sichuan University.[71] Tong Enzheng himself, however, ceased writing science fantasies and devoted himself to archaeology full time from the mid-1980s onward, spending much of his time in the United States (where he stayed after the 1989 crackdown on the Tiananmen protests), while Ye Yonglie turned to other popular genres. Others abandoned *kehuan* after the 1983 debates because they felt that it was too much trouble to go through the latest scientific literature and make sure that everything they depicted had a "scientific basis." Meanwhile, the tropes and conventions on which these writers had relied had exhausted themselves. This was a moment of generational change. It was only in the early 1990s, when younger writers emerged, that *kehuan* was revived—with works that were, in the view of many critics, more mature and sophisticated but that fall outside the scope of this book.

Conclusion

Science-related genres mediated visions of valuable knowledge, useful labor, and desirable futures in the late 1950s and in the late 1970s and early 1980s. Whereas Tian Han's *Rhapsody of the Ming Tombs Reservoir* extolled manual work and called for transcending the division of labor between mind and hand, post-Mao science fiction promoted new distinctions between those who did mental work and everyone else. The post-Mao emphasis on occupational specialization is well known, but the role that science-related genres played in naturalizing the distinction between manual and mental labor has so far been overlooked. Post-Mao science fiction provided a forum for addressing fundamental questions about the definition of human nature and human needs, the tensions between political commitment and technical expertise, and the value and function of different forms of labor. Even though these stories have been largely dismissed as naïve, they played an important role in pushing the boundaries of what was possible—without much consideration for what was plausible. They reoriented readers toward an open-ended future while helping to consolidate social and intellectual distinctions.

The stories discussed in this chapter by no means exhaust the diverse ways in which the future has been represented in Chinese science-related literature from the 1950s to the 1980s. I have focused on a few influential texts published in the late 1950s and from the late 1970s to the early 1980s because these two moments were similarly characterized by a forward orientation revolving around technological development and a radical transformation of nature—a theme that will be discussed further in Chapter 5. These texts reveal a tension between two meanings of the future: the first understood as the feelings of anticipation, the hopes and expectations that shape everyday life, and the second indicating a higher stage of history lying ahead. Nowhere in the texts examined do these two dimensions come together smoothly. These two dimensions remain largely unrelated to one another, calling attention to the difficulties in closing the gap between the present world and the one imagined. Tian Han's *Rhapsody* mostly emphasizes the anticipatory dimension of the future: an enduring condition of strenuous labor, which is then overcome in the utopian vision of the epilogue. Narratively, present anticipation and future world remain disconnected: it takes an explosion to leap ahead to a time of abundance and leisure. In the technological utopias of the late 1950s and in such stories as *Little Smarty* of the late 1970s, by contrast, the emphasis is on the future as an endpoint, and the labor that it takes to get there is only mentioned as an element to be superseded; history proceeds by way of leaps that do not lend themselves to a smooth narrative of becoming. In all these cases, the reader is asked to actively step in and make that leap possible: these texts were meant to mobilize readers to transform the world.

In Tong Enzheng's and Wei Yahua's stories, scientific knowledge leading to human happiness functions both as anticipation and end point. It would then appear that science comes to take the place of labor in propelling history forward, with the important difference that science is not expected to be overcome but rather to blossom indefinitely. Herein lies the potential for a less discontinuous tale of progress, one in which expectations and goals are seamlessly integrated. The main difference between science and labor, however, is that the first is not presented as a way of life that can be undertaken by just anyone. Science is mostly represented as arcane; when it is accessible, it is represented ironically, as in the long list of foods fed to the robot wife. Rather than being seen as everyone's labor or practice, then, science is the privilege of a small minority. Despite the rhetoric of science popularization, these stories do not invite readers to see themselves as active makers of the future. Rather, they promote a cautious and almost voyeuristic mode of anticipation, possibly eliciting the desire to be extraordinary scientists but ultimately leaving common readers in the position of spectators of others' greater deeds.

2

TRANSLATION ZONES

Anticipating World Literature in Socialist China

IN 1952, the prominent writer and editor Feng Xuefeng wrote: "Learning from the Soviet Union involves not only studying their most advanced science and technology but also their most advanced literature and art."[1] Literary translation played a crucial role in furthering cultural exchanges with the Soviet Union and the rest of the world, and it constituted an important if overlooked aspect of Chinese socialist literary culture.[2] But what exactly would be translated, and how? Cultural authorities attempted to regulate the work of translators through centralized planning and nationalized publishing, but in this as in other professions, daily work was never a matter of simply implementing a plan. Deciding what and how to translate involved complex debates concerning the relations between Chinese and foreign languages, literary form and historical time. Sketching the atlas of world literature in socialist China turned out to be a contested process that involved translators, writers, party authorities, and occasionally ordinary readers. At what scale should the maps be drawn? which regions should be put at the center? which texts should be included? and which styles should be adopted?—these issues were discussed at length.[3]

Much of the work of literary translators in the early 1950s aimed at providing Chinese writers with models from Russian and Soviet literature and introducing readers to the advanced world toward which they were heading: reading literature from the Soviet Union anticipated the experience of transformations soon to be realized at home. In addition, literature from other socialist countries was supposed to create a sense of solidarity with the socialist "brother nations."[4] But the range of texts available in translation was much broader than has often been assumed, and translation was not limited to texts from the Eastern Bloc. Translation from European and American literature continued as well, while that of Asian, Latin American, and African literature intensified, especially from 1957 onward.

During the 1920s and 1930s, debates on how to translate had crystallized around the tension between "sense translation" (*yiyi*) and "direct translation" (*zhiyi*), that is, between an elegant rendition in Chinese that would "domesticate" the foreign text and a faithful adherence to the structure of the original that would "foreignize" the Chinese.[5] In 1951, Mao Zedong designated "direct translation" as the preferred method to render Marxist-Leninist texts, and, according to Nikolai Volland, "foreignizing translation styles became the mainstream in the early People's Republic."[6] This was not, however, the last word on how literary translation was to be executed in the ensuing years. Several speeches delivered at the first National Conference on Literary Translation, held in August 1954 with the purpose of "elevating the quality of translation work," proposed various ways to harmonize the two approaches to translation as an alternative to unequivocally embracing direct translation. The conference was important not so much for the novelty of the translation strategies that it proposed—mediating solutions had been suggested in pre-1949 debates as well—as for its emphasis on the specificity of literary texts and on literary translation as a practice that could not be subjected to the same standards as other kinds of translation. However fraught by political constraints, the conference was partly an attempt to preserve a relative autonomy for the work of literary translators by keeping open the discussion of where to draw the limits on foreignization. Methods of literary translation were discussed by such influential writers as Mao Dun, Guo Moruo (who had translated Goethe's *Sorrows of Young Werther* and *Faust*), Lao She, Ye Shengtao, and by the head of the Central Propaganda Department, Zhou Yang.[7]

Guo Moruo, for one, criticized the notion of direct translation by emphasizing the need to recreate the "style and rhythm" of the original—that is, its "poetic elements"—in Chinese. "All good literary works are poetry," Guo claimed; therefore, "the mastering of poetry is essential."[8] Because few translators are as proficient in the foreign language as in their own, Guo Moruo suggested that they resort to collective translation (*jiti fanyi*) as it was practiced in the Soviet Union to help elevate the poetic quality of the translation:[9]

> When the Russian translators translate a Chinese poem into Russian, first someone proficient in Chinese renders its meaning, and then someone who under-

stands poetry enhances its poetic flavor [*jiayi shihua*]. Collective translation in the Soviet Union is already widely practiced, and I believe it is a method worth imitating. Here in China, the great majority of translators only go through the first step, the translation of the meaning, with very little polishing or often none at all. However, this second step is essential. We can't render "a cup of vodka" with "a cup of water." Only by changing it into a cup of Fen wine or Maotai can we be said to have completed the job.[10]

For Guo, a good translation had to account for a term's contextual use by rendering it with a corresponding Chinese term rather than with a calque conveying the word's etymology but not its actual meaning. Interestingly, Guo did not mention the possibility of rendering the term "vodka" directly in transliteration, as if this foreignizing option did not sit well with his idea of stylistic elegance. Indeed, he invoked Yan Fu's tripartite scheme of the qualities of a good translation—"*xin, da, ya*" (faithfulness, clarity, and elegance)—insisting that elegance was no less important a prerequisite than the other two. Guo also argued that knowing only one foreign language was hardly sufficient for a literary translator because one always needed to compare renditions in different languages.

Several other speakers, including Mao Dun, insisted on a blend of accuracy and creativity. The basic task of any translation was to convey the meaning of the original, Mao Dun argued, but this was insufficient when it came to literary translation, which had to recreate the artistic conception of the original. The translator had to identify with the author's creative process and "merge together [with him], as if the original author had written his work in a different language."[11] Mao Dun compared the translator to an actor and the author to a playwright: "This method of translation requires full creativity on the part of the translator, but also the intention of being absolutely faithful to the original, like an actor who has to create a character in a play: he would create the character on the basis of his own life and artistic training, yet the character that he creates must also correspond to the intentions of the playwright."[12]

As models of creative faithfulness, Mao Dun singled out Lu Xun's translation of Gogol's *Dead Souls* and Qu Qiubai's translations of Pushkin and Gorki. One wonders if Mao Dun was aware of the implications of selecting *Dead Souls*, which had been translated by Lu Xun not from Russian but from German and Japanese versions and thus involved a fraught encounter between various languages rather than a one-to-one transaction between a source and a target language. Lu Xun's style of translation by this time epitomized faithfulness to the foreign text and hence foreignization of the Chinese; however, by singling him out as a model of creative faithfulness, Mao Dun put a different spin on his approach. Meanwhile, deploring the practice of young translators who mechanically followed the original and produced unreadable texts, he emphasized that the Chinese language had to be protected from excessive foreignization.[13]

Debates held at the conference arguably say little of actual practices, but they do show that the very notion of a foreignizing, "direct" style of translation was a nebulous concept subjected to different interpretations rather than a clear-cut "mainstream" approach that all translators were to comply with. Notably, the debates were characterized by a rhetoric of mediation, which in turn revealed tensions between different understandings of the qualities and tasks of a good translator: one insisting on literary cultivation, multilingual competence, and creativity, the other capitalizing on language proficiency, specialization, and accuracy. By privileging the first over the second, Guo Moruo and Mao Dun were reclaiming the enduring relevance of the cosmopolitan writers-translators of their generation, who risked losing ground to an emerging group of translators who were being trained in Russian but, in their view, were not well-read in Chinese and world literature and not sufficiently talented in poetic composition.

Mobilizing translators for building a modern socialist culture involved reconsidering the nature of their work as well as their professional affiliations. Literary translators until then were primarily employed as teachers, academics, writers, cadres, editors, or journalists. Unlike other cultural workers, such as musicians, actors, painters, and writers, only a few noted translators were employed full-time at publishing houses or academic institutions. Translation continued to be thought of as a secondary activity, even as a "hobby;" as Mao Dun put it, translators were expected to contribute to socialism as "amateurs" (*yeyu*). At the same time, he lamented that good translators were so few. While arguing that collective translation per se was not an appropriate method of work because it rarely achieved stylistic unity, Mao Dun insisted that various forms of collaborative work should be explored: translators could discuss a text together, gain a "complete and unified" understanding of it, and then one of them would do the translation; when a first draft was completed, other translators would check it against the original and do appropriate revisions. Or they could "split the translation" (*fenyi*); after reaching a unified understanding of the text, they could each translate his or her portion, revise each other's versions, and then one person would unify the style. In the end, it was up to editors to check the text carefully, for they were the "ultimate guarantors of the quality of the translation."[14] Whereas Guo Moruo promoted collaborative work as a way to enhance the poetic quality of the text, Mao Dun seemed mostly concerned with devising an efficient way to use scarce human resources and to ensure a correct interpretation of the text. If the translator was an actor interpreting the intention of the foreign author/playwright, this very acting had to be mediated by a unified understanding, sought in collaboration with others. The criteria for such a unified understanding remained unspoken, and it is easy to see how such insistence on one correct interpretation could actually reduce the range of creative interventions and lead translators to opt for a flatter or relatively more literal rendition. Such tensions within Mao Dun's speech testify to the complexity of his institutional position—as a writer who saw translation as a means of preserving the voice of foreign authors, as an editor concerned with improving the quality of translations, and as a minister of culture who sought to regulate the profession and streamline the publishing sector at large.

Surely, the most important point on Mao Dun's agenda was the planned reorganization of publishing. He lamented that private publishers kept issuing translations "at random": works that were unimportant or harmful flooded the market, while those that ought to be made available to Chinese readers remained untranslated. For instance, there was no full translation of *One Thousand and One Nights*, Homer's epics, or the classics of the literature of India, a country with which China had had intense cultural exchanges. The *Manyōshū* and *Genji Monogatari* (The tale of Genji) were Japanese titles that Chinese people had barely heard of, and not even the Russian classics—Gogol, Chekhov, Pushkin, and Tolstoy—were fully translated. Mao Dun went on to complain that in the last few years a small number of unimportant texts were published over and over again in editions that differed only slightly from one another. Providing readers with truly diverse translations of the same text, Mao Dun noted, would not be a bad thing. However, in most cases publishers were simply reprinting the same version, at times even changing its title to dupe readers into believing that it was a different work. Publishers, after learning that that a certain text was in preparation for another publisher, would often hasten to produce their version first; thus, up to eight editions of the same work were issued, and more than twenty translators independently translated the same text.[15] To put an end to the malpractice of hasty translations—which in Mao Dun's view attracted the criticism of the socialist "brother nations"—the work of translators had to be thoroughly reorganized; nationwide translation plans should be drafted, and tasks would then be distributed to the various state publishing houses, to joint public-private publishing companies, and to the journal *Yiwen*.[16] Mao Dun's talk presented a striking plan of a total translation project that would introduce Chinese readers to the canon of world literature from antiquity to present. In many ways, this plan resumed the cosmopolitan editorial vision of his early years as editor at the *Xiaoshuo yuebao* (Short story magazine)—a vision that he had not been able to carry through back then, for in 1923 he had been replaced by Zheng Zhenduo, under whose editorship publication of foreign literature had dropped.[17] According to Mao Dun, translating the literary gems of the past would reveal a history of cultural exchanges in which China was embedded from early on as one of the world's oldest civilizations, while the classics of nineteenth-century realism would introduce readers to the giants of modern world literature. As for contemporary texts, Mao Dun noted that it was difficult to discern the good from the bad; efforts to translate them should be made; overall, however, contemporary writing was to take a back seat.

By 1956, publishing houses were nationalized and the publication of foreign literature concentrated at People's Literature Publishing House. In the two years following the conference, the number of literary translations dropped. As the translator Ru Long lamented, in the effort to eliminate multiple translations of the same text, all publication was concentrated in the hands of a single publisher, which was woefully insufficient.[18] Grand translation plans were made nationwide, hundreds of translators were put to work, but then their drafts got stuck in the editorial office of People's Literature Publishing House. This publisher's editions were seen as definitive, and no reprints were issued after they sold out. This situation was not conducive to improving the quality of the translations either. Ru mentions the case of an older translator who did not follow the word-for-word style of translation preferred by the publishing house. His work had been heavily revised by the editors, a fight had ensued, and eventually the book remained unpublished. Ru suggested that state publishers should "engage in friendly competition" with one another under the guidance of the Ministry of Culture. This would not affect central planning, he noted, for each publisher would still be assigned its tasks, but it would ensure that more translations of higher quality would be published. Ru Long's proposal did not have any practical effect, but it testifies to the alternative paths that some individuals deemed possible in the 1950s.

Mao Dun's emphasis on editors as the "ultimate guarantors of the quality of the translation" reflected the effort to implement a publishing system in which editors were assigned the role of arbiters of style, which often created conflicts with other professionals.[19] Nonetheless, influential writers and translators working at such journals as *Yiwen* could at times push for their favorite writers and texts and determine how to render them in translation.

Yiwen's Literary Internationalism

Founded in 1953 and named after the short-lived translation journal edited by Lu Xun in 1934, the monthly *Yiwen* was the main publication devoted to foreign literature from the early 1950s to the late 1970s.[20] Mao Dun was editor-in-chief until late 1958, when he was replaced by Cao Jinghua; deputy editor-in-chief Chen Bingyi, Dong Qiusi, and the poet Zou Difan were in charge of most of the editorial work until the mid-1960s. The journal reached a print run of 60,000 copies, with a staff of up to thirty translators.[21] Leafing through *Yiwen*, readers found a literary atlas that stretched from Cuba to France and from India to the Congo. A typical issue of the 1950s was divided by genres, including fiction, poetry, literary theory, reviews of recent translations, a section titled "News from Abroad" (*Guowai tongxun* or, in some issues, *Guowai tongxin*) and one called "Trends in World Art and Literature" (*Shijie wenyi dongtai*), which included short pieces on international news and events, ranging from the announcement of the publication of Tang poetry in Dutch translation (*Yiwen*, April 1956) to the invitation by a prominent Russian literary journal to writers from all over the world to nominate their favorite authors.[22]

Issue after issue, readers were presented with overviews of world literature in which some nations and forms were featured as more advanced than others. According to the Note to Contributors, the journal welcomed the following submissions: "(1) translations of modern literary works from the Soviet Union, people's democracies, and other countries that reflect the real life, thought, and struggles of the people, as well as representative classical works . . . ; (2) translations of articles on progressive literary theory and literary criticism from the Soviet Union, people's democracies, and other countries; reviews of studies, translations, and overviews of foreign literature; (3) news of artistic trends from all countries." In *Yiwen*'s early issues (1953–1956), Soviet fiction and criticism were given a prominent place; most would open with an excerpt from a Soviet novel or short story, followed by a text from some other Eastern European country. Contributions from other parts of the world would generally be included in the second half. In January 1957, however, "Soviet Union and people's democracies" was replaced by a more inclusive formulation, which emphasized the journal's reorientation toward "all the countries of the world": "(1) translations of excellent modern literary works from all the countries of the world and of representative classical works . . . ; (2) translation of articles on progressive literary theory and criticism from all the countries of the world."

The effort to widen the geographical scope of the journal reflected growing tensions with the Soviet Union. In February 1956, at the Twentieth Congress of the Communist Party of the Soviet Union, Khrushchev delivered his famous "secret speech" denouncing the lawlessness of Stalin's rule in a closed session to which the Chinese delegation was not invited. Mao Zedong and high party leaders read the speech later. In the following months, the Chinese Communist Party (CCP) held several meetings to discuss Stalin's shortcomings, which were mostly identified with his lack of commitment to proletarian internationalism. Mao, however, concluded that Stalin was still a great leader and that his mistakes only amounted to "thirty percent" of his work.[23] Disagreement between the Chinese and Soviet governments then arose over the handling of the Hungarian and Polish crises; even though Mao continued to publicly endorse the Soviet Union as the leader of the socialist world, on several occasions he suggested that the leadership was shifting to China. The relations between China and the Soviet Union became increasingly tense in 1959 for reasons that included the tensions between India and China following the rebellion in Tibet and the Soviet-U.S. rapprochement. Khrushchev eventually recalled all Soviet experts and reduced aid to China in July 1960, actions that Mao Zedong then used to deflect blame for the economic disasters of the Great Leap Forward. By 1964, the alliance had come to a formal end.[24]

Scholars have discussed *Yiwen* primarily because its translations of Soviet works portraying young idealists fighting against the bureaucracy provided inspiration for Liu Binyan and Wang Meng's critical short stories published in 1956. As Rudolf Wagner put it, *Yiwen* was "the only literary window to the outside socialist world, . . . a storehouse of alternative socialist options in literary form, quite apart from the often superior quality of the works translated."[25] From 1957 on, however, *Yiwen* published less and less recent Soviet fiction, shifting to earlier Russian works and considerably broadening its geographical focus. Whereas the 1954 issues introduced works from about fifteen countries, in 1959 the number of countries shot up to forty-five. The 1959 peak was an effort, celebrating the tenth anniversary of the People's Republic, to represent China itself as enmeshed in a vast network of cultural relations; in each of the following years, however, works from around thirty-five to forty countries were translated. Partly to ensure comprehensive geographic coverage, shorter fiction and poetry were now preferred over long excerpts from novels.

Yiwen's translations between 1956 and 1959 introduced a wide range of progressive writers from all over the world. For instance, the 1956 January issue included fiction by Miyamoto Yuriko, poems by Mayakovsky and Walter Lowenfels.[26] From February to June 1956 the prize-winning novel *Virgin Soil Upturned* by Mikhail Sholokhov was serialized.[27] The February issue also included fiction by Doris Lessing and poetry by Rabindranath Tagore and was illustrated with several woodcuts, one of which, an image from the Edo era by Japanese printmaker Suzuki Harunobu titled "Chrysanthemum Fairy," appears on the very first page (Figure 3). The only color illustration in the issue, this print of a young woman in kimono picking chrysanthemums along a creek reflects the call to draw on the forms and techniques of Asian arts, which was in turn related to the notion of cultural pan-Asianism that became prominent in 1957. In February 1957, Trends in World Art and Literature, included a report

FIGURE 3. Woodcut print by Suzuki Harunobu, originally published in color. *Yiwen*, February 1956.

of the Congress of Asian Writers in New Delhi (December 27–28, 1956) that claimed that in antiquity there were deep affinities between Asian literature and arts, which had then been destroyed by Western domination.[28] In August 1957, *Yiwen* devoted an entire issue to the literature of Asia, introduced by Mao Dun. The effort to configure an Asian literary community was reflected in *Yiwen's* enduring attention to Vietnamese, Thai, Korean, Indian, and Japanese literature over the following years. The attempt to revive pan-Asianism was short-lived, however; with the worsening of border tensions between China and India in 1959 and the many declarations of independence throughout Africa and Asia in the early 1960s, the emphasis on a cultural commonality rooted in an Asian past diminished in favor of building ties with newly independent countries in the name of anticolonialism.

Yiwen's translations in 1956–1957 are striking in their geographical variety, ranging from Icelandic writer Halldór Kiljan Laxness to Urdu writer Krishan Chandar (March and April 1956). The April issue includes a long article on Ethel Voynich's novel *The Gadfly*, a bestseller in the Soviet Union that had become an instant hit among Chinese youth when it had been translated from Russian in 1953; its film adaptation, the article announced, was about to be distributed.[29] In addition, special sections are devoted to the commemoration of the birth or death anniversaries of such authors as Rabelais, Montesquieu, Walt Whitman, and Heinrich Heine. Some issues include a literary heritage section that features such diverse authors as Munshi Premchand and Stendhal.[30] In May 1956, the section includes two short stories ("The Death of Archimedes" and "Alexander the Great") from the *Apocryphal Stories* by Karel Čapek, author of well-known science fiction books and the inventor of the word "robot." The June issue includes an essay by Jean-Paul Sartre; in July, short satirical pieces by Mark Twain; and in August, short stories by Alberto Moravia. The September issue includes Turkish fiction writers and an essay by Thomas Mann; in the literary heritage section, there are three short stories by Tagore and three by antimilitarist writer and intellectual Kuroshima Denji. The October issue is one of the most varied of the year, including short stories by William Saroyan, Heinrich Böll, Thomas Mann, Konstantin Paustovsky, and Mikhail Zoshchenko. That same year, Paustovsky had edited a volume with writings by authors suppressed under Stalin; Zoshchenko had been criticized by Zhdanov in 1946 and only partially rehabilitated. Editors at *Yiwen* regularly consulted Soviet publications, so they must have been aware that these were controversial authors. How far to go in following the Soviet "thaw" was still an open question in late 1956, and editors at *Yiwen* used the authority of Soviet sources to introduce alternative voices on matters of literary creation.

Several American and African American writers were introduced around this time, for instance, Erskine Caldwell, Arna Wendell Bontemps, and Anna Seghers, the noted author of *The Seventh Cross*. The main element these texts have in common is that they dealt with themes of social injustice, often in a rural setting. Some are excerpts from manuscripts that were to be published by People's Literature Publishing House. In this sense, *Yiwen* also functioned as a showcase for forthcoming books and was connected with a variety of other cultural events.[31] For example, a play by the Georgian playwright Georgii Davidovich Mdivani was included in the September 1956 issue, a few months before another of his play was performed at the People's Theatre in Beijing.

Internationalism and the effort to introduce Chinese readers to progressive writers of the world are the main editorial criteria that emerge in several of the 1956–1957 issues. As we shall see in the following section, editors often included foreign highbrow artworks and positioned them strategically to attract attention to controversial contributions. Although 1950s Chinese editors largely relied on Soviet selections, their inclusion of these images testified to an enduring cosmopolitan outlook harking back to the *Short Story Magazine* in the 1920s.[32]

Uses of Art

Yiwen's illustrations ranged from folk paintings to reproductions of Picasso, Monet, Manet, and other Impressionists; from scenes of industrial and rural work to Japanese woodcuts and images of "ethnic minorities" in the Soviet Union. The January 1957 issue, for instance, is dedicated to Egyptian literature and featured (mainly modern) fictional texts and poems, combined with ancient Egyptian art, such as a reproduction of a fresco with birds perched on a finely drawn locust tree (Figure 4). Other illustrations include drawings of slaves at work and are accompanied by the texts of "ancient work songs."

The texts and illustrations in this issue pay homage to Egyptian national heritage, and might have been a response to the Suez Canal crisis that was developing in those months. By reading Egyptian literature and looking at Egyptian art, the reader would be introduced to a nation that was engaging in an anti-imperialist war. The selections in this issue are largely based on assumptions of similarities between China and Egypt. The Egyptian poems celebrate

洋槐树与小鸟(彩色)　　　　　　　　　　埃及古代壁画

FIGURE 4. Egyptian fresco, *Yiwen*, January 1957.

affinities and bonds between the two nations and trace connections with other Asian "sister nations."[33]

In the following months, the "special focus" format was often used to pay homage to countries in the midst of wars for independence, but at the same time the journal continued to include works from a variety of geographic locations, dealing with a variety of themes. Illustrations often attracted the readers' attention to essays relegated to the last pages that dealt with questions unrelated to the focal theme of the issue. In February 1957, for example, a section was devoted to Latin American poets, including Miguel Ángel Asturias, Pablo Neruda, and Nicolás Guillén. Their poems sing of love for their nations, the fate of exiles, and the encroachment of U.S. imperialism. The issue is illustrated throughout with Pablo Picasso's paintings, which are unrelated to the Latin American poetry but call attention to Ilya Ehrenburg's essay "On Pablo Picasso," published on the last pages of the journal. The painting "Two Sleeping Peasants" (1919) is reproduced on the cover, showing two peasants sleeping on a heap of grain in the summer heat (Figure 5). The relaxed posture and the naked breast of the woman suggest sexual intimacy. Their bodies are plump, with none of the sharp edges that characterize Picasso's Cubist works. This is a friendly Picasso, even close to the models of socialist realism, certainly not in terms of overall composition, but in the ways in which some parts of the human body are represented, especially the man's big hands and feet.

Ehrenburg, one of the most prominent writers in the Soviet Union at the time, had visited China in September 1951, when he met with more than two hundred Chinese writers at the Beijing Hotel. By 1956, however, he had come under attack by orthodox Soviet critics for his novella *The Thaw* (1954), which gave the name to the period of cultural ferment following Stalin's death in 1953. Ehrenburg's essay presents Picasso as a controversial artist disliked by Hitler and Truman[34] and as an artistic genius who "always searches for forms that can convey his thoughts and feelings," who did not depict the world as he "saw it" but as "he thought it."[35] Ehrenburg's essay justifies the apparent complexity of some of Picasso's works by claiming that "new forms have always met with opposition," suggesting that some audiences might not have sufficient artistic training to appreciate him.[36] This was a controversial idea if one considers the emphasis on popularization in the revised version of Mao Zedong's "Talks at the Yan'an Conference on Literature and Art" published in 1953. As a whole, the February 1957 issue of *Yiwen* conveys a vision of anti-imperialist art that is geographically diffuse and in which personal vision and artistic form play important roles. The

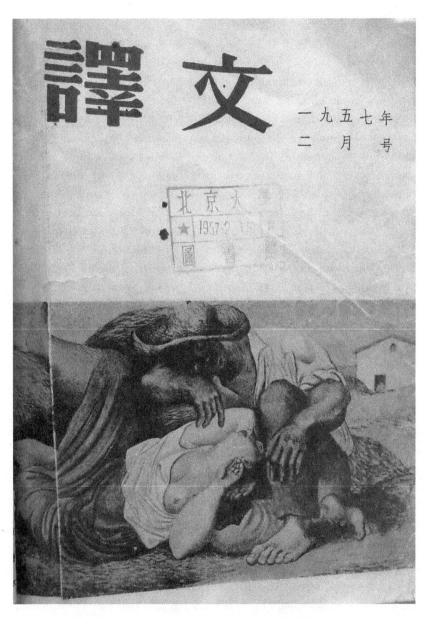

FIGURE 5. Cover of *Yiwen*, February 1957, featuring Pablo Picasso's "Two Sleeping Peasants" (1919).

illustrations call attention to Ehrenburg's article but, by showing a Picasso that is not too strange or experimental, make its content more acceptable to those who might have objected to Ehrenburg's emphasis on the subjectivity of the artist.

Aesthetic matters are also discussed in an article by the Czech minister of culture Zdeněk Nejedlý in the following issue (March 1957). Nejedlý was a well-known musicologist, notorious for banning most of Dvorak's works. Unlike Ehrenburg, Nejedlý can be considered a guardian of socialist realist orthodoxy, but his article is so long-winded that one could derive different meanings from it. It certainly makes a point about the necessity for socialist realist art to be able to compete—nationally and internationally—as "true art" and even proposes that artists adopt some "modernist" techniques. The Czech musicologist claims that the primary criterion to identify "true realism" is that it had to be art and not mere artisanal work. He urges writers to experiment with new forms. Although many elements in "modernist art" (*xiandaipai de yishu*) were "remote from reality, . . . so-called modernist art has much to offer to realist artists." Real life, Nejedlý argues, "has already entered the so-called stage of modernity; art, science, and the whole of culture are also going through this stage. Therefore, avoiding modernism, or thinking of eluding it and turning back to realism, is impossible."[37]

Modernity and modernism, for Nejedlý, were inescapable stages of development, and artists needed "to press onward through the jungle of modernist art."[38] Nejedlý emphasized that the kind of realism he was talking about was not *any* realism, but socialist realism, which ought to portray reality not as it was in the present but as it was developing toward the future. The techniques of modernism could therefore be used to convey a bolder vision of the future, which he conceived as a time in which what "needed" to happen would find its realization.

Nejedlý addressed important questions concerning artistic work: What were the forms that would best anticipate the future? How could "true art" be produced? Which techniques could enrich the work of the socialist artist? Even though from different perspectives, both Ehrenburg's and Nejedlý's articles addressed problems concerning the interaction of the political and the artistic that were widely debated in China in 1956–1957, and both suggested that technique and personal vision were essential aspects of progressive art. This meant affirming the specificity of the artist's work and articulating a view of "progressive art" in which the term "art" was given prominence.[39]

Diverse imaginary maps of world literature coexisted in the pages of 1956–1957 *Yiwen*, each showing a different aspect of literary internationalism. Some of these maps reproduced national borders and power blocs, while others did not. First, a map of "progressive" writers linked authors from different parts of the world, stretching from the United States to France and Latin America. These progressive writers were regarded as individuals sharing similar leftist concerns rather than as representatives of their national literatures, and the version of literary internationalism they embodied was unrelated to nation-states or to Cold War power blocs. Second, there was the Asian map, encompassing both literature and the visual arts, aiming at carving out a specifically Asian cultural community. Third, there was the aesthetic theory map, exemplified in the essays by Ehrenburg and Nejedlý, which mostly dealt with the relationship between art and politics, the forms and styles of socialist realism, and its relations with modernism and the avant-gardes; this map encompassed Soviet and Eastern European writers, occasionally stretched back to include the classics of Western aesthetic theory but rarely included authors from other places. It partially overlapped with the Socialist bloc map, encompassing all literature from countries allied with the Soviet Union. Finally, partly overlapping with the first (progressive writers) and the second (Asian literature and arts), there was the emerging map of anticolonial literature, which united Asian, African, and Latin American writers concerned with struggles of national liberation. The only map that foregrounded the author's nationality, it became more prevalent in 1959. Around this time, solidarity with anticolonial struggles became a more prominent aspect of the state cultural agenda, signaling the CCP efforts to position China as world power as it threw off the Soviet yoke and challenged the economic and political power of the United Kingdom and the United States. Yet, even then, other configurations continued to exist.

From *Yiwen* to *Shijie Wenxue*

"The backwardness of our literary undertakings cannot be denied. We still too rarely see literary creations that are truly moving, insightful, and beautiful in artistic form."[40] Such complaints on the deficiencies of Chinese contemporary literature were repeatedly voiced at the Second Conference of Delegates of the Chinese Writers' Association in February–March 1956, and they were often echoed over the following two years. In an effort to contribute to the "blossoming of a hundred flowers" in late 1956, *Yiwen* editors sent out a questionnaire asking readers to help improve their foreign literature selections and thus contribute to the flourishing of a Chinese socialist literature. The editorial board reportedly received more than 16,000 responses; as the summary of readers' views included in the May 1957 issue shows, dissatisfaction predominated, but suggestions on the direction to take were quite diverse. Readers urged editors to introduce a broader range of writing styles and works from all over the world, including capitalist countries. One reader mentioned that such writers as Hemingway should also be introduced, others requested more translations of works from African and Asian countries, yet others asked for more contemporary works from the Soviet Union, especially those "reflecting real life." A few readers suggested that writers from remote regions should also be represented, including ethnic minority writers from the Soviet Union. They also asked for more classics and for more diverse genres, including satire and comedy, better poetry, more theoretical introductions to recent foreign literary trends, and more special sections or special issues.[41] Although some of the readers who wrote these letters may have been staff of publishing houses and journals,[42] the variety of responses remains striking, and editorial selections followed up on some of them. In 1957–1958, such writers as Charles Baudelaire (July 1957), John Steinbeck (February 1958), Ernest Hemingway (February 1958). Giovanni Verga (March 1958), William Faulkner (April 1958), Gianni Rodari (June 1958), and Kobayashi Takiji (August 1958) were translated or discussed.

Among Western European writers, French authors were the most translated. In July 1957, a special section was devoted to Baudelaire, with nine of his poems translated into Chinese by the poet Chen Jingrong, a member of the Nine Leaves Group. Perhaps because Chen worked as an editor at the journal, she took considerable liberties in rendering these verses. For instance, she translated the fourth line of the poem "L'ennemi"—"Qu'il reste en mon jardin bien peu de fruits vermeils—as "zhi you hen shaode hongse guozi liu zai wo zhitou shang," rendering *jardin* as "branch," identifying the poet with a solitary branch, not a garden with only a few red fruits remaining, thus conveying an additional layer of isolation and dismay.[43] The translation of Baudelaire and other European and American writers in the late 1950s suggests that the dialogue with Euro-American literature was still seen as a precondition for Chinese literature to flourish. It is debatable whether writers who had come of age in or before the 1940s were ready to take anything but Euro-American and Russian works as their models, despite the rhetoric of brotherhood with other Eastern European, Asian, and African writers. "Nine Leaves" poet, scholar, and translator of Anglo-American literature Yuan Kejia, for one, lamented in an article published in *Literary Gazette* in December 1957 that "the neglect of Western literature is the reason the new Chinese literature has not risen to the level it ought to achieve."[44]

Such lamentations of inadequacy disappeared beginning in 1958, when editorial policies took a new turn. In late 1958, about two years after the start of the Hundred Flowers Campaign, Mao Dun was replaced in his role as editor-in-chief by Cao Jinghua; in January 1959, the name of the journal was changed into *Shijie wenxue* (World literature). As an editors' introduction explains in the first issue under the new editorship, mistakes had been made; from then on, more extensive editorial comments would be included to prevent readers from "misunderstanding" foreign texts. The journal's aim was redefined as "introducing works that reflect the real lives and revolutionary struggles of the people of all countries of the modern world."[45] A shift of emphasis from Russian toward Latin American, Asian, and African writers had already been underway, but in early 1959 the journal began to include long summaries and critical essays by Chinese translators, while translated excerpts became shorter.[46] The translators were to take a clearer stance toward the texts they introduced and thus mediate between texts and readers; their work was to be a combination of translation, editing, and criticism. From then on, translators' commentaries reflected three basic attitudes—endorsement, critique, and paternalistic support—often conveyed through temporal tropes; acclaimed works were those that anticipated the future, while those that allegedly returned to the past were criticized. In the late 1950s and early 1960s, while continuing to devote much space to Eastern European literature, *Shijie wenxue* devoted special sections to countries in which anticolonial struggles were underway, and the celebration of national liberation often overwrote literary concerns. In the February 1959, for instance, a special section titled "Hooray for the People of Cuba and Congo!" included poems by Cuban and Congolese authors, along with commentaries by such authors as Lao She, Ye Shengtao, and Yan Wenjing[47] that dealt primarily with the countries' declarations of independence rather than with the poems as such. Only one essay dealt with poetry, Xu Chi's "Cuban Thunders and Cuban Songs," which introduced José Julián Martí as the prophet of Cuban independence. Apart from the nation, Xu Chi claims, the other theme of Martí's works was poetry itself, which was to him "as dear as the fatherland, as precious as freedom, and as sharp as a sword."[48] Xu Chi presents Martí's work as a means to a revolutionary end; in fact, the poems selected are quite bombastic and arguably not the best Martí ever wrote, but Xu at least called attention to them.

Other Latin American authors, meanwhile, were contextualized within their literary traditions in separate essays, and works by such writers as Asturias and Neruda as well as by many other less famous writers from such countries as Columbia and Puerto Rico were introduced through extensive historical overviews, though only few of them were translated.

Besides revolutionary or leftist writers, *Shijie wenxue* discussed a variety of literary trends vaguely defined as "modernist" (*xiandaipai*); in this case, no translated texts were provided. As we have seen, Nejedlý viewed modernism as a set of techniques that could enrich socialist realist writing. In 1957, *Yiwen* had included several of Baudelaire's poems, although their protomodernist traits were downplayed in favor of a realistic reading. By 1959, however, *xiandaipai* was condemned as a remnant of the past. In the June 1959 issue, for instance, Trends in World Literature and Arts featured a report on modernism in Yugoslavia drawn from the Soviet journal *Foreign Literature* (*Inostrannaya literatura*), in turn translated from the journal of the Bulgarian Writers' Association, which deplores the "many deranged young poets and writers [who] are ideologically confused; they get all wrapped up in abstract concepts and claim that they don't need a plot to write a story."[49] These writers, according to the article, are stuck in the decadent atmosphere of the turn of the century. They "deny reality, deny humanity, and deny progress." The article concludes that the influence of bourgeois revisionism was hampering the "forward march" of Yugoslavian literature.

By 1959 "revolutionary" and "modernist" writing fell into opposite categories, one endorsed as vanguard and the other criticized for being passé. *Shijie wenxue* also kept up with young writers from Europe and the United States, introducing them through a rhetoric of paternalistic support. Rebellious youth was a frequent topic in the late 1950s, and the terms "lost generation" (*miwang de yidai*) and "beat generation"—variably rendered as *jidong de yidai* (excited/upbeat generation), *kuadiao de yidai* (fallen generation), or *bei gaokua de yidai* (ruined generation)—made their appearance. Editors emphasized that discontent and rebellion haunted the capitalist world and defined these writers as "rebels without a cause," who however deserved international support. In these cases, extensive editorial pieces were followed by texts in translation. The "angry young men," for instance, were introduced in November 1959 with an article by the translator Cao Yong, focusing on the book *Declaration* (a collection of eight essays by such British authors as Doris Lessing, John Osborne, John Wain, and Colin Wilson), followed by a short essay on Osborne's play

Look Back in Anger (1956) signed by Bing Xin, who was reporting from London, and by an excerpt from John Wain's novel *Hurry on Down* (1953).[50] Cao Yong pointed out that *Declaration* was in its fourth reprint within only half a year and deserved close scrutiny because of the sensation that it had caused in Britain and America. The "angry young men" did not have a common goal, Cao said, but they were all unhappy, disillusioned, and, of course, angry. Cao Yong endorsed them because they offered an insight into the depressed psyche of the British youth, highlighting the problems that intellectuals had to face in capitalist societies. In addition, they were talented and did not use modernist techniques, such as "stream of consciousness." They were to be appreciated because they epitomized a spiritual crisis caused by the Cold War and U.S. imperialism but were also to be criticized for their nihilism and "ultra-individualism." The article concluded by mentioning similar writers in France (Alain Robbe-Grillet and Nathalie Sarraute), Spain, and Germany (Siegfried Lenz). Cao Yong singled out writers from the United States (Jack Kerouac, J. P. Donleavy, George Mandel, and Allen Ginsberg) for particular criticism, claiming that "although they are dissatisfied with American reality, they wallow in drugs, sex, and alcohol, and therefore the decadent traits of their works greatly overwhelm the few elements of protest against bourgeois society."[51] All these "angry young men" were "Cold War martyrs," stuck halfway between the modernists of the past and the socialist revolutionaries launched into the future. "Progressive" intellectuals from all over the world had a duty to guide them toward a better grasp of reality.[52]

Although the commentaries that accompanied the translations of foreign texts have been read as dogmatic guides to correct interpretation,[53] they not only reveal that aesthetic considerations remained central to literary discourse for the entire socialist period but also show an ongoing engagement with Western literature. It is remarkable that, in the late 1950s, Chinese translators took over the dual role of censoring and endorsing Western texts rather than taking them as models or yardsticks for measuring Chinese writing and lamenting its inadequacies, as was the case in the previous years and once again in the 1980s. Their critique may have been formulaic, but independent of their intention and actual embrace of the discursive frameworks they deployed, it allowed them to momentarily undo the hierarchies that had until then shaped literary relations, situating them, the Chinese translators, as arbiters of literary taste. In his comparative study of censorship, Robert Darnton has argued that in eighteenth-century France "censorship was not simply a matter of purging heresies. It was *positive*—a royal endorsement of the book and an official invitation to read it."[54] In the different context of a literary journal of socialist China, editors and translators were expected to act as censors, but they primarily remained literary professionals who redacted not to expunge but to keep open the traffic of texts.

Translations of European literature continued well into the 1960s. In June 1963, a long article on the French *nouveau roman* introduced the writings of Robbe-Grillet, Sarraute, and Michel Butor.[55] The article offers a scathing critique of these writers and is more than twice as long as the excerpt from Sarraute's novel *Le planetarium* (1959) that follows it. It is exceptionally detailed and includes translated passages from Robbe-Grillet's novels and essays, with an unusual number of footnotes with references to *Le Figaro littéraire*, *Esprit*, and the *New York Times Book Review*. As was typical in commentaries on European and American authors, the justification for introducing them was that they had such impact on the rest of the world that they could not be ignored. The authors introduced Robbe-Grillet's and Butor's vision of the "novel of the future," illustrating the aesthetic implications of their "antihumanist" stance. Antihumanism resonated with the Chinese literary discourse of the time, for notions of "humanism" (*rendaozhuyi*) and "human nature" (*renlei benxing*) had been harshly criticized by Yao Wenyuan and Zhou Yang in 1960. But, in fact, the two antihumanisms were worlds apart: Chinese critics rejected humanism as an abstract concept that obscured the reality of class, while Robbe-Grillet's antihumanism resulted in a mode of writing about objects in their nonhuman otherness, a mode focusing on physical appearance and on the geometrical features shared by humans and things.

Liu and Zhu's introduction condemned these tenets as "sophisms," arguing that the *nouveau roman* writers were "extreme naturalists" who completely neglected the core of reality—social and class relations. Their works were the remainder of a past to be overcome, a "last-ditch effort of the reactionary and rotten modern bourgeois literature."[56] But to support their critique, the translators provided extensive excerpts in translation and detailed examinations of such formal features as manipulation of point of view, discontinuous chronological and spatial relations, lack of characterization and of linear plot. Furthermore, by pointing out that James Joyce, Franz Kafka, and Faulkner had already engaged in similar narrative experiments with much better results, the translators reminded readers of writers who were otherwise kept on the margins of literary discourse in the PRC. In other words, Liu Mingjiu and Zhu Hong's article was an "invitation to read" texts that were mostly unavailable.[57] A couple of short stories by Faulkner had in fact been translated in *Yiwen*; Joyce had been discussed before 1949 but not translated, and some of Kafka's short stories were translated in publications for "internal distribution." It is to these publications for "internal distribution" that I now turn.

Parallel Avenues

From 1956 on, what *Yiwen* did not publish might well have circulated in periodicals or books that were intended for "internal/restricted distribution" (*neibu faxing*). Initially aimed at keeping high party cadres, noted writers, critics, and scholars abreast of recent cultural and social developments worldwide, these publications ended up circulating more widely than intended, especially among young people who were sent for reeducation in the countryside in the early 1970s.[58] The existence of such texts had been mentioned in the *People's Daily* since the mid-1950s, and even though they were all "confidential," the actual restrictions to which they were subjected varied from case to case.

Many of the publications for internal distribution dealing with foreign literature were compiled in the editorial offices of *Yiwen / Shijie wenxue* under the supervision of deputy editor-in-chief Chen Bingyi. Their existence was closely related to the struggle against Soviet "revisionism,"[59] and much of their content was devoted to recent Soviet works and debates, such as Ilya Ehrenburg's *The Thaw* and Vladimir Dudintsev's *Not by Bread Alone* (1957; Russian publication 1956), whose depiction of Soviet bureaucracy had caused much controversy in the Soviet Union. Several of the debates—though not the actual works, for fiction was considered more threatening than theory—that were first published in the periodicals for internal distribution were later also reported in the "open" edition of *Yiwen / Shijie wenxue*, which suggests a porous system of publication rather than a strict division between internal and open channels. Initially, the *neibu* periodicals only offered overviews of recent literary trends, literary news, and work summaries, but soon they were accompanied by translations of works by authors ranging from Aleksandr Solzhenitsyn to Kafka, as well as issues devoted to single authors and translations of entire books, such as Vasily Aksyonov's *A Ticket to the Stars*, Yevgeny Yevtushenko's *Babi Yar and Other Poems*, and Ehrenburg's *The Thaw*. Translations of foreign literature were only a minor part of a large system of circulation of texts intended for internal distribution—a system that included "grey and yellow books" (named after the color of their covers), the first encompassing translations in the field of political and social sciences; the second, literary works.[60] These translations were produced extremely quickly and were often published only a few months after the original had come out.

Fast-Track Translation

"Internal distribution" was set up in the early 1950s to allow for the selective circulation of politically sensitive material among party elites and has hence been associated with censorship. Indeed, controversial texts such as Khrushchev's "secret talk" and Milovan Djilas's *The New Class: An Analysis of the Socialist System* (1955) were only distributed among high party leaders. Similarly, works by Chinese noncommunist thinkers of the 1930s and 1940s and by authors labeled as rightists in 1957 were only distributed internally. However, truly "restricted" documents constituted only a small part of *neibu* publications. One catalog compiled in 1988 lists 18,301 books for internal distribution, including drafts that were later revised for open circulation, collated material on specialized fields of knowledge, school textbooks, and periodicals.[61] Many Marxist-Leninist texts and even some of Mao's works apparently circulated "internally" before being issued in their final edition, which suggests that the internal distribution system had various aims. In addition to allowing for the sharing of politically sensitive material, internal distribution allowed for the circulation of provisional drafts, speeding up the sharing of knowledge among select professional groups at a time in which editorial requirements were high and the production of final editions slow. Teaching material and some high school textbooks were also distributed internally, which suggests that they might have been especially intended for educators. Another aim may have been to avoid international disputes concerning patents and copyright: almost one fourth of the total number of internal publications listed in the catalog dealt with "industry and technology" (*gongye jishu*), and it is likely that much of this material was directly translated from foreign publications.

About nine hundred of the books for internal distribution listed in the 1988 catalog are literary translations. Mostly issued by the People's Literature Publishing House and distributed by mail or through special bookstores, they had the words "internal distribution" (*neibu faxing*) or "this book is internal material, to be consulted by comrades of the literary world, please store carefully, do not circulate" printed on the cover. Qin Shunxin, an editor at People's Literature Publishing House, recalls a notebook with a list of the people who were entitled to purchase them. When a book was issued, the people on the list were contacted and asked whether they wanted to have a copy sent by mail. If they did, they or their work unit had to send payment first. This was the main route through which this material was distributed.[62] The first foreign book to be translated and distributed internally was Dudintsev's *Not by Bread Alone* (1957), and many more volumes were published between 1962 and 1965. Publication was then interrupted and resumed by the Shanghai branch of People's Literature Publishing House in 1971, when several of the editors who had been sent to cadre schools in the countryside returned to their workplaces.[63]

In the 1960s, material for internal distribution could also be purchased in two places in Beijing: the "Neibu fuwuchu" (internal service center) at Chaoyangmen, close to the Chinese Foreign Ministry, and the "Neibu faxingzu" (internal distribution group) at Dongdan ertiao, east of Wangfujing, the main shopping street. Although the first only served high party cadres, the second was also open to researchers and writers. Neither had any sign on the door. In the early 1980s, a bookstore for internal distribution opened at West Rongxian hutong, close to the central leadership's headquarters at Zhongnanhai. From the late 1970s onward, most bookstores had a "neibu" section that was accessible from a side or back entrance.[64] A letter of introduction was needed to purchase these books, but the majority of the literature books also circulated in other ways. During the Cultural Revolution, some book owners who feared persecution by the Red Guards sold them or gave them away as scrap paper. The books were then collected at recycling centers and often resold to students, reportedly for 0.26 yuan a kilo.[65] Some writers also recall how in the 1970s they went to *neibu* bookstores together with friends who were children or relatives of party cadres.

The history of the yellow books, as mentioned earlier, is closely related to the need to keep up with Soviet debates. When they attended the Third Soviet Writers' Congress in May 1959, Zhou Yang and other cultural authorities found it hard to follow the discussions because they had not read the works that had sparked them. Zhou Yang then held a meeting with editors at the Xinqiao Hotel in late December 1959, during which he urged them to publish translations that would help to fight revisionism and to critique ideas of human nature that were circulating in the Soviet Union.[66] Zhou Yang and Lin Mohan supervised the formation of an "antirevisionist team" that was divided into two groups, one focusing on the social sciences and the other on literature. The literature team, directed by Lin Mohan, was entrusted with drafting articles against revisionism and participating in the selection of revisionist texts to be published as yellow books. Many of the articles they wrote were first circulated in internal publications but were then republished in periodicals for open circulation, such as *Hongqi* (Red Flag), *Guangming ribao* (Guangming Daily), and *Literary Gazette*.[67]

Working in concert with the antirevisionist team, the Russian translator and deputy chief editor of People's Literature Publishing House, Sun Shengwu, was in charge of the selection of books to be translated. Sun would read the list of imported books that was periodically sent to the publisher, as well as several Soviet literary journals, and would select the works that were most controversial along with those that had received a prize. In addition to recent "revisionist" Soviet fiction, European, American, and Japanese works were also translated, some from Russian and others from the originals, purchased through "import-export agents" located in Hong Kong.[68] In early 1960, the Writers' Association held a meeting on the exchange with foreign literature in which new trends in Anglo-American and French literature were discussed. On this occasion, it was decided that such works as John Osborne's *Look Back in Anger* (1956), Jack Kerouac's *On the Road* (1957), and British working-class fiction, such as Alan Sillitoe's *Saturday Night and Sunday Morning* (1958) and John Braine's *Room at the Top* (1957), should also be translated. Thus, select books of English and American literature were translated into Chinese only a few years after their publication, sometimes earlier than into other languages.[69] Translations were occasionally spurred by specific events. The revival of Japanese militarism in the late 1960s and Yukio Mishima's suicide in November 1970, for instance, led to a translation of Mishima's collected works in four volumes.

Translators were expected to work fast and efficiently. To speed up the work, several translators would often collaborate; these collective translations would then be signed with such pseudonyms as "Siren" (This Person) and "Wutong" (Five Tung Trees) or with the name of the work unit or not signed at all.[70] Editors would often look over drafts, but time pressure and the editors' uneven competence in foreign languages meant that translators worked relatively free of external supervision. Shi Xianrong, for instance, disliked Jack Kerouac's *On the Road* and took considerable liberties when he translated it in collaboration with some other translators, omitting descriptive passages that they found repetitive and tedious.[71] In his son's view, "This wasn't because of any taboo but just because [my father and his cotranslators] thought that the structure and language was too rough and that it would be fine to publish it in an abridged version."[72] In 1984, when a few excerpts from *On the Road* were republished in the third volume of *Waiguo xiandaipai zuopin xuan* (Selected works of foreign modernism), Shi Xianrong considered retranslating the whole novel, or at least integrating the parts that were missing from the 1962 translation: "He leafed through the English book a few times but eventually set it aside," his son recalls. "I asked him why he had changed his mind, and he replied that the book was a mess, in translation it would be nauseating."[73] Not all readers, of course, would agree with Shi Xianrong: the poet Mang Ke, for one, recalls how much *On the Road* affected him and his young friends, and how in 1973 it inspired them to go traveling all over China.[74] Leaving aside generational differences in literary taste, Shi Xianrong's choice to abridge Kerouac is a reminder of the liberties that translators took, even as they were told to stay close to the text.

The publication of yellow books ceased in the late 1970s. From the mid-1970s onward, many new journals of literary translation were issued, and translations of all major Western writers were published, several of which were barely revised versions of the volumes that had been first issued for internal distribution. Writers from less prestigious literary regions, meanwhile, gradually fell off the radar.[75]

World Literature in the Chinese Literary Economy

Diverse visions of world literature and various avenues for its dissemination coexisted in socialist China, not thanks to the work of any writer, translator, or critic in particular, but as a result of the complex efforts that went into the building of a Chinese socialist literary culture. How then can the very notion of world literature in relation to the practices of translation discussed in this chapter be rethought, and what does "anticipation" have to do with it?

The concept of "world literature" has been a much-debated topic within Chinese and comparative literary studies since the early 1990s. Rather than a canon of works, for most scholars it denotes a mode of circulation and reading mediated by translation and an approach that focuses on the dynamics of literary exchange. But despite the global scope that the term "world" suggests, its theorization has largely focused on the circulation of genres and forms *from* and *back* to Euro-American literature. In most studies, Europe and the United States remain at the center as arbiters of taste and sources of cultural capital, as places of origin of forms and genres propelling literary change elsewhere, and as hegemonic institutions shaping a unified yet unequal space of literary exchange.[76] In *The World Republic of Letters* (2004), Pascale Casanova has proposed the notion of a "literary Greenwich meridian" with which writers in the periphery need to synchronize if they want to participate in the global literary arena. In her view,

> the unification of literary space through competition presumes the existence of a common standard for measuring time, an absolute point of reference unconditionally recognized by all contestants. It is at once a point in space, the center of all centers . . . and a basis for measuring the time that is peculiar to literature. . . . Literary space creates a present on the basis of which all positions can be measured, a point in relation to which all other points can be located. Just as the *fictive* line known as the prime meridian, arbitrarily chosen for the determination of longitude, contributes to the *real* organization of the world and makes possible the measure of distances and the location of positions on the surface of the earth, so what might be called the Greenwich meridian of literature makes it possible to estimate the relative aesthetic distance from the center of the world of letters of all those who belong to it. This aesthetic distance is also measured in temporal terms, since the prime meridian determines the present of literary creation, which is to say modernity.[77]

Casanova's discussion spans four centuries and locates Paris as the center of literary time "at least until the 1960s."[78] Her assumption that stylistic innovation radiates from the center to the peripheries, her insistence on the autonomy of the literary from the political, and her disregard for the hegemonic aspects of Parisian universality have been criticized.[79] But her proposal is helpful in that it calls attention to the chronopolitics of world literature and to the temporality of style. In her view, "time, the sole source of literary value . . . is also the source of the inequality of the literary world."[80] The struggle to gain recognition in world literature, in other words, involves an effort to be up to date.

This emphasis on inequality can also be found in Andrew Jones's essay "Chinese Literature in the 'World' Literary Economy," in which he writes: "World literature, more often than not, has served as a site for the (almost invariably unequal) exchange, appropriation, and accumulation of (financial *and* cultural) capital between the West and its others. These complex transactions, in turn, hinge on the practice of translation."[81] But what happens to such unequal transactions if, changing the order in Jones's title, we set out to explore

"world literature in the Chinese literary economy"? Once the "world" is reconceived as a site of transactions within the "literary economy" of socialist China,
the roles of those who appropriate and those who are appropriated are—or at
least appear to be—subverted. But then, does cultural hegemony—an important concept both in Casanova's book and in Jones's essay—provide a useful
lens to capture the mechanisms of literary cooptation, and if so, how should we
reimagine its center-to-periphery trajectory?

The selections in *Yiwen / Shijie wenxue*, as we have seen, reflect different notions of world literature: as a trove of classical and modern treasures, a
transnational alliance of progressive writers, the literary expression of national
liberation struggles, and the site of inquiry into the nature and aims of literature and the arts. Each of these notions presumes a discrepant view of the literary present, differently marked by literary and political expectations of how the
present itself is about to evolve. It is difficult to decipher what impressions those
fluid literary landscapes made on readers at a time deeply shaped by the Cold
War and by worldwide movements of decolonization. What remains is an en-
cyclopedic juxtaposition of texts. The table of contents of *Yiwen / Shijie wenxue*
always included, in parenthesis, the country of origin of the writer, and one can
surmise that part of the editors' task was to make the selections as varied as possible. The list of included works had to be geographically comprehensive and encompass a rich florilegium of national literatures. Never before had the Chinese
world of letters undertaken such a comprehensive cataloguing enterprise, and
in terms of sheer range of authors, the journal probably offered a much larger
variety than any English-language journal of literary translation at the time.

However, with the notable exception of Latin American literature, which
was indeed discussed in detail, there was surprisingly little engagement with
the literature of recently decolonized countries. Poems from Angola, Senegal,
or Congo were treated as self-explanatory evidence of national emancipation.
Writers of less prestigious literature, then, were included only as representatives
of the nation to which they belonged. European and American authors, meanwhile, were chosen because of their internationalist stance or their commitment to social issues or their perceived artistic merit or importance. They were
generally discussed in ways that emphasized their problematic relation with
the general ethos of the capitalist world—as rebels or victims, but above all as
outsiders who, to deserve inclusion, needed to be politically or aesthetically at
odds with their environment. One conclusion we can reach, therefore, is that in
the socialist version of world literature, writers from different parts of the world

belonged to political and literary categories that were incommensurable: they were not always identified with their nation and could not be encompassed by one single hegemonic vision or hierarchy of style. It was the incommensurability engendered by the tension between the aesthetic and the political that created a space for readers to pick and choose among the available texts.

Although time matters to the world literary system, such time is never fully unified but is fractured and variably imagined in different localities that aspire to be at the center. The alleged present of world literature is split by the co-presence of multiple centers of literary exchange. The inherent anachrony of the world literary system made it possible for translation in socialist China to function as an anticipatory practice, an active reconfiguration of global spatiotemporal hierarchies that went beyond a mere perception of Chinese belatedness. To be sure, belatedness was an important concern, as reflected by the complaints on the inadequacies of modern Chinese literature voiced by Chinese critics in 1956–1957. The same concerns emerged again in the 1980s, as we shall see in the next chapter. But anticipation from the 1950s to the 1970s also manifested itself as an imagined solidarity with other nations that were, like China, advancing rapidly toward the future. Anticipation thus affected the selection of translated texts both as perceived belatedness and as vanguardism, each of them more dominant at particular historical junctures but coexisting simultaneously, as well. It involved not only temporal but also spatial configurations based on varying degrees of imagined proximity and distance.

Yiwen / Shijie wenxue's selections of foreign literature were neither the mechanical effect of state planning nor the response to hegemonic definitions of what counted as the "literary present." What counted as "new" in Paris, London, and New York did affect translators' selections, but far from simply being subjected to hierarchies established elsewhere, Chinese translators in the socialist period momentarily became the arbiters of "literary time," for once indicting French or American writers for being remnants of the past. This is, of course, a globally less influential "centrality" than that envisioned by Casanova. As much as *Yiwen / Shijie wenxue* may have inverted the Eurocentric order, Chinese translators' indictments had no effect on foreign writers: none of them struggled to become famous in Beijing as they might have struggled to make it in Paris.

3

ACCELERATING LITERARY TIME

Metropolitan Editors at Work

DESKS COVERED WITH MANUSCRIPTS, jars with drifting tea leaves, ashtrays filled with smoldering cigarette butts, and, in dangerous proximity, envelopes torn open and newspaper scraps wrapping the shells of sunflower seeds. This is how we might imagine the editorial office of a literary periodical in 1980s China, the central setting for this chapter. Editors working at such journals as *Shouhuo* (Harvest), *Zhongguo* (China), and *Beijing wenxue* (Beijing literature) played a crucial role in making a writer's career in the years between 1983 and 1990. Editors cultivated modes of writing that would testify to brisk literary change and help Chinese literature "reach out to the world" (*zou xiang shijie*). Their practices illustrate a mode of anticipation understood as a concern with how Chinese literature ought to move forward, which was not solely an aspect of discourse but was felt, embodied, built into institutional arrangements, and enacted in a variety of collaborative endeavors. This concern affected the timing of publication and the formation of literary trends, particularly of avant-garde fiction, and significantly shaped the professional lives of writers, editors, and critics.

Late 1980s avant-garde fiction has generally been considered a form of modernism critical of the discourse of modernity or, alternatively, as a Chinese postmodern undermining of realism.[1] These appraisals, which largely reproduce the claims of critics involved in manufacturing the avant-garde as a literary trend, overlook the extent to which a developmental vision of literature (in itself an important aspect of the discourse of modernity) and a reliance on state literary institutions facilitated its emergence. The assumption of a developmental trajectory from realism to modernism, intimately linked to the work of translation and hence to local visions of world literature discussed in Chapter 2, shaped editors' expectations and guided their selections. A horizon of global comparison and a futuristic rhetoric formed the backbone of editorial selections, which aimed to foster forms of writing that were national in their features, future in their orientation, and global in their reach.

The emergence of avant-garde fiction reflected an effort to consolidate a space for "pure" (*chun*) or "serious" (*yansu*) literature relatively autonomous not only from political pressures but also from those of an incipient cultural market. By the mid-1980s, various genres of popular literature (*tongsu wenxue*) had reemerged, with several new journals devoted to them.[2] "Pure/serious" literature has generally been discussed in isolation from these popular genres, as if they were stable, distinct categories.[3] However, what constituted the difference between them was a much-debated question at the time, when a complex process of diversification was under way and new boundaries were drawn between as well as within these categories. We will begin with popular literature because a diffuse preoccupation with its effects shaped how editors, critics, and writers redefined the tasks of serious literature.

Popular as Anachronism, or What Makes Serious Literature Serious

What exactly "popular literature" meant was a controversial issue in the mid-1980s that confirmed its unsettled place in modern Chinese literary discourse. In late imperial times, *tongsu* generally referred to works that could be understood by less educated people and that were valorized for their simplicity.[4] In the writings of May Fourth intellectuals, *tongsu* took on negative connotations, indicating cultural forms aimed at sheer entertainment disseminated through commercial venues and media.[5] The term continued to have conflicting associations in the following decades, ranging from the idealized authenticity of popular forms of storytelling promoted by such writers as Lao She to the conservatism of feudal culture criticized by Qu Qiubai and Mao Zedong. When diverse popular genres reemerged in the early 1980s, several critics hailed the phenomenon as a welcome sign of the diversification (*duoyuanhua*) of the literary field. The newly reemerging entertainment culture entailed a redefinition of private leisure in more personal and individualized terms—specifically, of reading as the reflection of the readers' personality, experience, and taste. Assessments of popular genres ranged widely. Some critics hailed them as long-overdue responses to readers' legitimate demands for entertainment, others sternly condemned their frivolous traits. Most actually did both. Critics felt compelled to distinguish between healthy and harmful forms of the popular, and discussions were in general more open to popular fiction than the condemnations of the 1920s and 1930s.

A debate published in *Dushu* (Reading) in May 1985 offers a glimpse of how prominent critics saw the resurgence of popular literature.[6] For Liu Zaifu, it was a sign of the normalization of democratic life and of improved material conditions as well as a response to the aesthetic needs of the people, which "serious literature" was not equipped to fulfill. Dai Qing similarly noted that popular literature was not to be denigrated as a lesser mode of writing; it was not a matter of high and low but simply of serving different tastes. A market demand for this kind of literature, she argued, had been there all along—what had been missing was supply. Whereas Dai mentioned the storyteller Liu Lanfang (whose performances of episodes from traditional novels, *pingshu*, were regularly aired on radio and TV) as the new heroine of popular culture, an editor from People's Literature Publishing House saw considerable continuity with the literature of the previous decades, recalling how, immediately before the onset of the Cultural Revolution, successful novels had been published in more than 3,000,000 copies.[7]

Noting that it was difficult to draw a clear line dividing popular from serious literature, several contributors generally contrasted the fantastic or marvelous character (*chuanqixing*) of popular literature with the realism of serious literature. According to these assessments, *chuanqi* (the marvelous) fell outside the boundaries of serious literature. And yet *chuanqi* itself was perceived as a heterogeneous mode cutting through high and low: the stories in *Tang and Song Tales of the Strange*, edited by Lu Xun, were deemed positive examples, different from the extravagant fiction filling bookstalls in the mid-1980s. Li Zehou specifically contended that the main characteristic of popular literature was "that it leaves reality [*xianshi*] behind, that it engages in nonrealistic fantasies like convoluted and bizarre cases, wonderful martial arts [*wuxia*] stories, . . . things that in daily life one would not encounter or imagine, things we enjoy when life is dull or exhausting."[8] Li upheld popular genres as a welcome sign of pluralization but deplored their excessive simplicity: they were a product for immediate consumption of no enduring consequence. Although generally supportive of popular literature, most critics concluded with cautionary words. Liu Zaifu noted that some forms of popular literature were absurd and vulgar. Because they did not pay sufficient attention to interiority and were too centered on plot, they shared the characteristics of primitive thought: they were simplistic and weird and had little artistic appeal. The masses needed them only because they did not have the means to apprehend more sophisticated forms. Liu also lamented that too many Chinese literary works were packed with action and marvels, while too few works engaged with deep thought. Thus, he urged writers to elevate people's taste and stay away from popular genres. Other critics, such as Jiang Hesen, argued that popularity per se was not a sign of lack of literary value. What was problematic were not popular works as such, which included all-time masterpieces that could reach a range of readers, but rather the extravagant and erotic stories that were taking hold of the market.[9]

Such debates were not new, of course. They resumed discussions on the moral perils of nonrealistic elements in fiction and drama that had regularly resurfaced throughout the twentieth century. Perhaps more intensely than in past instances, however, the split between popular and pure literature was accompanied by a discourse that arranged them along the axis of developmental time. Several critics identified the popular with the primitive: popular forms were symptoms of atavistic, less evolved tastes. They were an anachronism unfit for the present: "If such sensational titles as *The Headless Woman Corpse* are revived, the effects will be even broader. . . . If some vulgar [*yongsu*] works appeared in antiquity or in the West, they had their historical and social reasons, but for the Chinese living in the twentieth century, why should we repeat the barbarism of those past times? Wouldn't we be committing an epochal mistake if we went after bizarre and strange things like they did?"[10]

Popular literature was anachronistic, for it appealed to primitive instincts, primordial tastes, and uncivilized states of mind. Forms of "serious" literature were better equipped to endure the test of time and to sustain the scrutiny of a global readership. One of the first to address the relation between literature and consumerism explicitly was Wu Liang, among the most active critics in promoting young experimental writers in the mid-1980s. Wu wrote extensively on roots-seeking literature and on the avant-garde and collected these works in several anthologies. An omnivorous reader who never received formal college education, he worked closely with other editors and critics in Shanghai to "speed up" the development of contemporary Chinese literature.[11] In a 1985 essay, Wu defines popular literature as a collective product entirely determined by readers' needs. He emphasizes its time-sensitivity: it is nothing but an opportunistic response to the fleeting tastes of readers. Its reemergence may be a "historical necessity," but it also ought to be controlled; otherwise, it would lead to the "exhaustion" (*shuaijie*) of literature and culture.[12] Wu further discusses how the emergence of consumption exerted a deep influence on contemporary social life and constituted a challenge for literature. This did not mean, however, that literature was to "surrender to commercialization." Rather, he urges critics and writers to acknowledge these transformations and reflect on (serious) literature's role: "How can literature remain serious and pure? Faced with the transformations engendered in social life and in people's behaviors by the consumption wave, how can one generate an autonomous aesthetic response and participate with one's specific stance in a movement of social change that is violent and yet subtle in its influence?"[13]

Wu Liang's questions were repeatedly echoed in the following years: How were writers to respond to the massive transformations in social life generated by new modes of consumption? What did autonomy mean, and what forms could it take under the circumstances engendered by the development of a cultural market? Even though, by the early 1990s, notions of seriousness and purity were lampooned by such writers as Wang Shuo and by several critics, the problem of generating an "autonomous aesthetic response" has remained an enduring concern in the Chinese literary field. Wu's essay, along with the debates examined earlier, reminds us that it was the reemergence of popular genres and of a notion of readers as consumers that prompted critics and editors to reflect on what "serious literature" ought to look like. Wu's essay testifies to how, even in the 1980s, the autonomy of literature was an aspiration and a horizon, not a stable condition that was later eroded by the marketization of culture.

Timing, Passing On

The editors who contributed to the emergence of Chinese avant-garde fiction adopted various strategies, which I somewhat schematically identify as timing, passing on, cultivating youth, creating models, and grouping. Editors timed the publication of works that they felt were innovative and relevant, which created a sense of progressive stretching of limits, while in fact different writing modes coexisted at the same time. Timing often simply meant deferring the publication of certain works, but it occasionally also involved passing them on to editors based in other cities. Speeding up literary time occasionally involved slowing down publication. In a 2004 account, Cai Xiang, who was deputy chief editor of *Shanghai Literature* in the 1980s and 1990s,[14] recalls an example: when Ma Yuan, a writer who is generally considered a precursor of the avant-garde, sent his "Gangdisi de youhuo" (Under the spell of the Gangtise Mountains) to *Shanghai Literature* in August 1984, the story elicited contrasting reactions among the editors.[15] The journal had just published Ah Cheng's "Qi wang" (The king of chess) in the July 1984 issue, and the view prevailed that it was better to wait before publishing Ma Yuan's story. Cai Xiang continues: "After we published 'The King of Chess' there was a sort of trend in the direction of 'roots-seeking,' and then suddenly we got Ma Yuan's work with its strong modernist features, so we kept discussing it until the Hangzhou meeting [December 1984]. On that occasion we asked Li Tuo and Han Shaogong to take a look at it and they were both very positive. So we published it in the February 1985 issue."[16] Cai Xiang suggests that the editors delayed the publication of this work because they wanted to give readers time to focus on Ah Cheng's story, which was acclaimed for its embrace of Taoist philosophy and Chinese native narrative technique, and postpone publishing a text that exhibited "modernist" (that is, foreign) features. The debates on modernism had just subsided earlier that year, and drawing on Chinese traditional forms offered a safer avenue for pursuing formal experimentation.[17] Ma Yuan has a slightly different account of this episode. According to him, after he heard that *Shanghai Literature* was not going to publish his story, he sent it to Li Tuo through a common friend. It was Li Tuo who then brought it to the meeting in Hangzhou and recommended it for publication.[18] The discrepancies between the protagonists' accounts, however, do not alter the fact that editors postponed the publication of Ma Yuan's story or that, in doing so, they allowed nativist texts to receive more critical attention, which contributed to the successive timing and drawing of distinctions between "roots-seeking" and "avant-garde." As critic Wang Yao put it:

> In the usual narrative, the development of New Period literature follows this sequence: scar literature, literature of self-reflection, reform literature, roots-seeking, avant-garde, and so on. Such a narrative reflects the characteristics of "modernity." However, if we take "roots-seeking literature" and "avant-garde literature" as examples, we cannot but acknowledge that such trends are neither linked by a chronological relation nor do they form a unilineal literary history; to the contrary, trends and schools often coexist in symbiotic relation, clash, and intersect in ways that are both necessary and accidental. Therefore, while emphasizing temporality, we should not overlook the spatial dimension of literary

history. Only by taking both into account can we hope to narrate and record the overall complexity of the practices of literary discourse.[19]

In terms of style alone, Ma Yuan's story could well be read as an instance of roots-seeking fiction, in itself a heterogeneous category, showing that the contrast between "roots-seeking" and "avant-garde" is not clear-cut. "Under the Spell of the Gangtise Mountains" is set in Tibet and is divided into sections, some of which are told in the first person, some in the second, and some in the third. The narration is interspersed with speculative digressions, self-reflexive authorial interventions, and intertextual references ranging from Tibetan myths to William Faulkner's fiction. The use of multiple narrating voices and various authorial alter egos make it a modernist work similar to other texts of Chinese avant-garde fiction, but episodes of hunting, solitary travels amid breathtaking landscapes, and an encounter with a yeti—as well as the celebration of local customs and a blunt contrast between the Han protagonist's "abstract logic" and the "mythic thinking" that allegedly pervades all aspects of Tibetan life—resemble aspects of roots-seeking fiction. In many ways, Ma Yuan's hybrid features anticipate the modernist primitivism of Gao Xingjian's *Soul Mountain* (1990).

The editors of *Shanghai Literature* decided to publish Ma Yuan's story only after receiving the endorsement of an influential critic and a writer who were not connected with the journal; the incident offers an indication of the collaborative networks among editors of different journals and writers and Li Tuo's prominent role among them.[20] Writers regularly sent him manuscripts; many of the texts that were later considered canonical were published thanks to his recommendation. At literary symposia organized by the Chinese Writers' Association and at official meetings organized to discuss emerging writers, he advocated for their work. For example, after Mo Yan's *Touming de hongluobo* (The crystal carrot) was published in *Zhongguo zuojia* (Chinese writers) in February 1985, the Writers' Association vice-president and *Zhongguo zuojia* chief editor Feng Mu called for a meeting in Beijing to discuss it, and Li Tuo together with the writer Shi Tiesheng intervened in support of Mo Yan's work.[21] Li Tuo also helped Can Xue and Yu Hua publish their stories. He read Can Xue's "Canglao de fu yun" (Old floating cloud) in early 1984 and kept it for about a year. It was only after Wang Zhongchen, an editor at the journal *China*, told him that chief editor Ding Ling wanted to publish avant-garde literature that Li Tuo recommended the story for publication. Li Tuo recalls: "When I heard that Ding Ling wanted to publish avant-garde fiction I could hardly believe it. I thought she was a big name, she could withstand [pressure], so I took out 'Old Floating Cloud' and told them, this story is excellent, if you really want to publish avant-garde fiction you have to publish this. I told them that in the whole history of Chinese literature, nobody ever wrote like her. *China* then published it. I think I dealt quite well with this: I kept calm, kept waiting for an opportunity. I was determined to get the story published."[22]

Deciding when was a good moment to publish a work, then, was an important aspect of an editor's work, but because professional boundaries were relatively blurry, editors greatly relied on the advice of prominent critics and writers. Ma Yuan, for one, explicitly commented on his peers' work. His letters to *Harvest* editor Cheng Yongxin include several suggestions on whom to invite to submit to special issues, on the length of the contributions he should solicit from specific writers, and even who was worthy of receiving a literary prize.[23] Avant-garde fiction was a collaborative endeavor in which the lines dividing writers, editors, and critics were not sharply defined, but in which editors ultimately had the important role of determining when to speed up or delay publication.

Cultivating Youth, Deprovincializing Style

Editorial work in the 1980s encompassed a variety of tasks, including soliciting submissions from specific writers, inviting them to workshops, and assigning literary prizes. After Yu Hua submitted three stories to *Beijing Literature* in 1983, the chief editor Zhou Yanru phoned him on a November afternoon in his hometown Haiyan in Zhejiang province, where Yu Hua worked as a dentist, inviting him to Beijing to revise one of the stories he had submitted; they would pay travel expenses, lodging, and a fee of two yuan per day.[24] Thus, Yu Hua went to Beijing to revise the story "Xingxing" (Stars), which was published in January 1984, winning the *Beijing Literature* "outstanding work" literary prize that year. A short essay published a few months later reveals the difficulties that he encountered at the beginning of his career and the support he received from the editors, who continued to invite him to workshops in Beijing for the next couple of years.

The critics' main complaint against Yu Hua's early stories, in his account, was that they dealt with small everyday events that were unworthy of literary representation. More generally, critics questioned whether he had the proper life experience to become a writer. Was such a young person, who had had an uneventful life when compared to the Red Guard generation, mature enough to write fiction? Was it possible at all to write fiction without having gone through any hardship? Yu Hua responds, defining his work in contrast to that of writers of a slightly older generation:

> I am now twenty-four years old, didn't go to the countryside, and was never a worker. No matter how hard I think back, I didn't have to go through twists and turns and didn't have to endure any frustration. Life is as clear as a bright sky, as quiet as water. I had, of course, little bits of anger, little bits of happiness, little bits of worry, little bits of ups and downs. Therefore, I felt that I could only write about these "little bits"; only by doing so could I feel comforted.
>
> So comrades who care about me have spoken up. They said I am too narrow-minded, urging me to observe society from different perspectives and calling for more depth. In their dreams they even hoped that I'd be banished to Siberia! Me groaning and moaning and then crawling up again: this is all they want to see. But I never wanted to grasp or interpret the world. I never wanted to have Tolstoy's vision or García Márquez's style [*qipai*]. When I opened my eyes to look, all I saw was a child: guests were coming, and when his father went to open the door instead of him, he cried with a broken heart. Or a countryside teacher who comes to the city and is enthralled by the notice "Disco Training Class." I'm so hopeless! But I also don't want a hard life—though, in fact, I am in no position to decide how my experiences are going to be. Therefore, I can only console myself: a turbulent life is meaningful, but a quiet life is meaningful too. . . . The late Tang poet Sikong Tu in his masterwork on aesthetics, *Shipin*, repeatedly emphasizes the concept of "flavor" [*wei*]. This "flavor" is not the "deep structure" of Euro-American narrative theory. "Flavor" can only be experienced through emotions and does not involve deep thought. Simply put, it is a "mood" [*qingdiao*]. . . . Sikong Tu's "flavor" includes a feminine and a masculine side. I know that I lack masculine vigor, and I don't dare rush into writing the "manly literature" that is popular at the moment. I very much admire Zhang Chengzhi and Deng Gang, but I am aware that I can't match them, so all I can do is to earnestly write about my "little bits."[25]

Yu Hua styles himself as a writer of small things with a "feminine" voice, remote from such writers as Zhang Chengzhi, who was soon to be associated with "roots-seeking" fiction. By appealing to late Tang aesthetics, he presents himself as a writer of emotions rather than a philosophically inclined author or a plot-oriented storyteller.[26] Furthermore, he argues against the idea, common at the time, that personal suffering is an important precondition for literary creation. He belonged to a generation of latecomers, and it was editors at *Beijing Literature*, he says later on, who helped him emerge as a writer of "little bits." The editors helped him become a writer by singling out those of his stories that were more "at the forefront" than others. Indeed, if the journal as a whole had an important role in his career, editors were by no means uniform in their assessment of his works. Li Tuo, who was appointed deputy editor of *Beijing Literature* in June 1985, later commented that he was not impressed by Yu Hua's early attempts, such as "Kan hai qu" (Going to see the sea), a coming-of-age story illustrating the inversion of roles that occurs between parents and children when the children grow up, which was warmly recommended by editor Wang Hao.[27] It was only in 1986, when the writer was once again invited by *Beijing Literature* to a workshop in Beijing and asked to bring his drafts along, that he met Li Tuo's enthusiastic approval. Li Tuo's reading of "Shibasui chumen yuanxing" (Leaving home at eighteen), a story of young man's trip that suddenly turns into senseless violence, was a true turning point in Yu Hua's career: "At that time, Li Tuo for us literary youth was a sort of spiritual master: once you got his attention, you were bound to become famous. After I arrived in Beijing, I gave my story to the editors who were collecting manuscripts for the January 1987 issue. Li Tuo read it only after some time and came to see me just two days before I left. He liked it a lot and flattered me so much that I thought he was drunk. He said to me: 'I can tell you quite clearly: you are already walking at the very forefront of Chinese literature'" [*ni xianzai yijing zou zai Zhongguo wenxue de zui qianlie de*].[28] In an interview, Li Tuo also said that it was only upon reading "Leaving Home at Eighteen" that he felt that Yu Hua was making a breakthrough: "As I read it, I felt extremely excited; at that time I thought that this was finally the "modern story" I had been waiting for so long. In a certain sense, for me roots-seeking fiction was not particularly satisfying. This story was really great, so I went to see Yu Hua and told him: this story of yours is very important. I might have put it too strongly at that time, but I said that this was probably the beginning of a new way of writing."[29] Li Tuo's words possess an awkward combination of surprise and fulfillment of expectations, expressing a state of anticipation—"waiting for so long" for a "modern story" to emerge.

In Yu Hua's account, Li Tuo was especially surprised that someone who came from a small town could have written such a story. Yu writes that when Li Tuo asked for details on how he had come to write it, "I said I didn't know. I only knew that writing like that made me happy. A few days later, we were chatting again, and he asked me which books I had read; when I told him, he said: 'Now I get it!' Basically, we had read the same books! He thought that since I lived in Haiyan, I read less than their Beijing writers. That wasn't the case, and therefore I think that being a reader helped me a lot in becoming a writer."[30] Yu Hua's comment refers to one of Kafka's short stories that, by his account, inspired him to write "Leaving Home at Eighteen." While visiting a friend in Hangzhou in 1986, he and his friend went to a bookstore and purchased the recently published Kafka's *Collected Works*. Just one copy was left and his friend took it. Only after promising that in exchange he would send him four volumes of Tolstoy's works did his friend agree to let Yu Hua have the volume of Kafka's works. The story that most impressed him was "A Country Doctor":

> When I read "A Country Doctor," I was amazed. For instance, the way [Kafka] wrote about the horse was very different from the literature I was familiar with back then. The horse in that story appears three times, and every time without any background explanation; first, he says that the horse is not in the stall; then, in the following passage, he writes that the horse is doing this and that. How could he write this way? The whole piece is about that horse. Kafka's stories are precisely like this; he writes without ever giving an explanation. . . . From that moment on, I went from reading freely to narrating freely. This is how I wrote my first story that attracted attention in the Chinese literary field: "Leaving Home at Eighteen." At that time I really wanted to write but didn't know what. Then I read a news item in a newspaper regarding the theft of apples on a highway in Zhejiang, and I thought I'd write about that. I began to write, and when I got to the point that "my" bag was stolen, it was as if the narrative were generating itself, naturally. After writing it I felt very excited, for the story was completely different from my earlier works. But I still didn't have enough self-confidence. At that point I needed much encouragement; for a young person like me encouragement was especially important. At that time *Beijing Literature* had already changed its team; Lin Jinlan and Li Tuo were now in charge of the journal. That was also an important time in my life because it was then that I met Li Tuo.[31]

Li Tuo, of course, did not tell Yu Hua what to read or how to write. But his statement that "this was finally the modern story I had been waiting for so long" suggests that his reaction entailed a process of recognition shaped by the reading of foreign texts. Li Tuo's appreciation of Yu Hua's story as simultaneously novel and familiar suggests a shared horizon of expectation that led to privileging certain stories over others. Although critics have emphasized the sudden and shocking nature of the emergence of avant-garde fiction, this anecdote suggests that it was also the result of feelings of anticipation rooted in shared experiences of reading. This was a particular form of reading: it was fragmentary, random, and rapid. It did not entail any deep knowledge of the complete works of any particular author, yet it shaped editorial attitudes and led to the immediate recognition of certain authors and stories over others.

The textual features that characterize Yu Hua's short stories of the second half of the 1980s have been amply discussed by critics.[32] I wish, however, to point out the process whereby he became this kind of writer, the personal encounters, institutional settings, and the readings that made his early career. Becoming an avant-garde writer, in Yu Hua's case, required his undergoing a process of "deprovincialization,"[33] in the sense of not only physically leaving his hometown and going to such urban centers as Hangzhou and Beijing but also leaving behind the quiet tone of his early works and learning to write in a cosmopolitan modernist style characterized by fragmentariness and juxtaposition of contrasting images, without logical explanation of cause and effect. Becoming an avant-garde writer meant learning to write of the minute events, family relations, and generational conflicts that he had depicted in his early stories in estranging ways, physically deforming objects and landscapes and revealing an uncontrollable violence erupting from routine gestures and apparently peaceful existences.

Editors often invited writers to participate in workshops organized by journals and by the Chinese Writers' Association, which were important avenues of professionalization. This is not surprising in itself: Michel Hockx has pointed out the importance of friendship and personal networks in early twentieth-century Chinese literature, and Perry Link has discussed how Chinese state literary institutions contributed to the professionalization of writers in the PRC.[34] It is striking, however, that several avant-garde writers were discovered in such contexts, suggesting that avant-garde fiction was a collective endeavor in which editors and state literary institutions played crucial roles. In this sense, avant-garde fiction did not appear suddenly. Rather, it was cultivated, manufactured, even expected. It was the result of close collaborations between editors and writers who were looking for ways to speed up "literary time" by drawing on a transnational repertoire of literary styles.

The writer Sun Ganlu was discovered by editors of *Shanghai Literature* and "cultivated" by the Shanghai branch of the Writers' Association, but in his case too Li Tuo played an important role. After graduating from high school in 1976, Sun attended the Technical Institute for Post and Telecommunication for two years and took up work at the Shanghai Post Office in 1979. He published some short pieces in 1982–1983, thanks to the help of friends who introduced him to some minor literary journals, and in 1984 he sent a story to *Shanghai Literature*. The editorial board invited him to talk to them: he was very talented, editors told him, but his stories were "too different from the normal way of writing" and could not be published. At this point Sun felt he had no perspective as a writer and tore all his stories into pieces.[35] Only a year later, however, the Shanghai Writers' Association invited Sun to participate in a three-month training course for young writers. In these three months, Sun joined in with thirty other aspiring writers from various professional backgrounds (Sun himself was still a postman) attending classes and meeting older writers, literary critics, and editors, such as Chen Sihe, Wang Xiaoming, Xu Zidong, Wu Liang, Han Shaogong, and Li Tuo, as well as representatives of the Writers' Association. At the end of the course, the participants were asked to turn in a story for publication in *Shanghai Literature*. Sun Ganlu submitted "Fangwen mengjing" (Visit to dreamland), which met with mixed reactions. When editors were still undecided on whether to publish it, Li Tuo took the story to Beijing where he recommended it for publication in *China*. The story was reportedly already in press when a phone call arrived from *Shanghai Literature*, saying that Sun Ganlu was *their* writer and that they had priority in publishing his story. The story therefore was mailed back to Shanghai and was published in a "special section" devoted to writers who had attended the course.[36]

"Visit to Dreamland" is a collage of narratives told by different personae, with allusions to real and invented texts and with several self-reflexive moments, the most hilarious of which is perhaps the "antinarrative festival" that takes place in a labyrinthine orange grove. The festival is described as a carnivalesque event celebrating freedom from the constraints of "narration":

> Throughout the past history of the orange grove, on the day of the antinarrative festival the dead used to come back from each corner of Paradise and Hell to take a cold bath in the pond of the paper-cut courtyard. Therefore, the antinarrative festival became the holiday when all the dead and the living would meet. Because the meeting took place in the bathhouse, both parties convened naked. The only difference was that the dead came with a bared soul, while the living came with a bared body. This custom has lasted to this very day, and for a young man like me coming from the outside and inexperienced in the ways of the world, the antinarrative festival meant revelation. In short, it was a sexy feast.[37]

The humor of this and similar passages in Sun Ganlu's fiction has generally gone unnoticed, as if "avant-garde" were incompatible with hilarity. In this story, deformed leftovers of the historical past reappear in an irreverent dream-like space. Sun Ganlu's writing relies on extended adjectival sentences, on elaborate and abstract wording that mocks well-established literary formulas and political jargon.[38] Some passages about ancestors are parodies of narratives of a glorious family past; others contain references to revolutionary history as well as to the discourse of eugenics. Humorous effects are created through the manipulation of set sentences and clichés (often literal translations of English idioms) and rapid shifts from the metaphorical to the literal, as in the parallel between the "bared soul" and the "bared body." The story is also rich in images of transformation, as in the sentence: "Her [the Goddess of Abundance's] breath became a dress with which I covered myself; in the darkness dimly lit by the moon and the stars, it protected me and also bound me."[39] Such quasi-mythological images are juxtaposed with trivial dialogues, which further contributes to the humorous effect.

Critics have frequently commented on the provocative character of Sun's linguistic experimentation. Chen Xiaoming, for instance, has called him "the most extreme provocateur of this age, who so stubbornly walks in a world of ornate diction [cizao], disdaining conventional life and paying no heed to traditional rules and norms."[40] Sun Ganlu thus epitomizes the self-reflexive play of signifiers that Chen attributes to China's avant-garde in general: the triumph of language over the world or, more precisely, the annihilation of the referential world by language itself. In Chen's view, Sun Ganlu's sentences "do not refer to the world; they have no connection with real life; they have lost the signified and only refer to themselves. These heavily loaded 'crowds of signifiers' are the grave of the story and the annihilation of reality." Sun Ganlu's writing, Chen goes on to say, is about nothing concrete; it merely illustrates the process of writing.[41] Although Sun's parodic use of language and his frequent references to illustrations and photographs attract attention to the intermedial character of his writing, one also finds mentions of the "heart" or "interiority" (neixin) of the narrator/writer, described as "dreamy," "dream-like," or "chaotic" and equated with the imagination. "Visit to Dreamland" thus raises a question about the relationship between literary language and the world of imagination.

In an essay titled "Writing and Silence," which includes quotations from Kafka, Borges, and Donald Barthelme, Sun Ganlu argues that "writing seems to be not the attempt to produce a voice but rather the attempt *not* to produce one."[42] The proliferation of images that characterizes his writing is aimed at silencing the writer's "ordinary" voice and at creating a lyrical diction that might approximate his interiority or provide a code for reading it.[43] Intertextuality, in this perspective, does not so much disconnect the signifier from the referent (as suggested by Chen Xiaoming) as aim at conveying a dreamlike interiority that constitutes the primary referent of literary language. "Visit to Dreamland" is not so much an affirmation of the preeminence of textuality over "experience" as it is an attempt to create an anarchic code through which the world of imagination and dream can be approximated.[44] In the final analysis, however, this attempt fails because, as stated by the narrator in "Visit to Dreamland," "imagination has its own language. We can only hint at its relations with the objects that surround it, but we cannot convey it. The objects in the imagination resist our ornate diction [*cizao*]."[45]

How to understand the relation between language and reality and between verbal expression and the writer's interiority was one of the issues of contention among avant-garde writers, editors, and critics. Sun Ganlu's formal experimentation was appreciated by several critics, but it appeared to some of his peers to be too disconnected from the "real world" and hence too bold. In his letter to *Harvest* editor Cheng Yongxin, Ma Yuan recommended "Visit to Dreamland" for a literary prize but also expressed reservations: "I just read Sun Ganlu's 'Visit to Dreamland'; it is really quite fine, I think I'd give my first prize to him, especially for its language. His imagination is quite something [*hen keyi de*]. However, if he keeps going on this way, he'll lead fiction into a blind alley [*ba xiaoshuo xiejinle si hutong*]. Why does he follow in Virginia Woolf's footsteps, why does he deliberately make things difficult for readers? Anyway, the quality is not bad, the feeling for language is good, what do you think? If you don't mind, give the five hundred yuan to him."[46]

Ma Yuan, a writer a few years older who had begun to publish a couple of years earlier than Sun, was generally quite vocal in his letters both in promoting his own works and in expressing opinions on his peers and younger writers. A few months later, in a letter commenting on Sun Ganlu's story "A Postman's Letter," Ma Yuan writes, "I couldn't actually read Sun's piece to the end. Even just saying it, I really feel I'm being unfair to my brother Ganlu. But there's really no way [I can read it]."[47] The differing reactions that Sun Ganlu elicited from editors, critics, and peers shows how controversial his role was within the emerging group of avant-garde writers. Some editors and critics endorsed Sun's texts, but their fragmentariness was considered extreme even by his peers. Even though editors supported formal experimentation, they were also concerned about not alienating their journal's readership; this concern was shared even by some avant-garde writers, thus limiting the space granted to such authors as Sun Ganlu.[48]

The 1980s literary journals and the various branches of the Writers' Association "cultivated" aspiring young writers through trips to the metropolitan centers of Beijing and Shanghai, personal conversations, and invitations to writing workshops, as well as literary prizes. Getting the attention of an editor was a crucial step in the process of becoming a writer. If Li Tuo had an important role in promoting Can Xue, Yu Hua, and Sun Ganlu, he was only one among several committed editors who endorsed young authors in the mid- and late 1980s, many of whom remain unacknowledged. For Ge Fei (Liu Yong, b. 1964), the first important publication came after a fortuitous meeting with editor Wang Zhongchen, who was traveling in Shanghai looking for manuscripts by young authors for the journal *Zhongguo* (China).[49] It is to this short-lived literary journal that I now turn, for it exemplifies the forward-oriented rhetoric that many editors adopted in justifying the publication of young authors. Its complex interaction with the Writers' Association illustrates the fluid and at times antagonistic relations between state institutions and editors committed to promoting young writers.

China: A Journal for the Youth

Many writers who emerged in the mid-1980s, including Ge Fei, Bei Cun, Can Xue, Liu Heng, and Xu Xing, started their careers by publishing in *China*, a journal especially devoted to the publication of young authors.[50] *China* started as a bimonthly in January 1985 under the editorship of Ding Ling; it became a monthly a year later but then was shut down in December 1986, a few months after Ding Ling's death. Though short-lived, the journal was quite successful, with a monthly distribution of 100,000 copies.[51] Initially, Ding Ling wanted to set up a "privately run and government funded" (*minban gongzhu*) publication, a journal initiated and managed by writers and/or editors rather than by party or state organizations, but still relying on public funding. The cultural authorities did not agree and decided that the journal would be under the direct supervision of the Chinese Writers' Association; it did, however, enjoy more autonomy than other journals and was apparently also looked on with more suspicion.[52] *China* published poetry, fiction, literary criticism, and translations of foreign fiction, as well as works from Taiwan, Hong Kong, and overseas Chinese writers.[53]

In the controversial memorandum published in the last issue of December 1986, the editors stated:

> In all conscience, we were engaged in a task that we considered sacred. . . . We received large quantities of manuscripts and devoted all our attention to discovering and cultivating promising literary youth. . . . Initially, we tried to get a grip on the developing trends of Chinese literature by focusing on poetry. . . . But when the story by the young writer Can Xue, "Old Floating Clouds," arrived on our desks after having passed from hand to hand and after many twists and turns, we felt that a phenomenon that contemporary literature could not avoid had already emerged; we had the responsibility to make space for it in our pages.[54]

China's editors justified their choices by appealing to the "inevitability" of literary phenomena. Much as Li Tuo had greeted Yu Hua's "Leaving Home at Eighteen" as a long-awaited "modern story," the editors understood their task as recognizing an announced future, catching writers who shared common traits with international modernism at the moment of their inevitable emergence. "Future" is a word that often appears in the editorial comments that prefaced each issue: "Our focus of attention [*zhuoyandian*] is the future: the future of literature, the future of the country, the future of the nation, the future of humanity. And the future rests on the shoulders of us all, especially on the shoulders of our youth."[55] The February 1986 issue, which includes this comment, contains Ge Fei's first short story, as well as poems by Duoduo, Jiang He, Bei Dao, and others. The almost equal space devoted to short fiction and poetry suggests close relations between the two genres at this time. The search for autonomy and professional specialization in the literary field meant a restructuring of the relations between literary genres, with editors and writers emphasizing affinities between fiction (especially short- and medium-length) and poetry, a development that will be discussed in Chapter 4.[56]

China was closed down after Ding Ling's death in 1986 not only because of decreased tolerance for literary experimentation but also because the Writers' Association cut back on publications devoted to short fiction and poetry in favor of those devoted to the novel. The editors' memorandum, which was published in most but not all of the copies of the last issue of the journal,[57] emphasized the political aspects of the dispute, suggesting that its closing was an act of political repression by the Writers' Association not too different from the literary persecutions of the past. The memorandum is frank and confrontational, and the complaints against the Writers' Association are explicitly stated. First, the editors pay homage to Ding Ling, recalling her efforts in setting up the publication. They acknowledge the Chinese Writers' Association's initial support but point out that increasing pressure was already put on their work before Ding Ling's death. After she died, the Writers' Association refused to appoint a successor to the chief editor, stopped financing the printing, publishing, and distribution of the journal, and just notified deputy editor Niu Han that a meeting would be held to discuss "*China*'s problem." The meeting did not take place, and the many letters the editors wrote to the Writers' Association "ended up like clay oxen in the sea—they disappeared into nothing, leaving people without a clue."[58] Eventually, *China*'s editorial board received a phone call from the Writers' Association, telling them not to sign the contract with the post office for the following year's distribution; another phone call a few days later ordered them to relinquish all rights of publication. The memorandum concludes in a tragic tone by quoting the line "I want to proclaim that we are innocent before we wither and fall" by the writer Ah Long, who had died in prison in 1967 but was then rehabilitated in the early 1980s.[59]

In response to the defiant tone of *China*'s editors and supporters, the Writers' Association issued only a brief statement, which formally announced that *China* was being "restructured" (*tiaozheng*) and that a quarterly for long fiction with the same name would be published by Zuojia chubanshe (Writers Publishing House) starting in January 1987. The decision was justified by emphasizing the need for a publication focusing on long fiction, including "biographical literature" (*zhuanji wenxue*). Furthermore, the statement suggested that *China* was redundant because the association itself already issued *People's Literature*.[60]

As noted earlier, *China* was closed down partly because of conflicts about which genres should be granted space and funding. The Writers' Association favored novels over short fiction and poetry. Other Beijing-based literary magazines that published experimental short stories by young writers also came under attack, however, between the second half of 1986 and the first half of 1987.[61] In the meantime, *Harvest* was establishing itself as one of the most prestigious journals in the Chinese literary field, thanks to the protection of the chief editor, Ba Jin. Editor Cheng Yongxin, who had worked there since 1983, played a central role in forming a group of avant-garde writers.

Creating Models and Grouping

The literary bimonthly *Harvest* resumed publication in 1979, with Ba Jin as chief editor and Ba Jin's daughter, Li Xiaolin, as de facto editor, and has since relied entirely on subscriptions and retail sales. The journal was initially successful in attracting readers, but by the mid-1980s *Harvest* found itself competing with a growing number of literary periodicals that published popular reportage literature exposing problems arising from the economic reforms.[62] According to Cheng Yongxin, it was Ba Jin, who did not engage in the daily routine of editorial work, who insisted that the journal should pursue the path of "pure literature" (by which he meant formal experimentation) rather than touch on contemporary political events or social problems.[63] Ba Jin's protection ensured that *Harvest* could publish formally audacious texts and be spared the criticism that several other journals incurred between 1986 and 1990.[64] In a published interview, Yu Hua comments on the importance of *Harvest* at this critical juncture: "I felt quite hopeless at that time. 'Leaving Home at Eighteen' had been published by Li Tuo in *Beijing Literature*, and I had also given them some other stories including '1986.' But suddenly the whole situation changed and in about a year's time all the writings I wanted to publish got rejected. . . . The good thing was that soon afterward, suddenly, it all changed back again. It was during this time of transformation that Li Tuo told me: 'What other journals do not dare to publish, *Harvest* probably will.' So he took all the texts that were rejected elsewhere and submitted them to *Harvest*, and they all came out."[65]

Cheng Yongxin took up his editorial position at *Harvest* in 1983, soon after graduating from Fudan University in Shanghai. In his first few years as editor, Cheng avidly read literary journals from all over China, looking for innovative stories by young writers.[66] At that time, he felt that a "literary revolution" was underway and was determined to make *Harvest* the key protagonist of that revolution. In addition to offering detailed advice on how to write, Cheng reached out to lesser known writers to solicit their submissions. He curated special issues that grouped writers together in distinctive new trends, creating the sense that brisk generational change was under way from one year to the next, and he collaborated with editors at different journals and publishing house to discover new talent.[67] Unlike other literary periodicals, *Harvest* did not assign editors to specific geographical areas, so Cheng and his colleagues found themselves working with writers from all over China. For writers, collaboration with Cheng not only ensured exposure to a national audience but also often led to better work arrangements at the local level. For instance, for the Jiangxi writer Ding Bogang, who wrote fiction in the little time he could take off from teaching, the publication of two stories in *Harvest* led to a three-year contract as a professional writer at the local literary institute of the Writers' Association, which allowed him to devote all his time to writing.[68]

Among the stories that Cheng read in the mid-1980s, he was particularly struck by those by Tashi Dawa (Zhaxi Dawa in Chinese) and other young Tibetan writers who appeared in the June 1985 special issue of *Tibetan Literature* (*Xizang wenxue*) on "magical fiction" (*mohuan xiaoshuo*). Cheng comments:

> Their works were not very well-written, they were immature and heavily imitating Latin American literature, but I thought that these writers had talent, and that if only they could find a Chinese way . . . China's own national way to express those things [*Zhongguo ren de fangfa . . . Zhongguo ziji de minzu fangfa lai biaoxian naxie dongxi*] they could certainly get very good results. So I wrote them a letter, saying that I had read their works, and that I urged them to find a more "Chinese" way to express themselves. I addressed the letter to Tashi Dawa, whom I knew personally, and he then passed on the letter to seven or eight other writers. They got very excited that we were paying attention to them.[69]

Tashi Dawa's writing was imitative, Cheng noted, but it provided a good starting point if it could be sinified. Cheng did not elaborate on what this would entail, but by writing this letter, the metropolitan editor urged peripheral writers to emphasize their local roots rather than their affinities with international trends.[70] In his response to Cheng, Tashi Dawa stressed that "magical realism" was merely a label tagged on by local editors, not something he or his peers identified with.[71] Subsequently, Cheng asked Li Xiaolin, the deputy editor, to let him collect a few works into a "special issue" (*zhuanhao*) that he would edit, to be published in late 1987. Li Xiaolin agreed, and Cheng solicited submissions from Ma Yuan, Ge Fei, Hong Feng, Tashi Dawa, and others.[72] Such special issues were published for three years, from 1987 to 1989. According to Cheng Yongxin, it was thanks to them that these writers quickly became famous; publishing in *Harvest* meant that all other literary journals competed for their works. In Ge Fei's words: "*Harvest* was a well-established journal. . . . Generally speaking, they were very selective and only published texts by famous writers. But starting from the mid-1980s, Li Xiaolin entrusted the last issue of each year to the young editor Cheng Yongxin. So, while the first five issues published works by very authoritative writers, in the last issue of the year Cheng Yongxin would collect texts by young writers. *Harvest*'s influence comes from these yearly last issues."[73]

Although the editor of *Harvest* claimed that those writers became famous because of the journal, Ge Fei suggests that the reverse was also true, that the journal became more influential because of them. Be that as it may, it is puzzling that nothing in the layout of *Harvest*'s year-end issues from 1987 to 1989 suggests that they were "special." Indeed, quite a few of the short stories by young writers who came to be considered avant-garde, such as Ma Yuan, Hong Feng, Yu Hua, Su Tong, Sun Ganlu, were already published in the fifth issue of 1987.[74] A letter by Yu Hua addressed to Cheng suggests that both the fifth and the sixth issues were special only in the sense that they were entirely edited by Cheng Yongxin, and not because of their design or content. Referring to the forthcoming special issue of 1988, Yu Hua wrote to Cheng, "I have been hoping that there would be such a collection of fiction—a collection of 'radical' fiction. It seems that all the anthologies of quality published in China now try to cover each single aspect and topic. I feel that the one you'll edit will be different: yours will not bother to offer an 'objective and complete' picture of contemporary fiction but will have to demonstrate a kind of force, an extreme force. Just like the no. 5 issue of last year. I'll be truly happy if I can be included."[75]

According to Cheng's own account, the special issues attracted more readers and writers to the journal, and in early 1988 writers specifically asked to be included in the last issue of the year. Other editors also reacted enthusiastically: "At that time, Li Tuo wrote me a letter saying 'with this plan of yours you are making the epoch.' At that time, his words were explosive, like cluster bombs."[76] The special issues were meant to provide models of brisk generational change. Yu Hua was featured in most of them, but every year a few new writers were introduced. In his correspondence with Cheng, Yu Hua expressed some preoccupation with the direction avant-garde fiction was taking in the writings of younger authors. In a letter dated June 9, 1989, the writer's advice to the editor conveys anxiety about the degeneration of literary language:

Hello Yongxin:

Thanks for your letter. In April I went to Xinjiang and Tibet, and in May returned to Beijing. On June 6 I escaped from Beijing and came to spend some time in Shijiazhuang. [The journal] *The Great Wall* arranged for me to live here, therefore I sat down to write a story for them.

I'd still like to be included in this year's issue no. 6, though the fact that you still want me in utterly surprised me. For you, for *Harvest*, I'll do my best to turn in a manuscript by the end of September.

Your plan to turn to another group of people is excellent. Indeed, now there's already a newer group of writers. But I worry that avant-garde fiction, which has only just emerged—you are the main manufacturer [*zhizaozhe*] of avant-garde fiction; I am your commodity [*shangpin*]—will be pushed into an odd corner because of the efforts of a group of vulgar critics and immature writers. The new generation of writers seems to be increasingly concerned about language— they seek to achieve a sort of delight by intensely pushing Chinese language to the limit. I am not opposed to this, but language exists to confront the world [*miandui shijie*]. Now the language of some texts seems to lack authenticity [*zhenshi*], which results in 'passing off fish eyes for pearls' within avant-garde fiction. It's also a real pity that some writers don't have much of a knack for narrative structure. That's why I like Ge Fei so much. I think that both in language and in structure, Ge Fei not only created a new attitude [*zitai*] in Chinese-language fiction but also found an authentic way of expressing [*zhenshi de biaobai*] his personal thought. Therefore, I think that your editing of this issue is probably going to be slightly more onerous. Now those who use the words "shallow and devoid of substance" to describe avant-garde fiction are not without their reasons.[77]

Yu Hua's tone in this letter is more intimate and self-assured than in his previous correspondence, testifying to a literary friendship that had grown over time. Like Ma Yuan, he offers his frank advice to the editor, showing that professional boundaries between editors and writers could be quite blurred. His preoccupation with language also recalls Ma Yuan's comments on Sun Ganlu's stories, while his use of economic terms ("you are the main manufacturer of avant-garde fiction; I am your commodity") suggests his awareness that their work was enmeshed in an emerging literary market. How the relation between language and reality should be understood and how far writers should go in constructing implausible verbal worlds were issues that were dividing experimental writers. For Yu Hua, the radical language game was not the direction Chinese literature should take. In many ways, his observations date back to the debates on modernism and obscure poetry of the early 1980s, but they seem quite at odds with Yu Hua's own experimental stories. Perhaps more than the rehearsal of a debate on literary language is involved: Yu's preoccupation seems to indicate a perception of an accelerated generational change—the anxiety of an avant-garde writer being superseded barely a couple of years from his emergence thanks to the same editorial strategies that had brought him to fame.

Although the late 1980s special issues of *Harvest* contributed to the making of an avant-garde, other anthologies and journals contributed as well.[78] Some of the writers included in the special issues were, in fact, never considered avant-garde. This does not detract from the importance of editors such as Cheng Yongxin and many others who carried out their work in relative obscurity and whose names survive only in the faded pages of journals. Compiling anthologies, as suggested by Yu Hua's letters, was an important part of editorial work. Cheng's activity of grouping writers continued with the publication of the anthology *Zhongguo xinchao xiaoshuo xuan* (*Selected Chinese new wave fiction*) in 1989,[79] followed a year later by the collection *Zhongguo xianfeng xiaoshuo* (*Chinese avant-garde fiction*), edited by Zhu Wei, a prominent editor and literary critic who wrote the monthly column "A Glance at the Newest Fiction" (Zui xin xiaoshuo yi pie) in the journal *Reading*.[80] While Cheng Yongxin had used the generic term "new wave fiction" and included a broad number of writers, Zhu Wei used the term "avant-garde" (*xianfeng*) and only included stories by Yu Hua, Ge Fei, Su Tong, and Ye Zhaoyan (two or three stories by each of them); furthermore, Zhu wrote much more extended commentaries than those that Cheng had included in his anthology. Although Zhu Wei's anthology had a circulation of only 1,500 copies, it contributed to determining who was avant-garde and who was not.

By no means did "avant-garde" fiction indicate a homogeneous style or ideology of language. As I have shown, editors and writers disagreed on questions of referentiality and on the extent to which they ought to reach out to readers. As the special issue format suggests, the avant-garde as an identifiable group of writers emerged out of editorial practices. At a time of accelerated succession of literary trends, distinctive positions consolidated quickly and were quickly superseded by new ones. Thus, editors helped establish an avant-garde canon at the very moment of its formation.

Conclusion

The interviews, letters, and oral accounts discussed in this chapter are at times contradictory; mostly from the 2000s, they are inflected by the professional anxieties of that era rather than from an earlier time. It is possible, indeed likely, that editors and writers nostalgically emphasize their own role and that of literary journals in the 1980s because this medium and the literary professions revolving around it are now perceived to be in decline. Nevertheless, the letters between Cheng Yongxin and writers as well as the writers' own recollections do testify to a literary economy based on intense collaborative efforts to make space for formal experimentation. This was a time of literary acceleration, and editors at major journals were the main force behind it.

Although the editors' tactics of timing publication, passing work on, cultivating youth, creating models, and grouping writers contributed to the creation of literary distinctions in 1980s China, the motivations behind specific choices remain elusive. Why did *China* editors write that Can Xue's "Old Floating Clouds" was "a phenomenon that contemporary literature could not avoid"? What was it in Yu Hua's "Leaving Home at Eighteen" that made it a long-awaited modern story? To some extent, these stories share stylistic traits, such as fragmentariness and lack of narratorial explanations, that make it possible to argue that these works represent a Chinese version of cosmopolitan modernism or, depending on how one understands the terms, postmodernism. In this sense, claims about their "inevitability" reflect a developmental understanding of literary history as it advances from realism to modernism. The observation that Chinese writers in the 1980s were catching up with literary developments that they felt had already happened elsewhere summons up the ghost of belatedness. Even though in terms of language and historical content there is nothing emulative in these stories, and even though modernist formal features were certainly not being introduced to Chinese language writing for the first time, a sense of having fallen behind permeates literary debates in the 1980s and contemporary discussions of Chinese modernism and postmodernism. Therefore, instead of sidestepping the problem of belatedness by stressing these stories' unique historical content, I suggest that belatedness itself can be productively rethought as a mode of anticipation. The notion of belatedness involves subordinating local temporalities to universal standards: it assumes that *elsewhere* things have happened or will happen on time. Anticipation, however, is unconcerned with punctuality but calls attention to the collaborative practices through which a literary form is recursively recognized as timely—that is to say, as the most appropriate response to the needs of a particular historical moment. Such a notion retains a sense of "not yet happened," but instead of suggesting a linear path along which Chinese writers and editors were trying to catch up, it foregrounds the processes of recognition of the new and revolutionary in the old and familiar, as well as the not-quite-conscious and unpredictable aspects of such processes.

Pierre Bourdieu has suggested that practice is *"protensive* in character," and that "a pre-reflexive—that is, unconscious—aiming at the forthcoming is the most common form of the experience of time."[81] The protensive dispositions and actions described in this chapter were shaped by experiences of reading and generated an acceleration of literary time, as well as the emergence of a new literary terminology through which editors and critics inaugurated a rapid succession of literary trends, or "newest certified present[s]."[82] Editors' efforts to create a specifically literary temporality was aimed at furthering the autonomy of the literary professions against both the market and the state. The struggle for autonomy involved seeking independence from institutions such as the Writers' Association while still relying on its initiatives and structures and also involved promoting "serious literature" amid rising commercialization while transforming the very features of what "serious literature" meant. In this context, the "autonomy" of the writer was not only a personal need but also one of the necessary preconditions for creating literary works that best represented the nation. For Chinese literature to "reach out to the world," it had to be "destatalized" and collectively individualized (in the sense that a unique, personal style became a requirement for recognition as a leading Chinese writer) at the same time that it was reinforced in its cultural traits. This process of destatalization was carried out by a handful of committed editors, who, paradoxically, worked mostly in state institutions.

The late 1980s was a period of transition in the economic lives of writers. High expectations mingled with a sense of impending crisis for professionals whose niches were potentially endangered, or at least not particularly favored, by the new market economy. Anita Chan has described how by the mid-1980s hopes placed on the economic reforms had turned sour, giving way to a widespread sense of frustration among urban dwellers, especially intellectuals, who felt that modernization had done little to increase their salaries and improve their living conditions. As we have seen in Chapter 1, writers and other intellectuals were particularly vocal in claiming that mental laborers deserved better compensation than manual workers.[83] There is no doubt that the marketization of literature intensified only after 1992, but even though there was no full-fledged literary market to speak of in the 1980s, economic considerations were the order of the day. A new voluntary copyright agreement, signed by forty-two literary journals in January 1985, is evidence of the competition among periodicals and efforts to regulate the economic dynamics of publishing. In the agreement (which came into force seven years before China joined the Berne

Convention), journals promised not to publish pirated versions from other journals and to resist reuse or adaptation by third parties without previous permission.[84] Furthermore, the question of what kind of economic compensation intellectuals could or should expect for their work was widely debated in the media. In this respect, discussions of how literature ought to address the transformations brought about by consumption proceeded in parallel with discussions of the future of intellectuals and their relationship with the emerging "commodity economy."[85] It is in this context that editors helped redefine literary value in ways that were ideally autonomous from both state and market.

To conclude with a caveat: attributing agency to any single professional group in the literary field inevitably raises the question that we encountered in Cheng Yongxin's and Ge Fei's contrasting views. Was it *Harvest* that made the writers famous or the writers who made *Harvest* relevant? It is important to reiterate that the literary professions were relatively fluid: the editors discussed in this chapter were also literary critics, and some of them wrote fiction and poetry. Established writers could respond to editors' recommendations with confidence and even assume the role of patron and protector for their friends. Rather than undertaking the impossible task of assigning a definitive point of origin for literary change, then, this chapter has foregrounded the social and institutional settings and the personal relationships that shaped 1980s literary production. Literary writing remained a solitary creative task, yet it was thanks to dense personal networks centered on editors and journals that manuscripts became published texts, and it was editors, more than anyone else, who determined which writers, texts, and trends were at the forefront.

4

FUTURES EN ABYME

Poetry in Strange Loops

IN GE FEI'S NOVELLA *JINSE* (Brocade zither, 1993), a literatus by the name of Feng Zicun goes to the provincial capital to take the imperial examination.[1] The year is 1586, and Feng has been preparing for the exam for more than a decade. The narrator comments: "Like many scholars who live in the sole company of books, Feng Zicun completely trusted the classics. To his mind, all the knowledge of his ancient country was excellent, perfect: it not only made you grasp the logic of things, gave you a thorough understanding of life and death, and made you aware of your role in society, but also offered refuge from dangers and disasters."[2] The irony of this passage becomes evident as the story unfolds: accumulating knowledge, of course, does not shield one from disasters. As Feng Zicun enters the examination hall, he begins to feel that those long years of study have been "an absurd mistake." To his dismay, the theme of the exam is the poem "Jinse." "Such a title is really out of place," Feng thinks. "Apart from the mediocre octave by Li Shangyin, which he knew very well, he couldn't recall any historical figure or event that could be related to it. . . . What kind of joke was this?"[3] His tutor had instructed him in Confucian teachings, expecting that the exam would revolve around such topics as human relations and celestial principles, the three cardinal guides and the five constant virtues. The rare times that candidates were required to write about poetry, they would be asked to comment on verses from the *Shijing* (Book of songs) or by the famous Du Fu and Li Bai. Feng Zicun concludes that his teacher was right when he said, "in today's academic circles there is no learning left to speak of," as was the prostitute who had told him that "the age of scholars is long gone."[4] In a daze, he rewrites the two final verses of Li Shangyin's poem, goes back to the temple where he lodges, and hangs himself. How this fictional representation of poetry rewriting should be read is the central question addressed in this chapter, which contrasts the rhetoric of the future in 1980s Chinese literary discourse examined in the preceding chapter with recursive temporal structures in short stories and novellas from the 1980s and early 1990s. The main mode of anticipation in these texts, I suggest, is anxiety, born out of feelings of loss and precariousness only partially soothed by the writing and reading of poetry.

Ge Fei's *Jinse* is not the only text of modern Chinese literature to allude to the late Tang poet Li Shangyin (813–858). He is, indeed, a favorite of several twentieth-century Chinese writers: Fei Ming (1901–1967) admired his poems and sought to imitate them in his writings; many essays and one novella by Wang Meng (1934–) are inspired by them; several of Ge Fei's (1964–) fictional works are interspersed with references to his poetry; and Li Xiuwen (1975–) wrote about Li Shangyin in a pamphlet in which he contrasted Li's depth of feeling to the shallowness of the writers of his own generation.[5] In addition, since the early 1980s, a remarkably large number of scholarly studies on Li Shangyin have been published in China, many dealing with his controversial "untitled" poems (*wuti shi*), particularly with "Jinse," which is perhaps his most famous poem.[6] Described in *Jiu Tang shu* (Old history of the Tang) as a precocious literary talent well-versed in ancient-style prose (*guwen*) and as an eccentric personality, Li Shangyin came from a family of petty officials, and although temporarily appointed to low-ranking positions, he spent much of his life moving from place to place and eventually died in poverty.[7] His poems were prized for their formal refinement and inspired imitators in the Song period; they were first collected by the editor Yang Yi (974–1020) but were extensively annotated only during the Qing dynasty.[8] He wrote about sensual love in a melancholic tone, and the evocative language of his verses, famously rich in images and allusions, led scholars to endless speculations on their meaning.[9]

In the 1980s and 1990s, several writers came to consider Li Shangyin's poetry as the epitome of "literariness," an aesthetic value that they invoked to counter a sense of cultural loss. Though generally prizing the difficulty of Li's verses, they traced the meanings and relations between Li Shangyin's poetry, literariness, and loss in widely divergent ways. Wang Meng, for instance, finds in Li Shangyin's poetry a quality that he attributes to Chinese literary language in general, a capacity to convey the "ineffable" meanings that are lost in conventional communication. Wang suggests that the aesthetic experience that one derives from this poetry can help heal the wounds inflicted by history and thus contribute to the renewal of national culture. Ge Fei, however, identifies Li Shangyin's literariness with a blurring of the boundary between the real and the imagined and with the conflation of different dimensions of time. Ge Fei associates Li Shangyin's poetry, which he reads as the expression of an inability to apprehend and control the real, with a wound that fails to become a scar—a transhistorical injury that underlies the human condition.

This chapter will consider how Li Shangyin has been appropriated in a variety of projects aimed at redefining what constitutes a "timely" literary form in the period of deep transformation during the 1980s and 1990s, and how these appropriations complicate the futuristic rhetoric of literary discourse examined in Chapter 3. As in earlier chapters, the materials I examine are diverse—fictional narratives, scholarly essays, speeches, and introductions to poetry collections—and reveal unexplored links between contemporary fiction, poetry, literary criticism, and Tang studies. Writing in multiple genres is, in fact, an integral part of the literary life of several contemporary Chinese authors. In the Chinese context this is nothing new: in the imperial era and in the early twentieth century, fiction writers often wrote personal essays and diaries as well as annotations about their favorite readings, and they often interspersed their novels with poems. Jaroslav Průšek has argued for a fundamental continuity between classical poetry and early twentieth-century fiction: the works of Lu Xun, Yu Dafu, Guo Moruo, and other May Fourth writers show more affinities with the "lyrical" tradition of classical poetry than with "the predominantly epic and objective character of folk literature."[10] These writers were burdened with the task of founding a modern national literature; therefore, they "unconsciously identified themselves with what they considered good literature and not with those genres which they felt were to a large degree folkloristic."[11] Similarly, in the 1980s, Li Shangyin's poetry helped writers redefine their task in opposition to the literature of previous decades, which they perceived, to borrow Průšek's term, as predominantly "epic" and hence lacking some of the qualities ascribed to a modern national literature, such as psychological analysis and depth. Reviving Li Shangyin's work can thus be connected with a concern for legitimizing ways of writing focused on interiority and with efforts to carve an autonomous literary space in the 1980s.

In his overview of the critical reception of Li Shangyin since the Song period, Stephen Owen has noted that Li Shangyin's "rise to fame was a complex history of changing values."[12] This statement refers to what is probably the central controversy in the studies on Li Shangyin: whether those poems apparently alluding to love ought to be read as political allegories that refer to specific historical figures. The Taiwanese writer and scholar Su Xuelin was perhaps the first to grant legitimacy to the theme of love in Li Shangyin's poems in the late 1960s. Contesting all previous allegorical readings, she claims that Li Shangyin's romantic life was their central theme and reconstructs the identity of the lovers who had, in her view, inspired them.[13] Su Xuelin portrays Li Shangyin as a romantic hero involved in passionate and often tragic love affairs with courtesans and nuns. Her appreciation for erotic themes is shaped by the emphasis on individual feelings in the May Fourth intellectual discourse. Her efforts to link poetry to precise biographical events, however, do not significantly differ from the work of those commentators who, reading the poems allegorically, have sought to identify the political personalities to whom the poems supposedly referred.[14]

The question of how to interpret Li Shangyin's richly allusive verses has continued to divide scholars in more recent decades. Although the studies published since the mid-1980s generally avoid overtly politicized readings, very few of them emphasize, as does Su Xuelin, the theme of love per se. Rather, most of them valorize the semantic indeterminacy of Li Shangyin's poetry, which Stephen Owen has variously described as a "poetics of the clandestine" and a "poetics of blurriness."[15] These studies have increasingly sidestepped interpretations that insist on direct links between poetry and life events—whether political or sentimental—and have instead laid stress on the radical ambiguity of Li's verses. An overview of commentaries published in the 1980s will illustrate this point, showing how the valorization of Li Shangyin's hermeticism contributed to the legitimization of *menglong shi* (misty poetry), which was initially criticized for its alleged lack of communicative clarity.

Reevaluating Li Shangyin: Ambiguity, the Role of the Reader, and the Meanings of *Menglong*

The late 1970s and early 1980s editions of Li Shangyin's poetry generally emphasize its sociopolitical implications and the contradiction between his "progressive" personality and the "feudal" times in which he lived.[16] A selection published in 1978 by a research group at Anhui University, for example, introduces Li Shangyin as "a poet who cared for reality, politics, and the destiny of the feudal state." Its editors read "Jinse" as representative of "the tragedy of a progressive literatus in feudal society" who was limited by his times and by his class background and could not recognize the causes of his misfortune.[17] The editors acknowledge the literary importance of the untitled poems and, following the Qing commentator Feng Hao, divide them into three groups: those expressing deep love and conveying clear allusions to the political misfortunes of the poet; those that are ambiguous and may or may not be allegorical; and those that only express sexual desire and hence are clearly not allegorical. The commentators claim that the untitled poems do not represent the height of Li Shangyin's achievements and that his merit lies in his denunciation of the "corruption and decadence" of his times, which he expressed in his political poems.[18] A similar view is presented in a book on Li Shangyin by scholars Liu Xuekai and Yu Shucheng, who praise some of the poems in the conventional mode of *yonghuai* (expressing one's feelings) because they convey the poet's "democratic thought."[19] The untitled poems are appreciated from a formal viewpoint and again divided in three groups, the least worthy of which is represented by poems expressing "superficial, vulgar feelings, the sensual passion for prostitutes," which clearly do not imply any allusion at all.[20] The editors compare Li Shangyin to Li Bai unfavorably, criticizing him for being much weaker, more passive, and pessimistic than Li Bai.[21] These early 1980s editions focus on debates that had divided Li Shangyin's commentators since the Southern Song period concerning the poet's use of figurative language—in particular, the relationship between love themes and the poet's social and political concerns.[22] These commentators imply that a clear line could be drawn between poems expressing deep feelings and those referring to ephemeral love affairs; political allusions and aesthetic value are associated with the first, whereas the second are dismissed as frivolous pastimes.

Subsequent editions of Li Shangyin's poetry reflect the growing emphasis on the expression of individual subjectivity that characterizes literary criticism in the mid-1980s. They focus less on political context and more on the psychology and feelings of the author. A 1985 reprint of a small Qing edition annotated by the Confucian Jiang Bingzhang explicitly takes issue with previous scholarship. The poems are preceded by a lengthy preface by Hao Shifeng, a contemporary scholar of Tang poetry at Nankai University, who points out that the edition did not enjoy much popularity when first printed in 1755, and that Jiang Bingzhang's commentary is biased: as a Confucian scholar, he looked only at the content of the poems and failed to take into account their aesthetic features. Hao argues against the tendency to portray Li Shangyin as if he were a second

Du Fu—a poet mostly concerned with the fate of the country—and criticizes allegorical readings of the untitled poems.[23] He defines their ambiguous mood as "spring sadness" (*shangchun*), "not mere sorrow but rather a complicated feeling of the interpenetration of hope and despair, in which longing and loss are intertwined with one another."[24] Echoing Su Xuelin, Hao Shifeng reprimands earlier commentators who discredit love as a worthy poetic theme and insists that Li Shangyin's poems express a "desire for free love . . . respect and sympathy toward his companions . . . mutual love between equals." The poet's unique respect for women greatly diverges from "feudal morality . . . and somewhat resembled the modern meaning of love."[25] Hao points out, of course, that this did not mean that the poet was completely "modern"; he was limited by his times and hence his aspirations never found full realization. In Hao's view, however, the very contradiction between Li Shangyin's desires and the limits of his epoch constitutes the point of departure for his aesthetic quest and is at the basis of the recurrent dream images in his poetry: for Li Shangyin, dreaming was not escapism but symbolized his yearning for beauty, love, and a happy life. Dreams were an imaginative space encompassing memories of the past and aspirations for the future.[26] Hao concludes by insisting that Li Shangyin's poetry can be enjoyed even if it is "misty": the appreciation of beauty does not depend on the understanding of meaning. In support of this view, he quotes Liang Qichao: "I cannot figure out what [the poems] are about. When I try to interpret them line by line, I do not even understand their literal meaning. And yet, I feel that they are beautiful, and in reading them my soul gains a fresh feeling of joy."[27] Hao Shifeng prizes ambiguity, which he associates with depth of thought, complexity of feeling, and literary modernity. He also claims that the political views that previous commentators attributed to Li Shangyin were overly reductive. Instead, he values the contradictory passions expressed in Li Shangyin's untitled poems. A similar valorization of complexity is found in an essay on "Jinse" written by Huang Shang in 1988. After offering an overview of several interpretations of the poem, Huang argues that no matter how difficult the poem, every reader can enjoy it in a personal way. Hailing Li Shangyin as the "greatest misty poet of Chinese antiquity," he calls "Brocade Zither" a "tower made of seven treasures" (*qibao loutai*): "By looking from the angle they prefer, visitors can have their own perception and knowledge of it. Such impressions may not be complete, but they cannot be wrong."[28]

Several commentators in the 1980s reevaluated Li's untitled poems. Granting more importance to emotional response than to rational understanding, they claimed that their difficulty should not prevent readers from appreciating them. The targets of their critique were socialist literary discourse and the didacticism they broadly identified with Confucian heritage. These writers conflate Confucian norms and Maoist prescriptions, condemning both as obsolete because they were excessively rational and ultimately unsound in literary matters and contrasting them to reading practices based on spontaneous enjoyment and interpretive autonomy. These commentaries make various assumptions about Li Shangyin's modernity: he was ahead of his time, a romantic precursor of the modern poet. Remarkably, the valorization of literary intricacy went hand in hand with ideas of moral autonomy, irreverence toward social constraints, and even, for Hao Shifeng, sexual freedom and gender equality.

The Li Shangyin revival helped promote reading practices based on personal creativity and a concept of the reader as an active contributor to the production of the meaning of a text. This epitomizes a reaction against the 1960s and early 1970s insistence on one correct interpretation and can be connected with the various attempts during the 1980s to configure the aesthetic as a realm in which a renewed "subject" could flourish, whose agency might then transcend the boundaries of the aesthetic and express itself in the sphere of politics in autonomous ways.[29] These commentators sought to redefine the autonomy of the aesthetic sphere by insisting on the semantic indeterminacy of Li Shangyin's poetry; at the same time, they emphasized the necessity of a more "scientific" approach to the study of poetry. Incidentally, the theorization of the aesthetic subject by the literary critic Liu Zaifu that was so influential in the mid-1980s represented an attempt to divorce literature not only from the sociopolitical realm but also, more in general, from the domination of instrumental reason.[30] In contemporary scholarship on Li Shangyin, however, a focus on the subjectivity of the writer, an emphasis on textual indeterminacy, and the claim to a "scientific" approach to literature often coexist in the work of the same critic, as in the case of the scholar Dong Naibin. Dong presents his work on Li Shangyin as a contribution to the strengthening of literary history as an "autonomous discipline" centered on the "spiritual exchange between the writer and the reader," granting central importance to the creative aspects of reception. He dismisses as unscientific and obsolete all interpretations aimed at ascertaining "one objective and incontestable literal meaning" and at connecting figurative language with specific historical referents. The multiple layers of meaning in Li Shangyin's poetry, he claims, were to remain veiled and ambiguous (*yinhui*).[31] Inspired by system theory, Dong holistically connects the "linguistic images" of

Li Shangyin's poetry not solely to the poet's psychological world but also to the whole of Chinese culture.[32] An analysis of the diachronic and synchronic relations between such images as the butterfly and the dream would shed light not only on the "psychological laws" of literary creation but also on the sedimented meanings of a cultural system, revealing the deep psychological pattern of Chinese culture itself.[33] Although he proposes a "systemic" approach to poetry, Dong argues that one could only "relatively approximate" its original meaning. To interpret means inscribing the subjectivity of the reader/interpreter onto the texts of the past in an open-ended process of subjective re-creation.[34] In another essay, Dong emphasizes the subjective aspects of literary creation but adds that the individual creative "I" is "at the same time . . . a constitutive part of a nation, a culture, and a certain class."[35]

Through their interpretations of Li Shangyin, scholars supported newly emerging practices of reading and writing that prized personal creativity as a means to strengthen Chinese national culture. Dong Naibin, in particular, emphasizes the interdependence between individual and cultural identity. These commentaries can also be read as defenses of menglong poetry. The word *menglong* (misty or obscure), which at the beginning of the 1980s was used as a derogatory term, appears in several of these commentaries as a positive literary quality.[36] In fact, menglong poetry was from early on associated with late Tang poetry, and Li Shangyin was often mentioned—sometimes together with the poet Li He—in essays on young menglong poets, such as Bei Dao, Gu Cheng, and others, published in the first half of the 1980s.[37] The poet and scholar Xie Mian was among the first to emphasize the modernist features of Li Shangyin's poetry. To mediate between a few young writers who took a radical antitraditionalist stance and their critics, Xie made modernism appear less foreign and therefore more acceptable by claiming that it was already practiced by Li Shangyin and Li He.[38]

Although Li Shangyin was often mentioned as an example of native modernism and as a precursor of menglong poetry, his name was used in conflicting arguments, reflecting the great variety of understandings of modernism and of the term *menglong* itself. Zhang Ming, for one, contended that most of Li Shangyin's untitled poems were not *menglong* at all; rather, they left the reader with a "bright, beautiful, and deep feeling." The only reason they were considered "ambiguous" (*yinhui*) was that it was unclear whether they were political or love poems. Li Shangyin could not be compared with or seen as a precursor of menglong poetry, which made people feel thoroughly "vexed" (*qimen*); his poetry, therefore, should not be used to promote the contemporary "menglong style," which Zhang despised.[39] For Zhang Ming, *menglong* meant not so much ambiguity and lack of clarity as a pessimistic and passive mood, which left the reader with existential confusion or outright depression, and which was not to be found in Li Shangyin and in the Chinese tradition in general. Tao Wenpeng, however, criticized Xu Jingya's notorious claim that the Chinese poetic tradition was inadequate to modern times by referring to Li Shangyin's poem "Yeyu ji bei" (Night rains: To my wife up north). In these verses, the poet imagines a future moment of happiness in which, reunited with his wife, he will remember his unhappy present as the past.[40] Tao sees this as an example of a "multilayered spatiotemporal structure" (*duo cengci de kongjian, shijian jiegou*) and thus, again, as a precursor of modernism. By pointing out that elements deemed Western were in fact already present in Chinese classical literature, Tao suggests a notion of modernism disconnected from conventional periodization: modernism consists of a set of textual features that might occur at any time and place and is not necessarily linked to the modern condition.[41]

Overall, scholarly work on late Tang poetry indirectly contributed to the legitimization of menglong poetry and of modernist writing in general. In the literary debates of the early 1980s, Li Shangyin was often presented as a native precursor of menglong poetry and modernism, even though his name was sometimes also invoked to discredit menglong poets. The writer Wang Meng, as we shall see in the discussion that follows, played an important role in these debates, bridging the diverse institutional fields and writing genres of classical poetry scholarship, literary criticism, and contemporary fiction and poetry.

Reconnecting with the Past: Wang Meng's *The Strain of Meeting*

The title of Wang Meng's novella *Xiangjian shi nan* (The strain of meeting, 1982) is based on the first verse of one of Li Shangyin's untitled poems, "Xiangjian shi nan, bie yi nan" (The strain of meeting equals parting).[42] Commenting on this verse in a later essay, Wang emphasizes that it not only alludes to the difficulty of meeting because of external circumstances but also to the difficulty of communicating even when a meeting actually takes place:

> Separation is painful, difficult . . . and yet, to meet is also difficult. For one thing,
> the opportunity to meet is rare, but even when one finally meets, what then?

If one meets, one should then connect and speak to the other. What I mean is: How can one meet and really communicate? To meet and not communicate is even worse than not meeting at all. . . . This poem is about love and yet goes beyond love. Think of all that is precious, all that one longs for and yet often risks losing or has already lost. . . . Isn't this often "the strain of meeting that equals parting"?[43]

What do the protagonists of this novella "long for and yet often risk losing or have already lost"? In the early 1980s, Lan Peiyu, a woman who migrated to the United States in 1948, is invited by the Chinese government to return for a belated memorial service for her father, who committed suicide at the onset of the Cultural Revolution. Described as a tormented Chinese in exile who feels left behind by history and estranged from her country, Lan returns, determined to reestablish a connection with her past and be readmitted to her national community. Above all, she looks forward to meeting her old friend Weng Shihan, a Communist Party member who had always considered himself to be a loyal revolutionary but was sent to the countryside during the Cultural Revolution and rehabilitated only in 1979. Like Wang Meng, Weng Shihan likes to read Tang poetry. In their youth, Lan and Weng were neighbors; he was involved in party activities, and she was starting to get involved. After missing an important appointment, however, she was accused of being a traitor. A few weeks later, she heard about the opportunity to study in the United States and reluctantly decided to leave. Having returned to China, she hopes to explain to her old friend what happened thirty years before.

Lan and Weng had radically different lives and yet were both labeled traitors—she for leaving the country, he for allegedly keeping in touch with her and acting as an agent for foreign powers. Both think of themselves as "survivors" of their "previous selves." At the ceremony for her father, for instance, Lan Peiyu thinks that she "had spiritually died an unjust death in America."[44] Weng Shihan, however, felt that something in him was dying in 1979 when he was leaving the village where he had spent his last ten years. While Lan is prone to self-analysis and somehow manages to come to terms with her past, Weng appears unable to mediate between the different voices that haunt his mind. He seems to finds momentary comfort in formulaic narratives about the achievements of the Chinese revolution, but the opportunistic behavior of some colleagues and the bureaucratic excesses of the party (a recurrent theme in Wang Meng's fiction) have dampened the political fervor he professes in theory. In addition, when questioned by Lan on the relation between his ideals and the Cultural Revolution, he is unable to come up with a definite answer.

One of the central issues of the novel is the death and destruction brought about by the Cultural Revolution, which emerges from Weng Shihan's account as an aberration, a usurpation of power by a small group, a break in the tide of progress. In short, Weng is the loyal party member to whom the Cultural Revolution only brought pain and destruction, a type that appears in several other Wang Meng stories. At the same time, he also asks himself whether his ten-year immersion among the peasants has been "a disaster or the best of luck."[45] Now that Weng has left the countryside, he has to rebuild his life and contribute to the construction of a new society in the urban environment where he belongs. He badly needs to believe in a brighter future, but the party narrative no longer convinces him. His trust in rationality and historical progress wavers, and he can only find consolation in a declaration of faith—"But I still believe in the self-confidence and cohesiveness of the Chinese people!"—as a response to the questions that plague him. At the center of this story lies an unresolved tension between historical necessity, human agency, and chance. This tension, however, is not fully explored but rather dissolved in the sentiment of trust in fellow countrymen through which what appears lost may be partly recovered—certainly not the past, but perhaps some of one's ideals through the feeling of belonging to a national community.

The epilogue to the story brings us back to the motive of the meeting. After a first brief encounter, Lan writes a letter to Weng expressing her hope of having a more in-depth conversation with him. At this point, Weng invites her for dinner but is forced to cancel it because of the intrusion of the second wife of Lan's late father (a greedy and vulgar woman). He finally sends Lan a farewell note, which includes the quatrain "Ye shan" (Visit to the mountain) by Li Shangyin,[46] and she goes back to the United States without having talked to him in any depth.

Before venturing any hypothesis on their narrative function, let us look more closely at the two poems by Li Shangyin referred to in the novella. Through the complex images in the first couplets, "Xiangjian shi nan" alludes to the inevitability of the passing of time and conveys a sense of sad resignation. This mood is overturned, however, in the last verse, in which the poet summons a mythical messenger, the blue bird, to do what he cannot with his all-too-human means: overcome distance and all other barriers and visit his beloved (a cold comfort indeed, but the point is that a supernatural being can achieve what humans cannot). No supernatural element intervenes in the "Visit to the Mountain" quatrain which is a more straightforward expression of disappointment at the inevitable passing of time: when the poet attempts to "buy the ocean" (suggesting eternal life) from the immortal Magu, all he gets is "a small cup of spring dew cold as ice."

The two poems thus convey different moods, including anger, resignation, hope, and disappointment. They express the sense of regret and disorientation felt by the protagonists, as well as the frustrated wish to reverse or undo the events that changed their lives. But they are not the only literary texts featured in this story: novels, poems, songs, and movies are mentioned as elements that define the characters' backgrounds and mold their attitudes, expectations, and beliefs. Books create similarities and distinctions among people; they bring them together and pull them apart. In one of their conversations back in the 1940s, for instance, Weng and Lan discuss the books they like and Weng warns her that the drama *Ye weiyang* (On the eve)—one of her favorites—is an expression of "petty bourgeois nihilism," not the best reading for a young revolutionary.[47] The drama is set on the eve of the 1905 Revolution and focuses on a small group of young Russian activists who sacrifice their personal lives to their political beliefs. Described by Ba Jin as one of the major influences on his life as a teenager, *On the Eve* must have struck quite a different note in the 1940s, at a time when party discipline was emphasized and political acts based solely on personal initiative were reprimanded. Not long after this discussion, Lan Peiyu misses the crucial appointment that would have transformed her into a revolutionary because she is absorbed in reading Xu Xu's sentimental novel *Jibusai de youhuo* (The lure of the gypsies).[48] Reading such works signals Lan's increasing insubordination toward party discipline. More generally, Wang Meng's novella shows that references to works of twentieth-century literature imply a specific political stance. Modern literature creates distinctions in terms of degrees of revolutionary fervor and can strongly affect the course of one's life. But the novella also reveals how such distinctions are time-sensitive: as the case of *On the Eve* exemplifies, the cultural and political significance of literary texts is susceptible to substantive revision over time.

What is it, then, in Chinese culture that remains unscathed by such recurrent revisions and that can reconnect Lan to her friend and her country? The spoken Chinese language does not constitute much of a common ground: Lan observes that the spoken language has undergone transformations over time and that the language she remembers from her childhood is no longer heard in Beijing. It is, instead, pre-twentieth-century literature (including vernacular fiction and drama) that brings together people of diverse political experiences and backgrounds: Lan Peiyu can talk about *The Romance of the Western Chamber* with another overseas Chinese, even though their political views were on opposite ends of the spectrum. While modern literature, language, material goods, and money are markers of class and nationality, classical literature is recuperated as a suprapolitical element that unites Lan with other overseas Chinese, with Weng, and with China.

Li Shangyin's poetry, in particular, can apparently convey the pain, sadness, and powerlessness of individuals who were confronted with historical events that were beyond their control and that caused disruption, separation, and loss of any coherent sense of self. The "Visit to the Mountain" quatrain that Weng rewrites in his farewell note to Lan comes as a possible solution for a question to which the story has no answer: "one meets, but how can one communicate?" The poem is a lament, and if taken literally, it would seem to convey Weng Shihan's disappointment at their inability to reverse the course of events. On the narrative level, however, it does reestablish a tenuous contact between the two protagonists. In this respect, the quatrain corresponds to the "blue bird" in the poem "Xiangjian shi nan," acting as a "supernatural agent" that intervenes in a situation in which direct human contact has failed. Patterned on the final verse in the poem, the quatrain functions as a magical solution, offering imaginary relief from an inevitable separation.

Written at a time when people were setting aside the struggles of the recent past, Wang Meng's novella suggests that Li Shangyin's poetry may help heal the wounds inflicted by recent history precisely because it dwells on feelings of loss and uncertainty. Wang's insistence on cultural communality, however, implies the centrality of a specific type of intellectual background and knowledge. If, as this story suggests, the discourse of class led to social disruption, and if it therefore needs to be replaced by an emphasis on culture, it is also true that the apparent cohesion created by a shared cultural competence is based on obvious distinctions between the elevated and the low, the refined and the vulgar. Two uses of "culture"—one in the sense of cultural capital, the other in the sense of common background—are conflated in this context.[49] Culture in the first sense is characteristic of particular social groups or classes. Culture in the second sense is "Chinese culture," imagined as shared by all Chinese and coextensive with the Chinese nation as a whole. Weng and Lan are united by culture in the first sense, a specific form of cultural capital, which, incidentally, is also what distinguishes them from the "opportunists" who blindly follow the party line, on the one hand, and from the "materialists," on the other—people such as the ex-wife of Lan's father who are only interested in expensive foreign goods. But the text passes culture off as Chinese culture in general, equating a certain form of literary competence with Chinese identity. The conflation of this class-bound notion of culture with a supposedly classless Chinese culture reaffirms the urban intellectual as a figure organically connected with the peasants and at the same time provides Chinese communities abroad with a source of self-identification.

In Wang Meng's *The Strain of Meeting*, Li Shangyin's poetry serves to convey a complex message in a situation in which conventional language has failed. Poetry overcomes the barriers put up by history, represented as capricious as nature itself. An unsettling parallel emerges between the valorization of a kind of poetry that demands abandonment to aesthetic appreciation and a notion of national identity according to which one does not need to understand recent history: just love your fellow countrymen and that will do. But can the imagining of a sentimental cohesion really heal all rifts? The story does not provide a clear-cut answer; Li Shangyin's quatrain, after all, expresses nothing but disappointment. But Lan reads it as an expression of hope and later feels that "her country's dense, collective life . . . had changed something in her."[50] If Wang Meng's story leaves things unresolved, his essays on Li Shangyin, which were mostly written in the late 1980s and early 1990s, are more straightforward, and it is to these that I now turn.

Poetic Language and Communication

In his essays on Li Shangyin's poetry, Wang Meng argues that everyone, not just scholars, should be able to appreciate Tang poetry. In contrast to such authors of the early twentieth century as Hu Shi, who emphasized the discrepancy between classical Chinese and colloquial language, Wang Meng understates this gap. Addressing the common perception that "Brocade Zither" is one of Li Shangyin's most difficult poems, for instance, Wang claims that its vocabulary is actually simple: "almost every character and word can be used in the vernacular, without altering them at all."[51] And yet he also argues that this poem—and classical poetic language in general—occupies a completely different linguistic plane because it serves no specific communicative function: "To buy things, to lecture children, to apply for a job, all this requires that you speak clearly, requires that language is standardized, universalized, and made to sound logical. . . . So what we mean by 'language' in these cases is the superficial language of communication. Poetry is language that seeks the ineffable and that seeks to directly reach the 'idea' [*yi*]; this is 'deep language' [*shenceng yuyan*],[52] characterized by syntactical discontinuity and illogicality. Wang Meng insists that each word and character in Li's poems (and again in Chinese classical poetry in general) is "extremely important and relatively autonomous," emphasizing the rifts between words, verses, and especially between couplets.[53]

Deep feelings, Wang argues, are beyond the reach of an overly logical language; the power and beauty of Li Shangyin's poetry, thus, lies exactly in its syntactical and logical discontinuity and hence in its ability to express the inexpressible. Li Shangyin's language, writes Wang Meng, "is not a normal narrative language" that follows grammatical rules and logical progression but "is rather an interior lyrical sublanguage or metalanguage [*neixin de shuqing de qian yuyan, chao yuyan*]."[54] In other words, it has the properties of "a primary language, . . . a language of the heart—a language that has not fully undergone symbolization and standardization."[55] Wang even rewrites some of Li's poems, disrupting the sequence of the words and rearranging them in several different combinations to show that shattering syntactic relations does not affect the overall feeling conveyed by the poems and that such a rewriting could even enhance understanding of the original.[56] Wang's "writerly" view of Li Shangyin's poems leads him to conclude that, "as to the famous 'card game fiction' [*pukepai xiaoshuo*] of the modernists, isn't it the case that our ancient China already had it?"[57]

Li's poetry epitomizes the original characteristics of the Chinese language, which does not follow strict grammatical rules and hence is able to capture the ineffable feelings that escape "superficial language":

> This kind of poetry demonstrates that human thought and feelings at their outset do not take the shape of linguistic forms that can be used on the surface. The so-called perceptible but ineffable is exactly the meaning that cannot be easily expressed by the "superficial language" [*biaoceng yuyan*]. To seek for the language of the "ineffable," this is what "Brocade Zither" is about. . . . At the same time, this kind of poetry is also an illustration of the marvelous nature of the Chinese language [*hanyu de qimiaoxing*]. Chinese is not characterized by a strict subject-object structure and a rigorous grammar but rather takes as its special characteristic the depiction of an affinity of scenery and sentiment.[58]

Wang Meng's essays downplay the importance of parallelism, rhyme, and tonal prosody in Tang poetry and their effect on the overall cohesiveness of the poem.

Indeed, syntactic discontinuity is what made Tang poetry attractive to Anglo-American modernist poets of the 1920s who were "impatient of the logical connectives which thwart the achievements of a language of pure sensation."[59] In this sense, Wang's views recall Ezra Pound's notion of ideogrammatic writing as "a possibility inherent in all verse—a sort of deep structure or primitive substratum of poetic utterance that is prelogical, pregrammatical."[60] Semantic ambiguity and syntactic discontinuity may indeed characterize Tang poetry,[61] but it is debatable that Chinese poetic language can function as a universal model for a "language of pure sensation," or a "language of the heart," as Wang Meng calls it, if only because of the different "referents, implications, and associations of words" and the more or less conventional uses of images and allusions.[62]

More important than the accuracy of Wang Meng's ideas on literary Chinese is his recuperation of Li Shangyin's poetry as the crystallization of the supposedly universal qualities of the Chinese language and as an example of native modernism. Like Tao Wenpeng, Wang suggests the possibility that modernism might be a set of formal features recurring at different times and places, hence disconnecting it from a Western origin and from the modern condition. The features that Wang Meng emphasizes are those that Anglo-American modernists read into Chinese poetry. Even though Wang does not mention them, he seems to imply that because Tang poetry traveled abroad and inspired foreign writers, it could also function as a native source for literary experimentation at home.

The Future of the Past

Li Shangyin's poetry is central to Wang Meng's aesthetic vision. In an open letter titled "Guanyu 'yishiliu' de tongxin" (Communication on 'stream of consciousness,' 1979), in which the writer explains his use of the techniques of *yishiliu* (stream of consciousness) in the story "Ye de yan" (Eyes of the night), he singles out Lu Xun's collection of prose poems, *Yecao* (Wild grass), and Li Shangyin's poetry as native sources of inspiration.[63] Wang describes "stream of consciousness" as a mode of writing that privileges free associative thinking and image over predetermined concepts and fixed content, its aim being to capture the "raw" human perceptions or affects, which "some people call artistic intuition. From a materialist viewpoint, they indicate the first immediate reaction to the world, to life, to objects."[64] Wang Meng explains his argument by resorting to two familiar notions of Chinese traditional aesthetics, namely *xing* (affective image) and *bi* (comparison). *Xing*, in his view, is a form of associative thinking, and hence a pristine form of stream of consciousness. In *xing*, he claims, the point of departure for writing is the image, which inspires a plurality of thoughts and emotions in the writer. The image is the source and origin of meaning. In Wang's view, after many decades in which an emphasis on *bi*—the exposition of a predetermined idea or concept—dominated, it was about time to recuperate *xing* to give full rein to the "flux" of contradictions that characterizes the human experience of the world.[65]

Although the stories by Wang Meng that several critics[66] consider as early examples of *yishiliu* do not allude to Li Shangyin, a brief discussion of two of these stories will help clarify his idiosyncratic appropriation of the Tang poet. "Ye de yan" (Eyes of the night, 1979) and "Hudie" (Butterfly, 1980) exemplify the author's bent for investigating the multiple facets of an individual psyche, even though the psychological discourse is contained within a predictable set of contradictions that generally find resolution in a hopeful, if rather incongruous, epilogue.

In "Eyes of the Night," the perceptions and thoughts of a middle-aged writer who returns from the country to the city after an absence of two decades are presented in "free indirect discourse," mostly unmarked by any introductory sentence that would clearly delineate them from the narrator's voice. An abrupt shift from the third to the first person reveals the intimate feelings of the protagonist at a difficult moment, heightening the effect of psychological introspection. Nevertheless, the various sequences of associative thoughts that cross his mind are ultimately logical and coherent.[67] "Butterfly" consists of a long flashback reconstructing the life of the protagonist, a successful cadre who has gained respect and privileges thanks to his commitment to the revolution but has also lost his first wife and a son because of it. The narration shifts seamlessly from the thoughts of the protagonist (associative interior monologues) to descriptions of the setting; often the sight of an object (an "affective image," as in the notion of *xing*) evokes the memory of some person or past event. As in several other of Wang Meng's stories, we find an exploration of the conflicts between various personae within the same character, conveyed in this novella through an allusion to Zhuangzi's allegory of the dream of the butterfly. But whereas Zhuangzi wakes up from his dream wondering whether it was truly himself dreaming the butterfly or whether he is but a butterfly's dream, thus leaving the question of his identity unanswered, Wang Meng's story ends with the protagonist coming to terms with his internal contradictions and reaffirming his identity as a cadre fully devoted to his work.

Wang Meng's own writing practice, then, reflects a rather cautious appropriation of Li Shangyin's figurative language. His short stories adopt the "associative" qualities that he detects in Li's poetry only insofar as they illustrate the characters' heightened perception of an unsettling environment and the tension between their private and public roles. In this respect, Wang's fiction does not fully enact the shift from *xing* to *bi* that he advocates in his essays: the contradictions explored through associative thinking (*xing*) end up being contained and resolved by epilogues that confirm a predetermined idea or concept (*bi*). Perhaps the most successful of Wang Meng's experimental stories is "Laijin" (Thrilling, 1987), a humorous account of the tragicomic adventures of a character called Xiang Ming (whose name appears variously in a range of homophone Chinese characters, and a couple of instances even in pinyin).[68] At several crucial moments, multiple possibilities of events and actions are juxtaposed. The story makes no allusion to Li Shangyin and conveys a playfulness that is alien to the poet, but like Wang's own rewriting of Li's verses in random order, it invites the reader to creatively recombine fragments of text.

Considering his creative writings alongside his theoretical essays, we can see that, for Wang Meng, Li Shangyin's poetry represents a model of allusiveness and psychological complexity, a source for cultural cohesion that could help overcome recent historical traumas, and a native example of "associative" writing. A slightly different vision of Li emerges, however, from one of Wang Meng's later talks, which transcends his preoccupations as a writer who sought to legitimize experimental forms in the context of major socioeconomic and cultural transformations. As the honorary president of the Society for Li Shangyin Studies (established in 1992), Wang Meng delivered a talk at the third meeting of the society in 1996, in which he welcomed the resurgence of interest in Li from "all sectors of society" as an indication of the broadening of the concept of literature. Like several other critics before him, Wang Meng conflates traditional literary exegesis with the literary practices of the Mao era. Traditional Chinese literary thought, he claims, privileged content over form, public affairs over sensual love, optimism and grandeur over melancholy and sadness. Because of this tradition, which continued after 1949, Li Shangyin did not receive enough critical attention, a regrettable trend that was finally being reversed in the present. Although his poetry does not convey any clear ethical message, Wang notes, it has an educational value in the present time of reform, opening up, and fast economic development because "it might help reinforce an elevated [*gaoya*] aesthetic taste, valorize our national cultural treasures, and develop an interest in China and Chinese literature."[69]

Once again, Wang emphasizes the poetic characteristics of the Chinese language, equating Chinese language, poetic value, and Chinese culture. Perhaps also because of the public, institutional nature of the talk, he links passion for Li's poetry unequivocally with the survival of Chinese national identity: "by reading Li Shangyin's poetry and Chinese classical literary works, we can savor the characteristics of the Chinese language and appreciate its charm, so that we may have 'Our Chinese Heart,'[70] and this heart will live forever." In short, the eternal life of poetry ensures that "Chinese culture will not perish; China and the Chinese nation also will not perish."[71] Finally, Wang explains that Li's poetry poses a challenge to Chinese literary history and to both Chinese and Western literary criticism because the categories and critical tools they offer are not adequate to analyze it. Li's poetry—which can be intuitively apprehended, appreciated, and enjoyed but not fully understood—has survived, when so may other things have perished. Its complexity reminds readers of the incommensurable depth of the Chinese past, of a Chinese culture that is to endure in the future. To abstract from the flow of time a space where things neither change nor perish, to "recognize" one's own "deep language" in it and thereby contribute to the strengthening of the national self: these are, in Wang Meng's view, the ends of literary education, and this is the role of the writer, literary scholar, and public intellectual that Wang Meng envisioned for himself in his writings on Li Shangyin.

Ge Fei's *Brocade Zither*: Poetry in a Strange Loop

Although none of Ge Fei's essays focuses exclusively on Li Shangyin, a reference to the poet appears in his study of Fei Ming in a section comparing the Fei Ming's treatment of time in the novel *Qiao* (Bridge, 1932) to the structure of Li Shangyin's poem "Night Rains: To My Wife up North," which depicts the present as the object of future memory, anticipating the time when the "now" of writing will be a memory of the past:

> You ask how long before I come. Still no date is set.
> The night rains on Mount Ba swell the autumn pool.
> When shall we, side by side, trim a candle at the West window,
> And talk back to the time of the night rains on Mount Ba?[72]

Ge Fei comments: "In the poem 'Night Rains: To My Wife up North,' the poet's time of writing is when 'the night rains on Mount Ba swell the autumn pool,' while 'When shall we, side by side, trim a candle at the West window, / And talk back to the time of the night rains on Mount Ba?' represents the imagined future of the writer, the time when he will talk with his beloved at the western window at night and recall the continuous autumn rains of 'now.'"[73] Ge Fei writes that, whereas in these verses the object of future memory is an actual atmospheric event, the rain, the object of the anticipated recollection in several passages of Fei Ming's *Bridge* is itself a fantasy—what the protagonist imagines he will recall at some later time is a flight of the imagination, in which past and future are experienced as a continuum.[74] The last couplet of Li Shangyin's "Brocade Zither" ("Did it wait, this mood, to mature with hindsight? / In a trance from the beginning, then as now")[75] is precisely an example of this kind of recollection. Ge Fei does not elaborate on these verses, but by mentioning them in this context, he seems to read them as suggesting that it is difficult to recollect past feelings clearly because they were already mingled with blurred fantasies when they first emerged. More precisely, past feelings cannot become the discrete memory of an isolated moment because, already at the time in which they were "present," they were tainted by the "anticipation of retrospection"—the imagined future in which they would become a memory.[76] In Ge Fei's view, Fei Ming's narrative style, Western modernist fiction, and Li Shangyin share such instances of "synchronicity" (*gongshixing*).[77] This focus on the temporal dimensions of Li Shangyin's poetry suggests similarities among the perspectives of Ge Fei and the critics who saw Li Shangyin as an example of native modernism, but Ge Fei's emphasis on feelings of anticipation sets him apart. To learn more about his reading of the poet, we need to turn to his fictional works.

Ge Fei's novella *Brocade Zither* can be read as an extended fantasy on Li Shangyin's poem of the same title. Described by the author as a "dream in a dream,"[78] it consists of four puzzling tales about a man called Feng Zicun. In each story, Feng dies, but before dying, he tells a tale or dream about another character bearing his name, which constitutes the following story in the novella.[79] The cycle of rebirths that takes place thanks to the act of storytelling recalls Jorge Luis Borges's short story "The Garden of Forking Paths," about a book attributed to T'sui Pen full of contradictions: "in the third chapter the hero dies, yet in the fourth he is alive again." In T'sui Pen's text, there are "'several futures,' several times, which themselves proliferate and fork."[80]

Each of the tales in *Brocade Zither* is set in a different place and presumably in a different period of imperial China.[81] In the first, "Butterflies," Feng Zicun is a solitary man whose tranquil life in a village is shattered by the sudden death of a woman and is then executed for unclear reasons—probably because he has attempted to open her grave. In the second, "In a Daze" (mentioned at the beginning of this chapter), Feng is a scholar who, after years of study, fails to pass the state examination and hangs himself. In the third, "Story of a Tea Merchant," he is a wealthy merchant who is invited to attend a ceremony at court; he then falls ill and, after a period of confinement to his bed, dies. Finally, in the fourth, "The Dream in the Dream," Feng Zicun is the sovereign of a state called Canghai who is unable to defend his country from the army of West Chu and migrates with his people to the land of Lantian. He knows that his son is about to kill him, and when asked by his gardener why he does not escape, he replies that a dream he has had the night before suggests that, even if he were to escape, he is doomed to die soon anyway. The king then starts to tell the gardener his dream, in which a Feng Zicun hears about the death of a woman. The end of the fourth story thus brings the narrative back to the beginning. Only in this fourth tale—which is a dream itself—does the reader realize that the first story is also a dream. To recapitulate: the first tale is the dream of the Feng Zicun of the last story; the last story, in turn, is the dream of the Feng Zicun of the third story, which is narrated by the sister of the Feng Zicun of the second story, which is narrated by the Feng Zicun of the first story, which is the dream of the king in the last story, and so on.

Gérard Genette defines any violation of narrative levels as metalepsis, a "deliberate transgression of the threshold of embedding" resulting in "intrusions [that] disturb, to say the least, the distinction between levels."[82] And this is what we have in Ge Fei's story: the last story, the lowest embedded unit, reveals itself to be the frame of the whole narrative, en abyme. The text could thus be read as an instance of the "strange loop," a figure explored in Douglas Hofstadter's *Gödel, Escher, Bach: An Eternal Golden Braid* (1979). The strange loop indicates phenomena that advance by going up and down through a multilayered system and recursively end up at their point of departure. Hofstadter argues that such recursive structures can be found not only in mathematics, the visual arts, and music but also in more elementary realms, such as grammar, the geometry of tree branches, and particle physics. What they all have in common is "nesting": a process in which distinctions between the outside and the inside or the background and the foreground melt, with several units propping up or generating one another, and the smallest embedded unit sometimes expanding to encompass the largest. These structures may break out of predetermined patterns, generating unpredictable outcomes.

After its abridged Chinese translation was published in 1984, *Gödel, Escher, Bach* (*GEB*) prompted vigorous debates in such fields as architecture, literature, psychology, and advertisement. The works of M. C. Escher were often alluded to in literary texts. His lithograph "Drawing Hands," for instance, is depicted in Sun Ganlu's "Visit to Dreamland" (discussed in the preceding chapter), where it serves as a comment on the self-contained aspects of storytelling.[83] Articles on psychology drew on *GEB* to suggest new therapeutic methods focusing on breaking the "strange loop" (*guaiquan*) of the patient's fear, pessimism, and despair.[84] Philosophy of mathematics scholar Zheng Yuxin emphasized Gödel's incompleteness theorems while also noting that the main contribution of the book is that it reveals the underlying similarities between cultural, scientific, and natural realms that seem remote from one another.[85] For Zheng, the book's central concept is that of "levels" (*cengci*), which indicate the various components of complex objects as well as the subject's different modes of engagement and layers of understanding. These different levels are connected through "leakages" or moments of mutual permeation and intertwining, forming "strange loops" or "braids." Zheng goes on to explain that Gödel's incompleteness theorems have important implications for the understanding of cognitive processes; beyond their applications in the field of artificial intelligence, he finds the very notion of incompleteness attractive because it implies that no system can ever be grasped in its entirety. Zheng's account suggests that *GEB* offered a way to appreciate the complexity shared by diverse fields of human creativity and the natural world, while at the same time accounting for their inbuilt unpredictability. It was thus in accord with a general trend in mid-1980s Chinese cultural criticism to elaborate methodologies that were holistic but not deterministic. In the field of art history, *GEB* inspired reflections on how tradition was an open-ended process oriented toward the future rather than an ossified totality established once and for all in the past.[86] For the literary scholar Wei Chongxin, it offered a way to rethink the complex dynamics of character personality and fate in the famous novel *Jin Ping Mei* (The golden lotus). The discussion of *GEB* even extended to the emerging field of advertisement, where the concept of "isomorphies" (*tonggou*) between objects was introduced as a new method of graphic representation.[87]

Even though Ge Fei's *Brocade Zither* was published a few years after *GEB* was translated into Chinese, and even though there is no proof of a direct connection, there are affinities between the debates generated by Hofstadter's work and Ge Fei's novella. The story narrativizes a "strange loop" of fear into which the diverse protagonists fall and from which they are unable to escape. All four episodes depict a man who, in the moment he is about to achieve success or self-realization, is struck by a twist of fate that reveals the illusoriness of the stability he has achieved. All the Feng Zicuns recite or rewrite Li Shangyin's verses and are differently affected by them, even though some of them appear to live in times preceding the date of the poem's actual composition. The "chronological displacement" of the poem—its anachronistic appearance at times when it had not yet been written—suggests a downplaying of historical difference. Historical periodization is subordinated to fictional framing and recursive reading. All this contributes to the sense of "synchronicity" in the novella, which displays a tension between recursiveness and unpredictability.

The embedded structure of the novella suggests that none of the Feng Zicuns could exist without the others because each of them inhabits a tale or dream told by another, although they all appear to be self-deluded about the autonomy of their existence. This is the result of forgetfulness. Perhaps because the figure of Feng Zicun lacks both a fixed identity and an autonomous existence, *Brocade Zither* has been read as a postmodern allegory deconstructing the notion of autonomous subjectivity. Xiaobin Yang has emphasized an uncertainty that is at the same time epistemological and ontological and that would be equally detectable from Ge Fei's and Li Shangyin's lyrical voices. In his view, "Li Shangyin's poem predetermines the lyrical voice of Ge Fei's narrative, since Feng Zicun, like Li Shangyin, dwells on his speculation on the feeling of being lost in his memory/anamnesis. The speculative subject, like Zhuangzi, becomes an unstable and self-questioning one." This instability is mainly conveyed by blurring the line between dream and waking; as Yang notes, "the mutual entanglement of reality and dream in narrative is part of traditional Chinese mysticism, which Ge Fei invokes against the linear, grand narratives."[88]

Whereas Yang's reading illuminates a possible philosophical implication of the novella, I would like to account for the specific functions of dream in Ge Fei's narrative in relation to its heterogeneous uses in Chinese classical literature. The multiple traditions of dream coexisting in Chinese classical literature have been subsumed under two main categories: dream as prophecy and dream as illusion. In a narrative text, a dream might offer insights into how things will evolve, solve a mystery or personal dilemma, provide fulfillment for a protagonist's desires, or reveal their illusoriness. Although the time-honored notion that "life is as illusory as a dream" dates back to early philosophical texts and is rehearsed in several famous narratives, in late imperial fictional narratives the very illusoriness of dreams serves as a literary device leading to unexpected twists, often subverting the philosophical tradition itself.[89]

What do dreams do in *Brocade Zither*? On a basic level, dreams are the source of the narrative, which thus rehearses the trope of life as a dream. As noted earlier, the novella also includes several dreams in a dream that anticipate the character's fate but do not help him escape it. For instance, a dream warns the king in the fourth story that he will soon be killed, but it does not help him change the course of events. Dreams within the dreams that constitute the narrative, therefore, function as unhelpful prophecy and convey dread, anxiety, and fear of death. These are the anticipatory affects that torment an uprooted subject, isolated and deprived of any meaningful historical context but nonetheless, perhaps all the more, viscerally attached to life. This is particularly true for the first tale, in which Feng Zicun is introduced as a man without a past. No one, not even he, knows who or where he was before coming to the village: "Some years ago, when Feng Zicun moved to this remote village, no one knew his true identity [*zhunque de shenfen*], . . . as for himself, he too was completely in the dark about his past experiences. Those trivial events seemed to have suddenly vanished behind time, and his searching for them had been fruitless. He knew that this unknown village not only corresponded fully to his aspirations but to a certain extent even surpassed them. Its mild climate, its distance from the city clamors, and the silent eremitic life very soon appeased his heart."[90] Feng has long renounced excavating his past, and his very amnesia allows him to live well, at least for some time. It is not the fragility of his memory that vexes him but rather the anxiety about what is going to happen to him. As suggested earlier, by the second paragraph of the story this very concern shapes his ensuing reveries: "Since the day he had been locked up in the stable, he had kept making conjectures about his unpredictable fate. He did not know how those refined villagers would punish him. At the same time, he was not quite prepared to face the dangers that were lurking in the silent sunlight."[91] The reasons for Feng's confinement in a dark stable are initially unclear. We next read about his sensations—the sights, smells, and sounds that assault him the moment he is freed—and his fears about what will follow. When he asks a man to give him water, the man responds:

> "Whether you drink or not, it no longer has any consequence."
> What did he mean? An ominous premonition nearly choked him. He carefully pondered the words of that young man and their strange overtone: perhaps he just wants to scare me? They won't go so far as to kill me.

Tufts of sophora flowers drifted on the river, emitting a sweet fragrance; butterflies fluttered their colorful wings, lingering where the smell was more intense.

Feng Zicun thought again of Zhuangzi's famous allegory of the dream of
the butterfly. . . . Could it be a dream? The confusion of time often blurred the
boundary between reality and dream. He had dreamt several times that he had
woken up in the stable, his face smothered with horse shit. Often, waking up
from the nightmare would bring him relief: as his spirits slowly regained lucid-
ity, danger would quietly flee in the dark and everything would become peaceful
again; he could then drink leisurely a sip of tea, leaf through ancient texts, im-
merse himself in his reveries under the dull blue light.[92]

Is the danger only in the dream or is it real? Hard to tell, and given that the two
dimensions are often indistinguishable in the novella, this very question is less
relevant than the panic that generates it. The possibility that this might be a
nightmare occurs to Feng as a reaction to his "ominous premonition." The blurring of dream and reality comes to his aid as a distancing device, a fragile refuge
before the real hits again in all its violence. The ensuing narrative consists of a
jumble of excursions into the past and the future, the first are flashbacks to the
events that have led to Feng's confinement in the stable (he has tried to open
the grave of a woman he was in love with), and the second are his thoughts anticipating what will follow. Even as narrative time goes back and forth, however,
the tale offers no description of Feng's memory processes, no searching for the
past. It is the narrator who reconstructs the recent events, while what mostly
occupies Feng's mind is the uncertainty about how the villagers will deal with
him: "He tried to guess his unforeseeable fate, envisioning all sorts of bizarre
endings; the only one he did not think about was death, not because he believed
that his crime did not deserve it but because he just didn't want to consider
this hypothesis."[93] Hence, the story features a split between the narrating voice
proceeding backward to reconstruct the events that have led to the present im-
passe, and the protagonist's thoughts and emotions, which are mostly projected
forward. This split is central to the fictional reenactment of the synchronicity
that Ge Fei observes in Li Shangyin's poetry, providing a dialogic rendition of
classical poetry into contemporary prose. We do find, in the third and fourth
tales, Feng's own attempts to reconstruct past events, but even then the primary
focus of recollection is the past omens of looming events rather than past events
proper. Throughout the four tales, it is the presentiments of loss and death that
mostly occupy the mind of the protagonist. Interior time is depicted as chaotic
and nonlinear, but a predominant perception of time rushing forward provokes

feelings of anticipation. Occasionally, the imagination of something good about to happen momentarily projects the character beyond a predisposed sequence in which he feels trapped and as such has a consolatory effect.

The novella's response to the literary tradition of dream tales is not merely a reiteration of the blurring of the line between what is dream and what is real. Even though the illusoriness of reality is an important premise of the narrative, this very illusoriness serves to illustrate the condition of anxious foreboding that characterizes all the Feng Zicuns. Dreams illustrate the futility of human efforts to predict, interpret, and control what is about to happen, even though they occasionally offer momentary refuge. They provide a series of fictional contexts for the recursive (re)writing of Li Shangyin's poem, reimagining the circumstances in which "Brocade Zither" might have been and will be written and read, fictionalizing an exegetic tradition that sought to reconstruct the contexts and personalities of poetic writing and performance and opening up the poem to further readings.

Feng Zicun is portrayed as an alter ego of the poet, occasionally writing the poem as if it were the first time, as if it were his own. The identification between reader and poet suggests an affective model of reading that avoids reducing the poem's emotional impact to allegorical meanings and that emphasizes its materiality: the paper and silk on which Feng Zicun the literatus and the king rewrite the verses and the tears that the lines bring to their eyes. Li Shangyin's verses are scattered throughout the narrative and repeated as if they were incantatory spells: the various Fengs rewrite them verbatim, ponder their words, but are generally unable to paraphrase them. Feng Zicun the hermit, we are told in the first episode, tells his interpretation of the poem to the village teacher, yet we never learn what this interpretation is. Li Shangyin's poem thus remains a heterogeneous space that does not serve a clear narrative function but never fails to elicit emotional responses from the protagonists. Like a dream, poetry has an ominous quality. In reading Li Shangyin's "Brocade Zither," the Feng Zicun of the first story "had the presentiment of a fear never felt before. . . . In his view, this poem contained a terrifying allegory; in its depth, there was an impenetrable emptiness."[94] In the third story, when the tea merchant rereads Li Shangyin's poem on his deathbed, he feels that the poem expresses the feeling of being entrapped in time rushing forward: "One could see that Li Shangyin and he were one and the same: trapped in the rigid pattern of time, with no way of getting out."[95] The reading of poetry, then, offers precarious access to the vertiginous state of a subject nearing death: a bundle of forward-oriented affects that transcend the

particularities of one's personal identity, the naked essence of humanity that supposedly emerges once historical belonging and experiences have been peeled off,
a hypothetical condition beneath the layers of status and class, as if they were
ever disposable and as if the task of fiction were to reimagine this very possibility.

Unlike Wang Meng's *The Strain of Meeting*, Ge Fei's *Brocade Zither* does not
simply embed the poem but reenacts it, adopting its structure and borrowing its
evocative language. The poem begins with the word *wuduan*, which means "no
beginning," "no end point," or "no reason." In the story, the beginning and the
end coincide, and there is no apparent external referent apart from the narrative
performance of the protagonists. The story and poem are also linked by thematic threads: the central verses of the poem refer to legends of the transformation of things or people and evoke feelings of longing and loss that return in the
story. Both poem and novella are composed of elements that are only loosely
connected, and both are interspersed with intertextual references. Some of the
words of the poem are used in playful ways. For instance, the words *canghai*
(ocean, vast sea) and Lantian (Blue Mountain) become the names of the realm
of the king of the last story and of the place where he goes in exile with his
people, respectively. Finally, some of the poem's sensory images, such as mist,
smoke, and heat, give rise to chains of associations in the fictional text.[96] In the
second tale, in which Feng Zicun is a scholar residing in a monastery outside
the city of Jiangning (Nanjing), the view of the mist on the river mingled with
the smell of rouge precipitates a trance of "empty fantasies." The smell of rouge
then mingles with the aroma of the jasmine tea that his sister put on his table,
calling to mind the face of his sister, which in turn blurs into the image of his
mother and of yet another woman. Visual and olfactory perceptions merge into
one another, giving rise to one fancy after the other. These flights of imagination
often seem to interrupt the sequence of events that lead the protagonist to his
death, but in fact they are the very cause of his ruin. The workings of imagination and dream and, above all, the desires they engender rob the various Fengs
of their hard-won stability, but this very loss and the anxiety about what might
come next compel and enable them to tell their stories.

Conclusion

In Wang Meng's *The Strain of Meeting*, Li Shangyin's poetry reestablishes a tenuous contact between the protagonists and provides a possible element of cultural cohesion for a national community that is seeking to recover from years

of political violence. Wang's essays, meanwhile, establish affinity between the Chinese poetic tradition and modernist literary practices: the reading of classical poetry provides an element of cultural and linguistic continuity that is retrieved from the past to be projected onto the future.

In Ge Fei's *Brocade Zither*, Li Shangyin's poem shapes the narrative on multiple levels; the novella provides in turn a context in which the poem is reread and rewritten and in which it continues to invite and elude interpretation. Ge Fei's story reenacts the layered temporal structure of Li Shangyin's poem, offering a reading of that last cryptic couplet that has puzzled readers for centuries ("Did it wait, this mood, to mature with hindsight? / In a trance from the beginning, then as now") and suggesting that the confusion they express is caused by feelings of anticipation. And yet, unlike Ge Fei's brief discussion of Li Shangyin's poetry in his essay, the moments of anticipation found in the novella do not refer so much to a time in which the present feeling will be a memory of the past as to the forebodings that catch the protagonists unaware as their lives unfold. Their content is not the present as an object of future memory (as in the "anticipation of retrospection") but the fears about what is yet to happen, which neither the narrator nor the protagonist have any way to predict or control.

Both Wang Meng and Ge Fei appreciate Li Shangyin's poetry primarily because of its hermeticism. Wang Meng's appropriation of Li Shangyin, however, presupposes the possibility of instrumentally selecting specific aspects of the literary past for present and future uses. Ge Fei's novella, by contrast, suggests a vision of literary history that is at odds with ideas of linear development and selective recuperation. Rather, the literary past emerges as a recursive yet unpredictable effect of reading and writing, as an integral dimension of the present that remains open-ended and partially inscrutable. Ge Fei's *Brocade Zither* seems to preclude the possibility of enhancing the future through the recuperation of a discretely defined past. Its experimentation with multiple temporal threads often culminates in moments of "achrony," conveying, as the narrator states, the feeling of being "out of time." These potentially liberating moments are subsumed, however, under a scheme of anticipated decline (the "rigid pattern of time"), which the protagonists attempt in vain to escape. Achrony itself—a momentary suspension of time—confronts the protagonist acutely with his impending death, a mode of anticipation that we will continue to explore in Chapter 5.

5

A CLEAN PLACE TO DIE

Fog, Toxicity, and Shame in *End of Spring in Jiangnan*

POPULAR SCIENTIFIC ACCOUNTS in the 1950s, as we have seen in Chapter 1, predicted that the weather of the twenty-first century would be entirely subservient to human wishes. Gone would be sudden August hails and disruptive May frosts; moderate rain and generous sunshine, appropriately distributed to suit different productive needs, would alternate within each single day. Overcoming the precariousness of life through the elimination of contingencies constituted the core promise of socialism, and controlled weather would be one of its tangible manifestations. But if in these predictions the weather featured as an essential condition of life and production, in other discursive realms atmospheric states were mostly invoked as allegories of political situations or human qualities. In the visual arts of socialist China, elements of the sky were the expression of class power, a temporary challenge to humans' triumph over nature, or the conveyors of an impending threat: think of the red radiant sun in Maoist iconography or the gales bending the apple trees just planted in the desert and the nightly storms in which enemies would come out of their dens in socialist movies. In the post-Mao period, terms related to the air have often been used to suggest certain literary qualities or feelings or a shift in the boundaries of political discourse: "misty" in "misty poetry" (*menglong shi*) alluded to a lack of communicative clarity and a depressive tenor; images of blue sky in the short fiction of the early 1980s suggested hope and optimism; times of more liberal cultural policies were described with the attributes of spring, followed occasionally by abrupt gusts of cold wind.

In all these cases, atmospheric elements are the figural expression of human struggles and moods. Anthropologist Tim Ingold has noted that the social sciences rarely discuss the sensorial elements that make up the weather—the color of the sky, the movement and temperature of the air and the clouds.[1] Weather generally remains invisible in the background of historical and anthropological accounts, treated as an intangible abstraction, even though it affects much of our lives and actions. Ingold calls attention to the atmospheric flows in which humans are immersed to emphasize humans' permeability to their surroundings. Questions about the weather are anthropological questions because they pertain to the ways in which human bodies are dynamically embedded in, and vulnerable to, their material environments, but they are also historical and ultimately literary questions because they concern the contingencies shaping human action.

Ge Fei's *End of Spring in Jiangnan* (2011), which is the third volume of the Jiangnan trilogy, engages with fog as a material aspect of the environment, as a medium, and as a trope.[2] The novel centers on the question of how one can find a clean place to live and die within the pervasive toxicity of postsocialist capitalism, at the same time exploring what the very condition of postsocialism entails for individuals. Fog serves as a medium for four manifestations of toxicity: shame, sacrifice, surplus, and crime. But before illustrating these claims, let me introduce Ge Fei's novel in the context of his Jiangnan trilogy.

Apprehension, Residual Promises, Planning

Ge Fei's works published from the mid-1990s onward have received scarce consideration in English-language scholarship, despite the remarkable critical attention they have received in China. English-language criticism focusing on his earlier works has generally read them as explorations of the ways in which memory and narration constitute the fictional subject.[3] The lacunae in individual memory and in written historical records, the randomness of fate, and the absurdity of any concept of historical rationality surely constitute the main themes of Ge Fei's works. As shown in the preceding chapter, however, his narratives are equally concerned with capturing the states of apprehension that shape how characters act. This is epitomized by a minor episode in *End of Spring in Jiangnan*, in which the young woman Luzhu tells about her habit of lowering her head while walking under a bridge or a door that is in fact high enough for her to pass through standing straight.[4] This compulsive gesture performs an enduring condition of dread: "we're in constant fear of a danger that won't necessarily happen, wasting our entire life in worrying."[5] Such a fear of an undefined danger forms the core affective state of many of Ge Fei's protagonists, intellectuals in crisis who struggle to respond to contingencies in ways that ensure their well-being; at the same time, quite surprisingly, it is the object of subtle humor and self-irony, with the narratives often undergoing unexpected twists.

The Jiangnan trilogy departs from Ge Fei's previous works in the way it portrays the relationship between individuals and their historical contexts. In Ge Fei's early works, a fundamental incommensurability divides the well-known narratives of major historical events from concrete human experience, which is often motivated by sexual desire. In the Jiangnan trilogy, however, the gap between the historical narratives defining an epoch and the protagonists' vicissitudes narrows, and the characters' aspirations are more directly related to the collective expectations of their age. These characters are actively involved in the major transformations of their times and in some ways typify them. The trilogy thus investigates the emergence and shrinking of aspirations generated by specific promises, probing into the legacies of the utopian visions that nourished human imagination at different moments of the Chinese revolution rather than setting up counternarratives that question hegemonic historical accounts.

The three volumes are set around three important moments in modern Chinese history: the 1911 revolution, the early 1950s, and the early 2000s. Each volume offers an independent story but acquires additional layers of significance when seen in the light of the others. Although the main protagonists belong to successive generations of one family, the focus is not on extended family relations but on immediate kin and the broader social world, encompassing a vast range of unrelated characters in the third novel. The trilogy weaves together such diverse documents as local gazetteers, letters, and online chats and combines a variety of genres: the first volume adopts elements of martial arts fiction, the second mixes detective story and socialist realist novel, while the third ranges from melodrama to satirical essay. Throughout these combinations of genres, characters, and moods, place remains constant. This is primarily a work about Zhenjiang in Jiangsu province, where the author grew up; thus, it bears affinities with *xiangtu wenxue* (native-soil literature) and many other contemporary novels set in the author's home region. Mo Yan's novels set in Shandong province come to mind as a famous antecedent, although in the Jiangnan trilogy there is no heroic past or ancestor to look back to and no nostalgic storytelling. One of the goals of the trilogy is to undertake what Edward Said has called a "*working through* [of the] attachments" that define the author's relation to his native place, coming to terms with the "unexpected, unwelcome loss" that pervades the condition of exile, a point that will be addressed in further detail shortly.[6]

Why write a trilogy? What does this expanded form offer to contemporary authors, and what account can be given of a writing process that unfolds over nearly a decade? Narratives that extend beyond the length of a novel are fairly common in contemporary Chinese literary culture—an interesting phenomenon that has not been much discussed.[7] Market considerations may encourage some writers to conceive their works as a series rather than as unrelated volumes; trilogies, moreover, offer the opportunity to elaborate on a subject matter from a variety of perspectives and settings that would be difficult to compress in the space of one novel. The Jiangnan trilogy, for one, calls attention to the enduring consequences of ideas and actions that sediment in the soil and the sky despite a political discourse that insists on a fractured temporality of ever new leaps forward. In each of the moments it covers, it returns to aspirations that are never neatly fulfilled, questioning conventional narratives of overcoming. No character appears in more than one volume, however, suggesting historical changes so radical that they are not conceivable within one single consciousness. The expansive form of the trilogy foregrounds, then, the interplay of the enduring and the contingent at diverse historical junctures and the incompleteness of any process of prevailing over an uncomfortable past.[8]

The first volume interrogates the concepts of utopia that inspired revolutionary movements around 1911; the second engages with the vicissitudes of an idealistic communist cadre in the early 1950s; and the third offers a trenchant critique of capitalism that does not find resolution in a recuperation of leftist politics. One could read the three volumes as narrative musings on three different sociopolitical moments and modes of production: the first registering the crumbling of village life and the complex outcomes of the revolutionary movements of the early twentieth century, the second focusing on the dynamics of private and public life under the collective experiments of socialism, and the third lampooning a society torn apart by commodification and unequal mechanisms of exchange. The trilogy is not invested, however, in evaluating socialism and capitalism as contrasting economic and political systems but rather in reconsidering the nature of their promises, the needs and excesses they address and create, and above all the ways in which promises, needs, and excesses intimately propel individuals to act.

The core promise of Chinese socialism, the first and second volumes suggest, was to put an end to the precariousness of all aspects of human life through the redistribution of economic surplus and the rechanneling of emotional excess. Socialist planning aimed to end material scarcity and create forms of intimacy that would be more solid than other bonds, promising not only material abundance but also lasting affection and reciprocity, a solidarity that would replace all previous relationships. Socialism involved an erasure of the boundary between self and other; it was a form of sublimity that radiated outward toward the collectivity and stretched forward infinitely. The Jiangnan trilogy retells the story of these promises of intimacy and abundance, showing how fragile they were from their very inception. In each of the three volumes, planning is an important element of the plot, from the tentative planning of revolutionary action in the first novel, to planning as a feature of the centralized economy in the second, to the waning possibility of organizing one's life in the third. But in each of the volumes the possibility of planning remains unevenly distributed—by some taken for granted, by others arduously obtained, and simply unavailable to yet others—and subjected to contingencies and sudden twists that no one can control. If planning is always an elusive goal rather than a secured means, the sheer belief in the possibility of planning becomes unavailable in the third volume. Thus, the trilogy traces the waning of a belief rather than the exhaustion of an actual practice. In *End of Spring in Jiangnan*, rather than planning, various forms of interruption or blockage created by emotional or material excess constitute the main mechanisms regulating social and economic life.

An Experiment in Counterpoint

Stretching over a period of twelve months from May to April sometime between 2006 and 2009 and encompassing recollections mostly revolving around 1989, *End of Spring in Jiangnan* depicts a diseased social world that is the culmination of economic restructuring begun in the 1990s, characterized by real estate speculation, loss of lifelong employment, displacement of the weak, and commodification of life. These are transformations that obviously concern the totality of China; the area of Zhenjiang, however, where the novel is set, constitutes an extreme case of pollution and environmental destruction. The novel elaborates on aspirations eroded by the promises that nurtured them, registering the uncertain possibilities offered by this kind of present: more opportunities to reinvent oneself from scratch but less security, and an ultimate failing on the part of individuals to exert control over their bodies and surroundings. A diffuse precariousness is presented as a basic condition of human life independent of social status: the fatuous, often harmful restlessness of the middle-class is contrasted with the muffled voices of people who are deprived of their jobs and have no legal protection, within circuits of exchange that reduce even songbirds to commodities. *End of Spring in Jiangnan* traces a nearly total erosion of expectations of a better future life.

The story begins with a one-night encounter between the poet Tan Duanwu and a young woman named Xiurong in 1989 in Hepu, a fictional town in Jiangsu province. The two lose touch immediately but meet again in a department store a year and a half later and marry soon thereafter. The narrative present is set about twenty years later. Duanwu now works in a dusty office for the compilation of local gazetteers, whereas Xiurong has changed her ethereal name (Beautiful Glory) into the materialist-sounding Jiayu (House Jade) and has undertaken a successful career as a lawyer. They have an eleven-year-old son; much space is devoted to the pressures that the education system imposes on children and to the child's loss of a pet bird, sealing the end of his childhood. The main plot revolves around two events: the purchase of an apartment for Duanwu's mother and the onset of Jiayu's cancer. When Duanwu's mother refuses to move into the apartment, Duanwu tries to rent it out through a real estate agency, only to find, a few weeks later, that the agency has taken possession of it, rented it, and pocketed the rent. Unable to get in touch with the agency or negotiate with the tenant, Duanwu and Jiayu eventually evict the tenant with the help of a gang of thugs. The long process of attempted eviction coincides with the growth of Jiayu's cancer (revealed only later in the narrative), suggesting a connection between the house and her body, real estate speculation and cancerous cells. While Jiayu works as a lawyer, the illicit tenant is a doctor: law and medicine are equally powerless to evict invasive beings or curb the proliferation of toxic matter.

Each of the four chapters shuttles between past and present: the events are first provisionally introduced and later retold from the perspective of some other character. This design—a prism of individual visions—predisposes the reader to remain open to further counterpoints and to actively reconstruct a chronology that in the narrative is not always made clear. Seasons are more explicitly indicated than years, especially for events in the 2000s, not only mimicking the work of memory (it is often easier to remember the weather attending an event than the year in which it took place) but also contrasting an indistinct long present with the more punctuated, forward-oriented past. As the narrator puts it, having a child was "the only agreement they reached on their future destiny. After that, just as we all feel, time ceased to offer any valuable thing. It doesn't make all that much difference whether you live a hundred years or a day in this world. To borrow Duanwu's somewhat inflated poetic language, waiting for death had become the basic reason to continue living. Their mutual sense of estrangement multiplied, increasing at uncontrollable speed."[9] In this passage and elsewhere, the novel emphasizes the prospect of death as a paradoxical motivation to live on. In several instances, we find characters wishing to control the circumstances of their death, as if a proper demise were all they can aspire to, once expectations for a proper life have been disappointed. The narrative ends with Jiayu dying in a remote hospital and Duanwu setting out to write a novel based on fragments of lore reported in local gazetteers.[10] The writing of the novel turns out to be the only long-term project of his life besides having a child. For the rest, Duanwu does not make plans; a decent man with few qualities and weak desires, he is a loser in the eyes of his wife and a hypocrite according to his friend Jishi. His name suggests an affinity with the famous poet of antiquity Qu Yuan (whose death is commemorated on Duanwu Day), and indeed in his own self-perception, he is a poet who has chosen to be out of step with the times and who enjoys working in an unimportant work unit, reveling in "slowly decaying in that small building," as Jiayu sarcastically puts it. Doing the fittingly superfluous job of compiling gazetteers along with reading and listening to classical music affords him a refuge from a relentless system of exchange that promises happiness only to produce waste, ultimately granting him survival as well as stories to write about.

Xiurong/Jiayu, however, is terrified by the thought of being left behind. When Duanwu leaves her after their first night together she falls into a fever and becomes almost cataleptic, for she has lost not only her virginity but her natural inclination to trust and to assume a commonality of feelings with others. From that experience of being rejected she emerges heroically, renaming herself to start a new life as a lawyer, anesthetically attuned to the demands of the age. Going through the motions mechanically, Jiayu makes sure to do what needs to be done; however, her self-numbing is incomplete. The vicissitudes of her clients, ranging from laid-off workers to insane killers to whom the law has not much to offer, increasingly touch her. According to one of her colleagues, she is too thin-skinned to work as a lawyer. Cancer kills her, but she is also consumed by her inability to preserve a space that is irreducible to material concerns, work pressures, or the needs of others. The very first sentence of the novel is "I am now yours," spoken by Xiurong (Jiayu) while she is "lying on a mat on the floor, her head resting on a volume of *Selected Poems of Pablo Neruda*, looking up at [Duanwu] with her childish face, her eyes timid and innocent."[11] Her statement is not simply an expression of naive morality (it is September 1989 and she has just slept with Duanwu) but the epitaph of a bodily sacrifice—an expropriation that begins there and culminates with cancer. "Sacrifice" is a word that comes up often in conjunction with her, first appearing in the poem that Duanwu writes for her that very night.

Through the pair of Jiayu and Duanwu and their network of family and friends, the novel ponders how commodification saturates and erodes everything that keeps humans alive. But rather than reading this work as a rant against capitalist modernization, I will focus on the discrepant forms of exile through which the characters respond to the transformations of their environment, a territory that, though not quite effaced, has been awkwardly disguised: "Capital is like a hurricane blowing all over mid-spring Jiangnan, dressing up decay with coats that seemed fancy or trendy but were just pretentious and ill-fitting."[12] What puts the protagonists in the condition of exile is not displacement proper (though that too plays a role in the narrative and dramatically affects the lives of workers and farmers) but rather a "dressing up" of their environment that is too rapid to cover up all ruins and too vulnerable to a primordial wilderness that creeps back in, whenever the "fancy coats" are left momentarily unattended.

Edward Said warns against two dangers facing the exile: making a fetish of exile, "to live as if everything around you were temporary and perhaps trivial . . . to fall prey to petulant cynicism as well as to querulous lovelessness" and giving in to "the pressure . . . to join—parties, national movements, the state," which involves "a loss—of critical perspective, of intellectual reserve, of moral courage." Said speaks of exile "not as a privilege, but as an *alternative* to the mass institutions that dominate modern life. Exile is not, after all, a matter of choice: you are born into it, or it happens to you. But, provided that the exile refuses to sit on the sidelines nursing a wound, there are things to be learned: he or she must cultivate a scrupulous (not indulgent or sulky) subjectivity."[13] "Cultivating a scrupulous subjectivity," Said suggests, means developing a contrapuntal reading of the world. For Said this is a matter of overcoming narrowly conceived nationalist allegiances and producing an awareness of the ways in which metropolitan and colonial histories are shaped by each other, a stance that is more readily available to those living with the memory of an environment that they have left behind.[14]

End of Spring in Jiangnan tackles the sense of displacement that occurs not when one leaves one's country to go abroad but rather when facing a familiar landscape that has been utterly transformed. In response to a situation of rapid change in which fetishization of exile is not an option and all bodies that one could join—whether state organizations or communities of poets—are fraught, Duanwu simply refuses to move fast, looking for a discrepant rhythm unmoored from a fantasy of exile that the narrative itself proves to be a surplus of material accumulation, a luxury for the few. Throughout the novel, contrapuntal threads stitch together a tattered social totality, allowing for a resolute yet provisional authorial voice to emerge with particular clarity in the more essayistic moments of the narrative. The main characters too are only given provisional privilege, their perceptions continuously refracted through the words and gazes of others. Scraps of phone conversations show how stories of intellectuals and merchants, poets and lawyers, entrepreneurs and subalterns are mutually intertwined. Apparently minor characters prove to have multiple connections within the narrative: for instance, a laid-off factory worker who only receives the equivalent of 4,000 dollars as compensation for a lifetime of labor and goes to Jiayu's office for legal assistance later turns out to be one of the employees in the factory that Duanwu's friend Shouren plans to raze and transform into a villa, and possibly one of those who then beat up Shouren in desperate revenge.

The novel includes several of the legal cases in which Jiarong is involved—an artifice that calls attention to itself, for no lawyer could realistically be dealing with such diverse trials, ranging from laid-off workers to perverted killers. This idiosyncratic appropriation of legal cases allows the author to narrate a broad spectrum of stories without connecting them tightly, in an episodic fashion recalling a TV series. The narrative gropes through a myriad of distressing situations that find no resolution, which beg to be read as heterogeneous symptoms of the same malaise. And while an iterative, at times obsessive review of earlier events fills the story with new details on the past, a pervasive fog solidifies and obscures visibility in the present. The novel thus registers transformations that go beyond the razing of villages and the six-lane roads brought about by modernization: there is a thickening of particles that initially remains unnoticed or is passively perceived as an atmospheric event, but soon the toxicity of the particles is revealed, relentlessly seeping through the skin and tainting bodily organs. As we shall see in the next section, fog itself undergoes a process of material and metaphorical accretion from a translucent gauze allowing for a fleeting flourishing of the imagination to a toxic residue of unchecked expansion and an obstacle to communication and life.

Poetics of Mist

In the 1950s, forecasts of future life did not mention fog. But fog features prominently in *End of Spring in Jiangnan*, where it is the principal trope through which the interplay of human action and its material traces on the environment is explored. Fog hovers on the bank of the Yangzi delta where Duanwu walks with Luzhu, the melancholic young woman he has just met at a party in the villa where she lives with her uncle, the real estate developer Chen Shouren. Chen's manor, "Wuthering Heights," newly built near an abandoned dock, epitomizes the new economy of real estate development while also alluding to the socioeconomic conditions of nineteenth-century Europe and the fictions they generated. Having had an inkling of the city government's plans, Chen has bought land from the local fishermen for a ridiculously low price, dreaming of transforming dirty slums into an Italian-style coastal resort overnight. Delicately crafted rockwork and a garden enwrap his house in the calm idyll that is the privilege of the few:

> In the southeast corner of the garden there was a newly built octagonal pavilion, and next to it a rockwork [*jiashan*] of piled up *taihu* stone, which the just planted Chinese wisteria and cypress vines had not yet covered. Between the pavilion and the mansion ran a little pathway covered with cobblestones along which were even mounted mushroom-shaped lights. The lawn had probably just been mowed, as Duanwu could still smell the peculiar fragrance of sunrays on the grass. In the garden there was a little pool: Shouren had planned to build an outdoor swimming pool, bluestone had been laid on the sides, and lotus flowers were growing in it.[15]

The mansion hosts lavish parties attended by a political-economic-artistic elite of literary bureaucrats and academic painters, wealthy developers, dubious politicians, and thugs, whose favorite pastimes include discussing esoteric substances for enhancing one's health and prolonging life. Paulownia trees surround the villa—Shouren hopes that they will soon grow into a thick wood to separate it from the surrounding slums. As the narrator notes, "Shouren was obsessed with 'aesthetics' and 'empty tranquility.' The sheer presence of those barebacked poor wretches would ruin his 'tranquil cultivation.'"[16]

Just outside the villa, there is a desolate if blurry sight, a suburban "terrain vague" simultaneously preindustrial and postindustrial.[17] The fog enshrouds the deserted shipyard—a vestige of past days of maritime commerce—and blurs water and land, veiling the power plant chimneys on the other bank. Fog softens contrasts and muffles sounds, calling for a more intense effort of the senses, for eyes narrowing to capture shadows and ears pricking up to detect the origin of noise. It alters distances. Like ethereal gauze softly stretched over the wounded landscape, it occludes sight, confounds perception, but at least in this instance, it is not threatening.[18]

As they proceed hand in hand across the steel girders of an abandoned dock along the river, the air redolent of rust, Luzhu tells Duanwu the sad story of her life.[19] Groping through the fog, the two are afforded a moment of fantasy or suspension. Luzhu asks whether the lights in the distance might belong to fishermen about to cast their nets; they walk in that direction for half of the night, and when the fog dissolves over their destination, it unveils an enormous trash dump: an artificial mountain-in-the making that, like volcanic lava, deforms the soil. The counterpoint with the delicately crafted rockwork—graceful, complete—in Chen's garden is obvious, though only a few months later, after Chen's death, the villa will be abandoned and weeds will again take over. Growth cannot be tamed, as urban waste and weeds alike invade leftover spaces.

An enduring friendship begins as Duanwu and Luzhu smoke a cigarette, sitting on a pile of trash.[20] Luzhu stares blankly, with no apparent emotion. She tells Duanwu that even the trash workers—whom she deems "inhuman" because they do not enjoy the conditions that are appropriate for humans—are better off than herself: at least they have moments of laughter. Luzhu is convinced that her existence has no meaning or value, but her depression is not solely a personal matter; it is intimately related to the ruin of the landscape, for all she aspires to, she tells Duanwu, is "a clean place to die."[21] She had assumed that she had found such a place in a monastery in Dunhuang, but now that her uncle and aunt have forced her to return to the "real" world, she is left with the task of finding a clean place to survive within her toxic surroundings.

In this episode, fog works as both a distancing and a connecting medium: it temporarily separates the protagonists from their surroundings but also prompts them to move—if only to the trash dump. In the passage I shall discuss in the following section, fog becomes an essential part of the landscape. No longer solely a medium through which the characters move and breathe, fog becomes granular: a substance in which the medium and the object of the gaze coincide.

Fog's Intertexts, Pulviscular Prose

Through fog as landscape and as metaphor, *Late Spring in Jiangnan* engages its own literary genealogy and the material conditions of its writing. Water and dust particles hover in the air throughout the narrative, but it is only in the fourth and last chapter, "Night and Fog," that fog is explicitly thematized. The chapter begins with a disappearance: Jiayu departs from home on a snowy late February day, leaving no trace but a grainy black and white image on the building surveillance camera that, Duanwu notes, seems to cover up all recollections of the twenty years they lived together. It is only retrospectively that Duanwu realizes the portents of her leaving; after her departure, it takes him several online chats with her to realize that she is about to die. And just when he wants to visit her in the hospital in Chengdu, where she has spent the last few weeks, fog delays his departure. It is at this dramatic moment that he recalls the various textures of mist that have swathed his life and writing, from the ethereal haze of his childhood to the gritty fumes of his adult life:

> As a child, Duanwu loved fog [*wu*]. At that time they were still living in Meicheng, in an old alley close to Xijindu.[22] At the back of the street there was a wide reed bank, behind which flowed the mighty Yangzi. Along the river, steelgreen peaks surrounded a dense forest. A deserted Taoist monastery with a red wall was nested on the hill.
>
> In late spring or early summer, every time Duanwu woke up in the morning, he'd see clouds and mist resembling flying willow catkins, enshrouding the reeds just about to turn green, blurring the bold profiles of the temple walls and lush trees. After the rain, floating clouds [*yun'ai*] would rise between the mountains and the shadows of sails on the river. White and light, they'd linger for a while, fluffy and soft like cotton candy, pure and white like rabbit hair.
>
> His brother Wang Yuanqing, who was then in middle school, told him that it was neither fog [*wu*] nor clouds [*yun*], but that it had a special name, mountain mist [*lan*]. When he was going to college in Shanghai, it was exactly the time when "misty poetry" was the rage. In Duanwu's writings, *wu* was always combined with *lan* to form a disyllabic word: *wulan*, mist. This was his homage

to his brother. This word, which the latter cherished so much, endowed that bustling age with strong emotions and a sentimental atmosphere.

At that time, members of the literary association would often meet in a secret facility room of the audiovisual education building to watch the videotapes of banned foreign movies on a 29-inch Sony TV. Alain Resnais's 1956 [sic] famous film was the first to connect fog [*wu*] and crime [*zuie*]. It was after seeing it that Duanwu blurrily [*mengmeng longlong de*] began to say goodbye to his youth. Fog [*wu*] and mist [*wulan*] for a while disappeared from his works. He no longer liked the cloying style of misty poetry.

Today, whenever the image of fog [*wu*] reappeared in his poems, it had become a completely unconscious reflex. Whenever he raised his pen to depict the surrounding landscape, the first word that came to his mind was "fog" [*wu*], as if he were afflicted by an obsession. At the same time, the characters with which he'd combine *wu* had changed. For the people living in Hepu, the meaning of the words "mountain mist" [*lan*] had long been locked up in the dictionary, just like the proverb "being contented with poverty and living a spiritual life" had become an unlikely myth. Fog had now acquired a more appropriate partner, a more intimate companion: *mai*, as in *wumai*, "fog haze," the technical word that often swirled on the tip of the tongue of weather forecasters. Fog haze was one of the most typical landscapes of this age. . . .[23]

On windless days, the vapor rising from the ground would enwrap dust, ashes, carbon dioxide, invisible toxic particles, lead molecules, at times also the grey smoke coming from the wheat straw burnt by farmers. Day after day, the thick blanket thus formed covered people's heads and pressed onto their hearts. This fog haze nourished his poetry, at the same time as it posed questions.

These questions had nothing to do with how poisonous this thing called "fog haze" might be; rather, they had to do with the indifference with which everyone accepted it. As if it were not a new thing that had only appeared in the last few years. As if it were not an insult to nature, but nature itself. As if it hadn't already symbiotically conspired with the dark night, acting in collusion with it to let the sun die a slow death and time stop; as if it were neither a warning nor an allegory.

At this moment, Duanwu was pulling his suitcase, crossing the dimly lit street and the vulgar, gaudy square of which the city was so proud. Even in the haze, healthy-bodied people were still visible everywhere. . . .

The ashen, hairy, filthy fog [*zangwu*] ceaselessly bred crime [*zuie*] and shame [*xiuchi*] in his heart, unfolding in the dim light toward the depth of darkness.

In front of his eyes, in a messy alley with only a scant trace of human presence, the thick fog [*nongwu*] was brewing a sinister scheme. It was not only blocking the flight that in his imagination was leaving on time and the destination that he yearned to reach, but was also separating life and death.[24]

Various permutations of fog punctuate Duanwu's life and writing, accompanying a coming-of-age process that involves a growing awareness of evil as well as displacement from an idyllic neighborhood to an overbuilt city. In Duanwu's earlier poetry, mist (*wulan*) signifies the immaterial, the imaginary, purity, and heightened pathos; it is associated with nostalgia for pristine landscapes and childhood. That fine mist, reduced to an anachronism surviving only in a dictionary, has now been replaced by a granular substance that precipitates on the fictional page. The present "fog haze" is both a material aspect of the environment and "a warning, an allegory." The passage traces a repetitive relay between the experiential and the allegorical, with each new compound—*wumai*, *zangwu*, *nongwu*—denoting an accretion of substance that turns attraction into disgust, registering a shift from the soft mistiness enshrouding childhood recollections to a toxic dust that by itself, automatically as it were, seeps into the writing.

Fog thus becomes intertwined with crime. The connection first occurs to Duanwu after watching Alain Resnais's documentary *Night and Fog* in the late 1980s. Made in 1955, the documentary was commissioned by the Comité d'Histoire de la Seconde Guerre Mondiale to memorialize concentration camps and was coauthored with Jean Cayrol, who had been in one of the camps as a political prisoner. The title of the documentary draws on Cayrol's book *Poems of Night and Fog*, which in turn refers to Hitler's 1941 Night and Fog Decree (Nacht und Nebel Erlass) mandating that political dissenters ("communistic elements and other circles hostile to Germany") in countries occupied by Nazi Germany would be secretly arrested and deported to concentration camps and that no information on their whereabouts would be communicated to their families. Fog in the documentary evokes atrocities committed in the dark, willful repression of truth, and the shunning of accountability in postwar France.[25] Duanwu's mention of *Night and Fog* just after Jiayu has left home establishes a contrast between two different kinds of crime: the first involving brutal violence; the second, more hidden, but infiltrating the human body in more capillary and equally pernicious ways. The more diffused nature of crime in the present renders the issue of accountability even more fraught. Indeed, the ensuing reflections on fog transform the question of accountability raised by

Resnais's documentary into one that is more closely related to acquiescence: what strikes Duanwu most is how "fog haze" is accepted as natural. What kind of language, then, can adequately respond to such toxic opaqueness of air?

This is a question that animates not only Duanwu's own writing but also the novel as a whole. *End of Spring in Jiangnan* responds to this question through a form of writing that I would like to call "pulviscular prose." The term "pulviscular," from the Italian *pulviscolare* ("dustlike"), indicates particles of dust floating in the air that become visible when traversed by a ray of sun. I borrow the term from Italo Calvino's *Why Read the Classics?*,[26] although I am obviously concerned not with literary classics but rather with dusty pollutants and the ways they affect fiction writing, and with a prose that strikes mordacious attacks against quasi-solid air, reverberating with the gritty sound of silt stuck between the teeth. Pulviscular prose nourishes itself on poisonous dusts, for the residue that kills is also what instigates writing. No longer the realm of poetic invention and romantic recollection, pulviscular prose aspires to resemble the video-camera recording of Jiayu leaving home: an imprint that aggressively overwrites the translucent remainder of gentler mists. *End of Spring in Jiangnan* repeatedly depicts the granular texture of air to denounce not only the deterioration of the landscape but also the damage to the body. Ge Fei's pulviscular prose thus transfers opacity from the psychological depth of the self to the dynamics that attend to bodily transformations, from the ambivalence of feeling to the turbidity of matter. This matter encompasses the human and nonhuman, the organic and inorganic. Take, for instance, the words "the ashen, hairy, filthy fog ceaselessly bred crime and shame in his heart" at the close of the earlier quotation.[27] The hairy appearance of the fog suggests a growth in which the boundary between the inorganic and the organic is unclear. The fog itself retains an organic quality: it is the condensed residue of human actions, and it is this residual quality that allows it to enter into osmotic relation with the heart, infecting Duanwu with a sense of crime and shame. This sentence hints at a crucial movement of contagious circulation of *zui'e* ("crime," but also "evil") and *xiuchi* ("shame"), with fog serving as their substrate.[28] Fog, in sum, condenses and conveys affective states and behaviors. It works as an infectious agent at the same time as it makes contagion visible, thus calling attention to questions of accountability and acquiescence—both as a self-reflective commentary on the work of the writer and in broader societal terms. Finally, it nurtures enduring aspirations for a clean place, even as it obscures the landscape.

Shame

Shame is a slippery affect. What exactly causes it, and what does it prompt people to do? Drawing on Silvan Tomkins and Michael Franz Basch, Eve Kosofsky Sedgwick argues that shame is both "a disruptive moment"—that is to say, an interruption of communication—and "a desire to reconstitute the interpersonal bridge."[29] It emerges when a circuit of "identity-constituting" recognition is interrupted;[30] it is the physical (not quite conscious) reaction to a contact that has been broken and the manifestation of an inability to appeal to the other. Shame, in other words, emerges when a request for recognition remains unfulfilled by an other. It follows a request or expectation that may not be excessive in itself but that comes to feel excessive because the request has been denied; shame expresses the desire to reiterate that request, if in a more contained or less exuberant fashion. At the same time, shame "is both peculiarly contagious and peculiarly individuating"[31] and can easily drift from one individual to the next, as Sedgwick explains: "One of the strangest features of shame, but perhaps also the one that offers the most conceptual leverage for political projects, is the way bad treatment of someone else, bad treatment *by* someone else, someone else's embarrassment, stigma, debility, bad smell, or strange behavior, seemingly having nothing to do with me, can so readily flood me—assuming I'm a shame-prone person— with this sensation whose very suffusiveness seems to delineate my precise, individual outlines in the most isolating way imaginable."[32] The words "very suffusiveness" recall the trope of fog in *End of Spring in Jiangnan*. Fog not only conveys shame but also constitutes its visible manifestation as a suffusive substance that forces individuals to redefine their boundaries against those of other people and things, interrupting habitual trajectories and gestures, and making one aware of the daily efforts of identification and recognition that sustain social life. A look at the instances in which this emotion is invoked in the novel will help refine my earlier suggestion that we think of its main characters in terms of exile. Initially, I connected the condition of exile with the deep alterations of the landscape. The native soil appears alien, and its peculiar strangeness is conducive to shame as well: the sudden unfamiliarity of a toxic landscape produces an awareness of distance, a sense of disconnection that makes one want to turn one's gaze away but that might also generate efforts to reconnect with the environment and with others through a more scrupulous self-individuation.[33]

Shame epitomizes the moments in which immoderation suddenly appears strange and thus momentarily interrupts interest or joy. But understanding shame in Ge Fei's novel means being alert to its contradictory workings and nuances conveyed by the different terms employed, ranging from abashment to humiliation. Refracted through a variety of names, this affect is pervasive like fog, no less significant for being heterogeneous, fine-grained, elusive, and at times only implied. Feelings of humiliation and shame are a frequent topic of conversation between Jiayu and Duanwu. Jiayu mostly sees shame as a toxic component of her life that she hopes to excise, while Duanwu seems to accept it as an inherent part of their world. For Jiayu, it mainly emerges from interpersonal relationships—it is a response to the ways in which other people treat her or to her own unexpected behaviors. For Duanwu, it is a more general reaction to his surroundings and to the conditions of life and death of people he does not necessarily know. Thus shame is gendered: it is linked to intimate feelings of humiliation for the female protagonist, while it borders on indignation and becomes a theme of poetic composition and philosophical reflection for her male counterpart. Shame is not transformed into something else for either of them, unless perhaps, eventually, in Duanwu's writing. Jiayu asks "why, since birth, has humiliation [*chiru*] unceasingly entangled" her, to which Duanwu responds, "My dear, it is impossible for anyone to live without feeling humiliated in this world!"[34] Duanwu's response is enigmatic; he does not explain what makes it impossible to live without humiliation. If, in this context, for Jiayu humiliation is the result of a sense of diminished self-esteem stemming from her constant altercations with her mother-in-law, a more intimate and secretive sense of shame (*xiuchi*) emerges at moments when she admits to her greediness, through motions that betray pressure even as they register solace. In these instances shame is not unrelated to the transgression of a prohibition, but it mostly comes with the sudden awareness of an excess, as when she sleeps with a young man she has just encountered at a lawyers' training course in Beijing and realizes, though not for the first time, "the greediness and wildness [*kuangye*] of her body." In this instance, the narrator notes, "shame [*xiuchi*] not only couldn't hinder the emergence of pleasure, to the contrary, it became the catalyst of pleasure and release."[35] Only a few hours before this happens, Jiayu feels abashed (*xiukui*), quite strangely, when her lover displays more knowledge of classical poetry than she expected. She had shown off a couple of verses, but he turns out to know much more than she does about the setting of the poem. Her abashment is associated with being caught boasting or pretending but also with her realizing that she does not have the cultural advantage she assumed in comparison with someone of a younger generation, foregrounding her condition as a person who strives to keep up with times but is unable to secure a distinctive space for herself.

These instances suggest a fine line between humiliation and shame: if humiliation involves being debased by others, shame involves finding out or realizing something inadequate in oneself. But overall, shame is equally relational: it is often the result of a physical or verbal interaction that unveils properties (emotions, body parts, material goods, or cultural competence) that are excessive or insufficient, not in the quantity or measure one was hoping for, and therefore unsightly. The object of shame is what one wants to cover or wants others to divert their gaze from. Shame and humiliation are predominant affects in the novel and emerge from an interruption in the flow of communication between individuals and also between individuals and their environment, an interruption that is mostly caused by some form of verbal or sensory excess. For Duanwu, shame and humiliation traverse the boundaries of social class. His belief in the inevitability of shame is related to his concern for those who are sacrificed: the humiliation suffered by the sacrificial subjects translates (or should translate) into shame for those who enjoy the benefits of the sacrifice. It is in this transference of affect that a residual hope for a different ethics lies. Shame is important because it is one of the few affects left available for a postrevolutionary renovation of ethics—through poetry.

Sacrifice, Poetry, Excess

The term *xisheng* (sacrifice) first occurs when Jiayu sees the six lines Duanwu has written for her on that first night together in the late summer of 1989: "He left an incomplete poem, a mere six short lines, titled 'Moonlight over the Sacrificial Altar.' . . . It was only a confused mess of scribbles jotted down before leaving, no sublime words with deep meaning. . . . But the words 'sacrificial altar' made her realize that she had been the sacrificial victim [*xishengzhe*]: she had been cruelly discarded, and the poet who had probably disappeared forever was both the priest and the ancestor or deity who could directly enjoy the offer."[36] On this first encounter, a link between sacrifice, eroticism, and poetry is suggested. As noted earlier, the novel begins with the sentence "I am now yours," which can be read both as a promise and as a request to Duanwu to acknowledge and reciprocate her promise. But Duanwu turns away and leaves, and Jiayu feels humiliated for having been discarded: her gift has been ignored, her sacrifice is in vain. Although Jiayu reads the poem as a revelation of her own nature as a sacrificial victim, she does not seem to take the verses all that seriously: the six lines are not quoted; all that matters to her is the "sacrificial altar" in the title. Jiayu is characterized as an incompetent reader of poetry who only notes the details that she can relate to herself. Although on a first reading she identifies herself as the victim that has been sacrificed or discarded, she later comes to think of her husband, if not as a sacrifice proper, then certainly as a superfluous poet who has chosen to be discarded, and of poetry as a useless thing.

Poetry, however, has not always been useless to her: she only loses interest in it after meeting Duanwu. Indeed, a few months before, she had joined a group of students commemorating the poet Haizi, who committed suicide in late March 1989. The occasion is described:

> One poet after the other went up on the stage to recite poems written by Haizi or by themselves. Quite unexpectedly, Jiarong too felt a vague [*mengmeng-longlong de*] desire to write poetry. Of course, more than anything she felt ashamed [*cankui*] and guilty: such huge things were happening around her, but she turned a deaf ear to them and didn't have the slightest idea, while she would instead take to heart the case of a widow becoming pregnant. She felt she was too narrow-minded, too cold. At the end of the evening, she stayed on to help the leaders of the students' association tidy up tables and chairs and clean up the place.[37]

By the time Jiayu meets Duanwu, she has read all of Haizi's works and keeps dreaming of him walking alone on a stretch of railroad at Shanhaiguan, where the young poet threw himself under a train.[38] Jiayu responds to Duanwu as if he were a reincarnation of Haizi—the dead poet with whom she is enamored and who has achieved what she will later aspire to—finding his own place to die. Jiayu's sacrifice on her first encounter with Duanwu can be seen as the sacrifice of poetry as well because meeting the poet brings her passion for poetry to an end. The relation between poetry and sacrifice, however, goes beyond Jiayu's disillusionment, for there is some allusion to poetry every time sacrifice is mentioned. And yet this relation remains elusive: Is it that poetry can serve as a medium to acknowledge sacrifice, however momentarily or partially, or is it that poetry itself is sacrificed to something else?

Not solely limited to Jiayu and Duanwu's first encounter, sacrifice soon takes on a more explicit social significance. In the second chapter, which is mainly told from Jiayu's perspective, sacrifice is again discussed in conjunction with a poem written by Duanwu, which the reader does not get to read. What we get instead is an essayistic digression conveying Duanwu's thoughts on this theme:

> At that time, Duanwu had just finished a long poem titled "Sacrifice." For a while, he was simply bewitched by this word. According to him, every epoch has innumerable sacrificial victims. It was precisely the appearance of the word "sacrifice" that transformed and sublimated the actual meaning of ordinary death, for what "sacrifice" emphasized was not death per se but rather its goal and significance. Duanwu pointed out that in the religious and magic activities of ancient times, for instance, the sacrificial victim that was sent to the altar, whether animal or person, constituted a part of a solemn and mystical ritual. It was a price that had to be paid. The reason these sacrificial beings were picked was that they were immaculate and pure, and hence appropriate for the liking of the spirits. They were sent as gifts in exchange for favorable weather, harmony of yin and yang, and good luck throughout the year. Sacrifice itself was part of history, or part of civilization [*wenming*]. Even though in the revolutionary era, to reach certain concrete or illusionary goals, batch after batch of sacrificial victims were killed and buried leaving no visible trace, their names nonetheless endure because they have been included in the history of the victors. Even the nameless victims have been dealt with properly: they were incorporated in a conceptual symbol, such as a monument to revolutionary martyrs, thus obtaining recollection and commemoration and symbolically entering history.
>
> By contrast, those who are sacrificed today are bound to fall into oblivion.
>
> Individuals of all sorts, because of all sorts of circumstances, die for unknown reasons. Unfortunately, they die outside history. They are the consequence of some random accident. There isn't even anyone who requires them to be sacrificed: they automatically turn into sacrifice. As for the reasons this is so, it boils down to the fact that their behavior was improper or that they were unlucky.
>
> No commemoration
> No mourning
> No recollection
> No identity
> No goal or meaning.

In Duanwu's words, they would burst with a popping sound like bubbles on a water surface at the faintest breath of wind. At times one would hear no sound at all. Their sacrifice strengthens the luck of the survivors, and their disgrace and pain become topics of conversation [*tanzi*] for those who live on without a purpose [*tousheng*]. And all the sacrificed get is humiliation.

Duanwu thought that precisely because the sacrificed of the present have no value, they became sacrifice in the real sense of the word. This sentence was a little difficult to understand. Actually, Jiayu completely disagreed with her husband's opinion.[39]

For Duanwu, the sacrificed of the present are purely accidental. No historical agent requires them and no historical narrative or monument reclaims them. Their death is forgettable and leaves no traces. Why Jiayu disagrees with him remains unexplained. Later, she will choose to die in a remote hospital, cutting herself off from her family and friends. Community, let alone the rationalization afforded by historical narratives, has nothing to offer her. By escaping, she seeks to preserve the unreasonable excess of her suffering, the bare randomness of death. In contrast to Duanwu, she sees nothing recuperative in recollecting and mourning, as if the sacrifice of her body could not, or should not, be made sense of in any way.

In part, Duanwu's reflection on sacrifice recalls Bataille's notion of "accursed share": "The victim is a surplus taken from the mass of *useful* wealth. And he can only be withdrawn from it in order to be consumed profitlessly, and therefore utterly destroyed. Once chosen, he is the *accursed share*, destined for violent consumption. But the curse tears him away from the *order of things*; it gives him a recognizable figure, which now radiates intimacy, anguish, the profundity of living beings."[40] But the affinity is only partial: whereas Bataille's concept of sacrifice seems to valorize its "violent consumption" because it furthers the self-knowledge of humanity, Duanwu is particularly upset by the extent to which humans are sacrificed randomly and invisibly. Duanwu contrasts the ritualistic sacrifice of past societies, which involves the exchange of human lives for cosmic balance, with the sacrifice of the present, which is not ritualized and does not aim at anything in exchange. For Duanwu, the sacrifice of the present is true sacrifice precisely because it is unstructured, nonritualized, aimless, and ultimately invisible. What he sees as cruel is the very pointlessness of such sacrifice. Because the victims Duanwu talks about remain unrecognized, in Bataille's scheme their experience would not even constitute a sacrifice.

Paradoxically, then, Duanwu does not reject "the history of the victors" as inhuman or fake: even monumental history offers some kind of consolation compared to the lack of recognition in the present. But if those who are sacrificed are not included in a motivated narrative, if their corpses drift nakedly outside signification and reason, how should one talk and write about them? Would a heroic narrative or a new martyrs' monument offer them recognition and thus dissolve the excess of their deaths? Or does their very nakedness offer itself as a bounty to the poet, much more readily available than the former dead who were draped in the honors of monumental history? If so, what would their reinscription entail, and what form would it have to take? Would a poem such as Duanwu's have to denounce their death as pointless and excessive, thus still leaving the dead without a rationalizing narrative, or would any act of commemoration automatically deprive their death of its excess?

We do not know the words of Duanwu's poem or how he would respond to these questions. But his concern with recognizing, even valorizing, the pointless, profitless death of today's sacrificial victims is caught up in a paradox, for indeed, as Duanwu perceives it, "their sacrifice strengthens the luck of the survivors, their disgrace and pain become topics of conversation [*tanzi*] for those who live on without a purpose [*tousheng* (literally, *tou*, steal; *sheng*, life)]. And all the sacrificed gets is humiliation." The economic metaphors at work in this sentence are noteworthy, for what I translate as "topics of conversation" is *tanzi* (*tan*, talk; *zi*, capital). Thus, loss of human life is translated into social and cultural capital for those who survive. In other words, a pointless expenditure of human life is put back into circulation, converted into social and cultural fodder for those who *tousheng*—those like Duanwu himself who live on without a plan or "steal life."

It is the transfer of excess across the biological, economic, and sociocultural spheres that the novel attempts to make visible, documenting a ceaseless dynamic of exchange. In *The Accursed Share*, Bataille hints at a connection between "the movement of energy on the earth" and art and literature, saying that "even what may be said of art, of literature, of poetry has an essential connection with the movement I study: that of excess energy, translated into the effervescence of life."[41] Commenting on the structural analogy between sacrifice and poetry, Bataille has written that "a sacrifice and a poem alike withdraw life from the sphere of activity, they both *give* to be seen that aspect of the object which has the power to excite desire or horror."[42] Duanwu's poetry writing and frequent listening to classical music convey precisely such a wish for withdrawal. However problematic and, as it turns out in the novel, illusory such a withdrawal might be, it bears reminding that the wish itself constitutes a response to a particular sphere of activity: an unprecedented real estate expansion in the Zhenjiang area that has displaced tens of thousands of people, destroyed local economies and natural resources, created expectations of infinite economic growth, produced unspeakable pollution and waste, and engendered desires that no economy can fulfill. This is what meets Duanwu's eye as he drives to a poetry conference soon after Jiayu has left home:[43]

> Among the spring fields, flashing across, a few solitary houses. Some dirty shops along the sides of the road, and the remains of villages waiting to be torn down—collapsing roofs, gable walls pointing up, and exposed rafters silently lay in the rain. He knew that the countryside was vanishing. People said that farmers not only did not rebel against having their homes pulled down and being displaced, but they were also impatient for this to happen, stretching their necks in expectation. Whatever the case might be, the countryside was entirely disappearing.
>
> But spring farmland couldn't truly revert to wasteland. Capital is like a hurricane blowing over mid-spring Jiangnan, dressing up decay with coats that seemed fancy or trendy but were just pretentious and ill-fitting. What one would eventually see were high-grade six-lane roads and wasteful green belts; luxurious wedding cars one after the other, with red balloons attached on the reflectors and shining lights, striding ahead toward an imaginary happiness; and all along the way, enormous billboards advertising real estate and the "dream life" that they guaranteed.[44]

This passage is a snapshot of a dressing up in progress, of ill-fitting suits barely cloaking derelict bodies. The vision of tackily decorated cars speeding toward an illusory happiness occurs immediately after Duanwu and Jiayu's marriage has crumbled: marriage and capitalism both revolve around promises, figures of futurity waiting to be fulfilled. Throughout the novel, promise remains a crucial mode of anticipation and is intimately linked to the sacrifice of landscape.

Sacrifice and landscape come together also in another episode revolving around poetry. Duanwu is meeting his friend Luzhu at a restaurant, and while she discusses the feasibility of some environmental projects with a representative of the Nature Foundation, he starts reading a poetry book that he has taken (with her permission) out of her handbag. That very morning, he has similarly rummaged in his wife's handbag in search of her cell phone (without her knowing it), finding a used knotted condom with sperm in it. These two episodes featuring the poet's rooting around in a woman's handbag suggest an analogy between poetry and superfluous leftovers—bodily fluids that would normally flow through another body or be discarded but that are caught in some kind of blockage and contained. Luzhu's book is a collection of poetry by Wallace Stevens that Duanwu admired twenty years earlier but now finds trivial. Even "Death of a Soldier," a poem that had shocked him in the past, now sounds "as cloying as a lullaby," although the verses quoted in this episode allude to the kind of death that Duanwu regards as true sacrifice—a death that finds no commemoration and leaves no trace:

> Death is absolute and without memorial,
> As in a season of autumn,
> When the wind stops,
>
> When the wind stops and, over the heavens,
> The clouds go, nevertheless,
> In their direction.[45]

In these verses, the sudden occurrence of death in the battlefield is compared to the wind's ceasing on an autumn day. Although it would seem that life leaves no trace just as the wind leaves no trace, "over the heavens" clouds continue to move, despite the cessation of the wind and a life. But the very presence of drifting clouds strikes Duanwu as an anachronism and alienates him from his formerly beloved poet, even though "he knew it was none of Stevens's fault" for Stevens had simply "not anticipated that although death would continue to come, white clouds would actually become extremely rare. He had attended six funerals, and during all of them the sky was grey."[46] This sardonic observation calls attention to the connections between human sacrifice and the pillaging of the environment. A contemporary, post-Stevens poetry would have to account for this sacrifice as well and can no longer imagine white clouds that "go, nevertheless, in their direction." Indeed, in Duanwu's own poem that closes the novel—a completion of the six lines titled "Moonlight over the Sacrificial Altar" written for Jiayu on the day of their first encounter but now renamed "Water Lily"—the clouds mundanely "weave dirty underwear," the theme of sacrifice linking the consumption of sex with the unanticipated toxicity that grays the sky.

Excess, Shamelessness, Crime

Shame occurs when excess becomes inadvertently apparent. *End of Spring in Jiangnan*, however, also offers an explicit denunciation of excess through tangential episodes employing hyperbole and paradox, as in the case of a killer whom Jiayu represents as a lawyer. The killer is a lucid pervert who is not only uninterested in hiding the unsightly but also shamelessly amplifies it to horrific levels: he has murdered seven people (the boss of a company, his family, and a maid, whom he has also raped) as well as a dog, merely out of the suspicion that the boss might have slept with his girlfriend. When Jiayu goes to meet him, a policewoman warns her that they have never seen such a fierce criminal: "he simply doesn't count as human." The killer disdains the formalities of the law; when Jiayu tells him that having a trial and a lawyer are signs of civilization, he responds that they are mere ruses to mask the inevitability of his death:

> "Why do they want to [make me undergo a trial]?" Wu Baoqiang said with a cold laugh. "Is it to make fun of me? Are you kidding me? Since you fucking want to make fun of me, I won't object if you take me to be killed right now. Again you play tricks on me. Fuck, if one gets cancer, one can still have some illusion of getting better—one chance out of ten thousand, out of a hundred thousand! But I'll die for sure, right? I can die, so don't kid me with the law. To hell with the public prosecutor, witnesses, the judge, the lawyer."[47]

Wu asks to be shot, because only a violent and unadorned death is acceptable to him. He contrasts the brutal clarity of his destiny with the hopes that a cancer patient might still entertain.

Jiayu does not know that she is ill at this point, but the dialogue anticipates her own quest to control the circumstances of her death. In any case, she tells him that even for him the verdict is not final. She even concedes that his motivation for killing—his suspicion that his girlfriend might have slept with her boss—is understandable and presses him on why he did not limit himself to just one death: why kill to such excess? "How much of a need" [*duoda biyao*] was there to also kill the boss's parents and then hide in a wardrobe waiting till his wife, children, and maid would return from the movies and kill the four of them as well, all for a text message he found on his girlfriend's cell phone?" Killing one person out of jealousy, Jiayu implies, might be justified, but the assassin's excess explodes all congruity of cause and effect. The assassin chillingly replies that the question of need should have been asked not to him but to the boss himself:

> "You ask him, why does he need to earn that much money? Buy all that real estate? Keep so many girlfriends? He can't use all that money, can't live in all those houses; he also can't screw that many girls. How many of the things in this world are not superfluous [*duoyu*]? You ask me why I killed that many people, I simply respond with four words: 'the more the better'! I knew how many people were in

his home, and I couldn't stop before killing them to the very last. Because to me, the reason to kill people and earn money is the same! You can't use superfluous money. But if you deposit it in the bank, you'll feel good, right? With killing it's the same. How did that old saying go? 'If I kill one we're even, if I kill two I'll make a profit.' We're greedy in whatever we do. This is human nature. You find it strange that in our society there are so many cases of family extermination, don't you, but in fact it isn't all that strange, because killing is like making money, making a little more profit counts for some, and killing one more person also counts for some, . . . people always want to gain a little something, even if it's something useless."[48]

The killer shamelessly compares his excess in killing to superfluous monetary gain, calling into question the boundary between the monstrous and the human. His speech exemplifies the novel's strategy of drawing analogies that at first appear implausible (between earning and killing or money and murder) to defamiliarize the arbitrary equivalences established by money in a capitalist system of exchange.

Whereas the murderer singles out the desire for surplus as innate to human nature and as the cause of criminal accumulation, in most of the novel diverse manifestations of *duoyu* or superfluity recur to foreground the mechanisms of blockage and release that shape human communication as well as the broader economic context in which characters act. Superfluity also manifests itself at the level of narrative, as puzzling events that find no resolution. What should be made, for instance, of the used condom Duanwu finds in his wife's handbag? An object containing a bodily fluid—now superfluous because deprived of its reproductive potential—poses an unanswered question. One might infer that the condom confirms a neighbor's suspicion that Jiayu has slept with an official in the education bureau to have her son transferred to a better class, and that she kept the semen to blackmail the man. But all this is never confirmed elsewhere in the narrative, making it a detail that remains unaccounted for.

Duoyu would thus seem to encompass anything from immoderate greed and accumulation to the fluids expelled by the body. Superfluity, or excess, is a constitutive condition of humanity that transcends the boundaries between the personal and the public, the emotional and the material, the intimate and the economic. The gentle veils of mist, not immediately available for human use and therefore soothing, are also superfluous, along with the toxic particles that result from excessive use of resources, as well as human tears. The fact that the one term, *duoyu*, establishes a basic equivalence of these contrasting meanings calls attention to the osmotic flows connecting the outside and the inside of the human body. Superfluity, the novel suggests, becomes toxic when it ceases to flow—that is to say, whenever immoderation makes people hold on to things that should continue to circulate and thus be redistributed. Although blockages may create toxicity, both within the human body and in the broader social world, the potential for an ethics of redistribution nevertheless resides in the interruptions that generate such affects as shame.

Conclusion

In *End of Spring in Jiangnan*, fog serves as a medium that both nurtures and obscures the search for a clean place to die. Although the novel aspires to offer a systemic diagnosis of contemporary China, it does not provide too tight a system of analogies, letting chaos seep in through contingent details and provisional dialogues. Over and over again, we are drawn to look for analogies only to discover their fragility. By suggesting analogies but keeping them imperfect, the author brings forth a tension between determining causes and unexpected events that escape determination. By building a system that does not hold, the novel seems to mimic the tension between closure and open-endedness, blockage and flow, that characterizes the workings of capital. If capitalism is a totality in which everything is exchangeable and new forms of exchangeability are constantly sought in the realm of things not previously exchangeable, the novel represents a general economy—we might call it an ecology—in which many narrative threads remain loose, enveloping the landscape like a soft, toxic mist. The dystopic tenor of *End of Spring in Jiangnan* denotes a mode of anticipation encompassing the contrasting temporal scales of the environment and human life: the long-term scale of environmental devastation and its much more immediate, though often subtle and less obvious, effects on the human body. By way of its imperfect analogies, the novel seeks to rejoin these two dimensions of time, yet their incommensurability makes it difficult for individuals to fully acknowledge their connections. Mist, fog, and "fog haze" bind them materially and figuratively: lingering in them are residues of futurity.

Tales of Futures Past began with tropes of planning, purity, and control, and ends with an emphasis on insecurity, toxic excess, and a loss of foresight and insight because of the clouding of all lines of vision. Even so, the very act of writing about fog is animated by an aspiration to clarity, metaphorically and otherwise. The polarity of communicative clarity and obscurity, as shown in the preceding chapters, has been an ongoing issue of contention in contemporary Chinese literary discourse. This polarity also underlies the contradictory cluster of cultural expressions that go under the name of modernism. Much of aesthetic modernism has revolved around the aspiration to estrange the real by deforming the linguistic medium. Another vein of modernism, however, one that is more directly related to processes of modernization and standardization, has sought to clarify the lines of expression and reduce the media clutter to a minimum, insisting on the possibility of communicative immediacy. In Ge Fei's novel, fog itself is the reminder of the mediated nature of experience and communication. At the same time, the novel suggests that the poetic employment of a "misty" language is inadequate to the demands of the present. Hence, the novel is animated by an effort to communicate that is engendered by the ominous thickening of the air. Through its engagement with these environmental changes, *End of Spring in Jiangnan* confronts—in the remnants of promises of poetic emancipation and of economic development turned sour—the contrasting hopes of modernism that have been at the center of this book. Its "pulviscular prose" enacts not an embrace of excess but an aspiration to moderation, reduction, and clarity. Fog renews the desire for vision.

APPENDIX ONE

Literary Periodicals for Internal Distribution in the 1950s–1960s

Shijie wenxue cankao ziliao
(Reference material for world literature)

Started in 1955 as *Waiguo wenxue qingkuang huibao* (Report on the situation of foreign literatures),[1] the periodical was initially meant for open circulation, and only after the Twentieth Congress of the Communist Party of the Soviet Union and the Polish and Hungarian crises did it begin to focus on recent East European and Russian literature. From May 1956 on, "Internal Periodical, Please Do Not Circulate" was printed on the cover. The September 1956 issue introduced Ehrenburg's *The Thaw*, and the July 1957 issue dealt with the debates spurred by the publication of Vladimir Dudintsev's *Not on Bread Alone*. In 1961–1962 a special issue was devoted to Ilya Ehrenburg. Texts were drawn from the Soviet *Literary Gazette* and other Eastern European journals, and from such periodicals as the *Atlantic*, *Harper's Magazine*, *Saturday Review*, *New York Times*, and *The Worker* (United States), *Times Literary Supplement* and the *Daily Worker* (United Kingdom), *Les Lettres Françaises* and *Les Nouvelles littéraires* (France), *Iraq Times* (Iraq), *Bungakkai* (Literary world) and *Shinchō* (New wave) (Japan).

Shijie wenxue qingkuang huibao
(Report on the situation of world literature)

Started in 1962, the periodical was published irregularly, with the words "Confidential: Internal Material, for Leaders' Reference Only" printed on the cover. Sixty-four issues came out between 1962 and 1965. The publication included overviews of new literary trends, translations of essays and articles from foreign journals, and summaries of fictional works, and was introduced by an editors' note that provided contextual explanation for the texts, including additional news about authors or the source from which they were translated. Soviet and French periodicals were the main source for material.

Shijie wenxue qingkuang fukan
(Supplement to the Report on the situation of world literature)

Five issues came out in 1965, on irregular dates, with the words "Confidential: Internal Material, Store Carefully" on the cover. An editors' note said that, to meet the professional needs of some readers, the editorial board had decided to integrate *Shijie wenxue qingkuang huibao* with this supplement, which would "publish representative and influential reactionary works that leaders and literary researchers need to know." As for the general aims of the publication, "fighting revisionism is the first task, and criticizing bourgeois literary trends comes second; this is in support of the current international struggle against revisionism." The supplement published works by controversial poets and writers who were critical of Stalin, such as poems by Yevgeny Yevtushenko, short stories by Vasily Aksyonov, and essays by Aleksandr Solzhenitsyn, as well as some of Franz Kafka's short stories ("Metamorphosis," the "Chinese Great Wall," and "In the Penal Colony").

Xiandai wenyi lilun yicong
(Collected translations of modern literary theory)

The periodical was published irregularly between 1961 and 1963 and then bimonthly until 1965. The aim of the publication was to bring to "those who work in literary theory, teachers of literature, and workers in literature and the arts at large the latest articles in literary theory and criticism from all the important countries of the world, including modern revisionist and bourgeois literary theories and criticism, for reference, study, and criticism." In 1961–1962, there was no indication that this was an internal publication. In December 1962, its name changed into *Waiguo wenxue xianzhuang* (Current situation in foreign literature), and "For Leaders' Reference; Please Do Not Circulate" was added on the cover. According to an editors' note, the change in name reflected the effort to speed up the pace of publication and bring the latest trends in literary theory and criticism to readers' attention. It focused primarily on Soviet theoretical debates and drew on communist periodicals in France and Italy.

Xiandai wenyi lilun yicong fukan
(Supplement to Collected translations of modern literary theory)

The supplement was first published in October 1960 with the words "For Leaders' Reference—Please Do Not Circulate" printed on the cover. The early issues included many translated texts, while the later issues relied more on extensive summaries by the translators themselves and included integral translations only for the texts deemed more representative or important. Published through 1963, the supplement had a broad geographical focus and paid special attention to international Marxism and discussions on art and politics; for instance, it introduced writings by the British Marxist literary critic Arnold Kettle and essays on the debate on humanism and literature in the Soviet Union.

Waiguo wenxue xianzhuang fukan
(Supplement to Current situation in foreign literatures)

Probably a continuation of *Xiandai wenyi lilun yicong fukan*, six issues were published in 1964, with "'Top Secret" printed on the cover, in addition to the usual "For the Leaders' Reference—Please Do Not Circulate." The publication mostly reported on criticism against the Chinese Communist Party raised in the Soviet literary world, attacks against CCP literary policies and Chinese literature. The periodical also published writings by authors from Bulgaria, Czechoslovakia, Poland, who, "unwilling to lag behind," were also critical of the CCP. These articles had in fact already been published in other internal publications devoted to politics, but they were republished so that literary cadres and workers could consult them. Overall, these issues gave the impression that Chinese literature was under massive attack by the rest of the Socialist world. Titles of translated articles included "Combat Dogmatism and Vulgarization in the Arts," which had first appeared in the Soviet magazine *The Communist* and which was, according to the editors, "the most massive and vicious attack against our party's literary line and literary policy, as well as against Mao Zedong's literary thought."

Note

Compiled on the basis of publications consulted at the National Library of China and partly adapted from Gu Fan [Li Huifan], "Huangpi shu ji qita."

    1. The periodical changed its name to *Reference Material for Foreign Literatures* in 1957 and to *Reference Material for World Literature* in 1959.

APPENDIX TWO

Poems by Li Shangyin

无题
相见时难别亦难，
东风无力百花残。
春蚕到死丝方尽，
蜡炬成灰泪始干。
晓镜但愁云鬓改，
夜吟应觉月光寒。
蓬山此去无多路，
青鸟殷勤为探看。

锦瑟
锦瑟无端五十弦，
一弦一柱思华年。
庄生晓梦迷蝴蝶，
望帝春心托杜鹃。
沧海月明珠有泪，
蓝田日暖玉生烟。
此情可待成追忆，
只是当时已惘然。

谒山
从来系日乏长绳，
水去云回恨不胜，
欲就麻姑买沧海，
一杯春露冷如冰。

CHINESE CHARACTERS

Ah Cheng [Acheng] 阿城
Ah Long [Along] 阿垅
Ba Jin 巴金
ba xiaoshuo xiejinle si hutong
　把小说写进了死胡同
baofeng 暴风
Baofeng zhouyu 暴风骤雨
Bei Cun 北村
Bei Dao 北岛
bei gaokua de yidai 被搞垮的一代
bi 比
biaoceng yuyan 表层语言
Bing Xin 冰心
Cai Xiang 蔡翔
cankui 惭愧
Can Xue 残雪
canghai 沧海
Canglao de fuyun 苍老的浮云
Cao Jinghua 曹靖华
Cao Suling 曹苏玲
Cao Yong 曹庸
cengci 层次
Changping 昌平
Chen Bingyi 陈冰夷
Chen Jingrong 陈敬容
Chen Mo 陈默
Chen Sihe 陈思和
Chen Xiaoman 陈小曼
Chen Xiaoming 陈晓明
Cheng Daixi 程代熙
Cheng Yongxin 程永新
chiru 耻辱

chuanqi 传奇
chuanqixing 传奇性
chun 纯
Chunjin Jiangnan 春尽江南
Chun zhi sheng 春之声
cizao 词藻
Dai Qing 戴晴
Deng Gang 邓刚
Ding Bogang 丁伯刚
Ding Ling 丁玲
Dongdan ertiao 东单二条
Dong Naibin 董乃斌
Dong Qiusi 董秋斯
Du Fu 杜甫
Dushu 读书
duo cengci de kongjian, shijian jiegou
　多层次的空间、时间结构
duoda biyao 多大必要
Duoduo 多多
duoyu 多余
duoyuanhua 多元化
Fang Borong 方柏容
Fangwen mengjing 访问梦境
Fei Ming 废名
fenyi 分译
Feng Hao 冯浩
Feng Jicai 冯骥才
Feng Mu 冯牧
Feng Xuefeng 冯雪峰
Feng Zicun 冯子存
fengzi cun 疯子村
Gangdisi de youhuo 冈底斯的诱惑

Liang Qichao 梁启超
Liang Shiqiu 梁实秋
Lin Jinlan 林斤澜
Lin Mohan 林默涵
Lingyin 灵隐
Liu Binyan 刘宾雁
Liu Cixin 刘慈欣
Liu Heng 刘恒
Liu Lanfang 刘兰芳
Liu Mingjiu 柳鸣九
Liu Suola 刘索拉
Liu Xie 刘勰
Liu Xuekai 刘学锴
Liu Yisheng 刘逸生
Liu Yong 刘勇
Liu Zaifu 刘再复
Lu Xinhua 卢新华
Lu Xun 鲁迅
Lüse de shiti 绿色的尸体
Magu 麻姑
Ma Jian 马建
Ma Shunjia 马顺佳
Ma Yuan 马原
maipulun 麦普纶
Mang Ke 芒克
Mao Dun 矛盾
Mei nüshe qi an 美女蛇奇案
menglong shi 朦胧诗
mengmeng longlong de 朦朦胧胧的
Mengyouzhe 梦游者
miwang de yidai 迷惘的一代
miandui shijie 面对世界
minban gongzhu 民办公助
mohuan xiaoshuo 魔幻小说
Mo Yan 莫言
neibu 内部
neibu faxing 内部发行
Neibu faxingzu 内部发行组
Neibu fuwuchu 内部服务处
neixin 内心
neixin de shuqing de qian yuyan, chao
    yuyan
    内心的抒情的潜语言、超语言

ni xianzai yijing zou zai Zhongguo
    wenxue de zui qianlie de
    你现在已经走在中国文学的最
    前列的
Niu Han 牛汉
nongwu 浓雾
Ouyang Yuqian 欧阳予倩
Pan Jun 潘军
Pi Pi 皮皮
pianwen 骈文
pingshu 评书
pukepai xiaoshuo 扑克牌小说
qibao loutai 七宝楼台
qimen 气闷
qipai 气派
Qi wang 棋王
qiangu zhi mi 千古之谜
Qian Xuesen 钱学森
Qian Zhongshu 钱钟书
Qiao 桥
Qin Shunxin 秦顺新
Qin Zhaoyang 秦兆阳
qingdiao 情调
Qu Qiubai 瞿秋白
Qu Yuan 屈原
quanguo youxiu duanpian xiaoshuo
    jiang 全国优秀短篇小说奖
Rang womende shenghuo geng kexue
    xie 让我们的生活更科学些
rendaozhuyi 人道主义
renlei benxing 人类本性
Renmian taohua 人面桃花
renti teyi gongneng 人体特异功能
Rongxian hutong 绒线胡同
Ru Long 汝龙
Sha Hei 沙黑
Shanhe rumeng 山河入梦
Shanhudao shang de siguang
    珊瑚岛上的死光
shangchun 伤春
shanghen wenxue 伤痕文学
shangpin 商品
shenceng yuyan 深层语言

Shenmi yi 神秘衣
Shenqi de tongkong 神奇的瞳孔
Shibasui chumen yuanxing
 十八岁出门远行
shidai 时代
shijian de kejiu 时间的窠臼
Shijie wenxue 世界文学
Shijie wenxue cankao ziliao
 世界文学参考资料
Shijie wenxue qingkuang fukan
 世界文学情况副刊
Shijie wenxue qingkuang huibao
 世界文学情况汇报
Shijie wenyi dongtai 世界文艺动态
Shipin 诗品
Shisan ling shuiku changxiangqu
 十三陵水库畅想曲
Shi Tiesheng 史铁生
Shi Xianrong 施咸荣
shiyan 试验
shiyan wenti 试验文体
Shouhuo 收获
shushang 书商
Shu Ting 舒婷
shuaijie 衰竭
Sikong Tu 司空图
Siren 斯人
su 俗
Sulian wenyi 苏联文艺
Su Tong 苏童
Su Xuelin 苏雪林
Sun Ganlu 孙甘露
Sun Shengwu 孙绳武
taihu 太湖
tansuo 探索
tanzi 谈资
Tang Xianzu 汤显祖
Tao Wenpeng 陶文鹏
Tian Han 田汉
tiaozheng 调整
Tong Enzheng 童恩正
tonggou 同构
tongsu 通俗

tongsu wenxue 通俗文学
Touming de hongluobo 透明的红萝卜
tousheng 偷生
Waiguo wenxue qingkuang huibao
 外国文学情况汇报
Waiguo wenxue xianzhuang
 外国文学现状
Waiguo wenxue xianzhuang fukan
 外国文学现状副刊
Waiguo wenyi 外国文艺
Wanzhu 顽主
Wang Hao 王浩
Wang Jiaxiang 王家骧
Wang Meng 王蒙
wangran 惘然
Wang Shixie 王士燮
Wang Shuo 王朔
Wang Xiaoming 王晓明
Wang Yao 王尧
Wang Zhongchen 王中忱
wei 味
Wei Yahua 魏雅华
wenming 文明
Wenrou zhi xiang de meng
 温柔之乡的梦
wenxue jiu shi renxue 文学就是人学
Wenyi bao 文艺报
Wode Luotuosi 我的罗陀斯
Wo jueding yu jiqiren qizi lihun
 我决定与机器人妻子离婚
wu 雾
wuduan 无端
Wu Jianren 吴趼人
wulan 雾岚
Wu Liang 吴亮
wumai 雾霾
wuti shi 无题诗
Wutong 伍桐
wuxia 武侠
Xijindu 西津渡
xisheng 牺牲
Xizang wenxue 西藏文学
xiandai 现代

Xiandai wenyi lilun yicong
　　现代文艺理论译丛
Xiandai wenyi lilun yicong fukan
　　现代文艺理论译丛副刊
xiandaipai 现代派
xiandaipai de yishu 现代派的艺术
xianfeng 先锋
xianjing 仙境
xianshi 现实
Xiangjian shi nan 相见时难
xiangsheng 相声
xiangtu wenxue 乡土文学
Xiao Lingtong manyou weilai
　　小灵通漫游未来
Xiao Lingtong sanyou weilai
　　小灵通三游未来
Xiao Lingtong zaiyou weilai
　　小灵通再游未来
xiaopin 小品
Xiaoshuo yuebao 小说月报
Xie Mian 谢冕
xie yi ye, pai yi ye 写一页，排一页
xin, da, ya 信、达、雅
Xin shitou ji 新石头记
Xinshi zhi han 信使之函
xing 兴
Xingxing 星星
xiuchi 羞耻
xiukui 羞愧
xuanxu 玄虚
Xu Chi 徐迟
xuecai 雪菜
Xuehua nage piao 雪花那个飘
Xu Fang 徐芳
xuwu 虚无
Xu Xing 徐星
Xu Xu 徐訏
Xu Zhimo 徐志摩
Xu Zidong 许子东
Yan Fu 严复
yansu 严肃
Yan Wenjing 严文井
Yang Yi 杨亿

Yao Wenyuan 姚文元
Yecao 野草
Ye de yan 夜的眼
Ye shan 谒山
Ye Shengtao 叶圣陶
Ye Shuifu 叶水夫
Ye weiyang 夜未央
Ye Yonglie 叶永烈
yeyu 业余
Yeyu ji bei 夜雨寄北
Ye Zhaoyan 叶兆言
yi 意
Yilin 译林
yishiliu 意识流
Yiwen 译文
yiyi 意译
yin 隐
Yin Chuanhong 尹传红
yinhui 隐晦
yingyi 硬译
yonghuai 咏怀
yongsu 庸俗
Yu Dafu 郁达夫
Yu Hua 余华
Yu Shucheng 余恕诚
Yuxisheng 玉谿生
Yuanfang lai ke 远方来客
Yuan Jie 元结
Yuan Kejia 袁可嘉
yun 云
yun'ai 云霭
zangwu 脏雾
Zhaxi Dawa 扎西达娃
Zhaiyi 摘译
Zhang Chengzhi 张承志
Zhang Guangnian 张光年
Zhang Jie 张戒
Zhang Ming 章明
Zhang Mingmin 张明敏
Zhang Xian 张献
Zhang Zhimin 张志民
Zhao Botao 赵伯陶
zhenshi 真实

zhenshi de biaobai 真实的表白
Zhenzhong ji 枕中记
Zheng Wenguang 郑文光
Zheng Yuxin 郑毓信
Zheng Zhenduo 郑振铎
zhiyi 直译
zhi you hen shao de hongse guozi liu
    zai wo zhitou shang
    只有很少的红色果子留在我枝
    头上
zhizaozhe 制造者
Zhongguo gudai shehui yanjiu
    中国古代社会研究
Zhongguo ren de fangfa
    中国人的方法
Zhongguo xianfeng xiaoshuo
    中国先锋小说
Zhongguo xinchao xiaoshuo xuan
    中国新潮小说选
Zhongguo ziji de minzu fangfa lai
    biaoxian naxie dongxi
    中国自己的民族方法来表现那
    些东西
Zhongguo zuojia 中国作家
Zhou Libo 周立波

Zhou Yanru 周雁如
Zhou Yang 周扬
Zhu Heling 朱鹤龄
Zhu Hong 朱虹
Zhu Wei 朱伟
zhuan 专
zhuanhao 专号
zhuanji wenxue 传记文学
Zhuangshi 装饰
Zhuangzi 庄子
zhunque de shenfen 准确的身份
zhuoyandian 着眼点
zitai 姿态
Zou Difan 邹荻帆
zou xiang shijie 走向世界
zui'e 罪恶
Zuihou yige aizheng sizhe
    最后一个癌症死者
Zui xin xiaoshuo yi pie 最新小说一瞥
Zuojia chubanshe 作家出版社
Zuoxie Shanghai fenhui qingchuanghui
    shoujie xueyuan xiaoshuo zhuanji
    作协上海分会青创会首届学员小
    说专辑

NOTES

Introduction

1. Ye Yonglie, *Xiao Lingtong Manyou Weilai*. It was then republished as palm-size "serial picture booklet" (*lianhuanhua*) in 1980.

2. Průšek, *The Lyrical and the Epic*, and Xiaobing Tang, *Chinese Modern*, respectively. Maghiel van Crevel's terms "elevated and earthly" (*Chinese Poetry in Times of Mind, Mayhem, and Money*, esp. 24–27) parallel Tang's "heroic and quotidian."

3. Fitzpatrick, *Everyday Stalinism*, 9.

4. For a nuanced discussion of the term "postsocialist," see McGrath, *Postsocialist Modernity*. For McGrath, postsocialist modernity is a global condition emerging from "the collapse of the 'alternative modernity' of communism," namely, "a fundamentally new stage of capitalist development, not just for China but for the world" (14–15).

5. Raymond Williams, afterword to *Modern Tragedy*, 97.

6. Levin, "Farewell to *Modernism*," 90; Bauman, *Legislators and Interpreters*, 130; Jameson, *Postmodernism*, 48, 99–100.

7. T. J. Clark, "Origins of the Present Crisis," *New Left Review*, 90–93.

8. For works that emphasize the notion of the future in the field of postcolonial studies, see Scott, *Conscripts of Modernity*, to which I will turn shortly; in queer studies, Muñoz, *Cruising Utopia*. For works that forcefully embrace a presentist temporality, see Berlant, *Cruel Optimism*, and Edelman, *No Future*. For a reflection on the politics of temporality in contemporary philosophy, see Reynolds, *Chronopathologies*. On narrative anticipation in Anglophone contemporary novels, see Currie, *About Time*.

9. Koselleck, *Futures Past*, 258–259.

10. Ibid., 59–60. Peter Osborne has also argued that modernity was premised on "a reorientation towards the future" ("Modernity Is a Qualitative, Not a Chronological, Category," 70).

11. See Ricoeur, *Time and Narrative* 3:212–214.

12. Scott, *Conscripts of Modernity*, 44.

13. See ibid., prologue and chapter 1.

14. Ibid., 114–115.

15. On the future as a category of historical inquiry, see Panchasi, *Future Tense*.

16. Adams, Murphy, and Clarke, "Anticipation: Technoscience, Life, Affect, Temporality," 247, italics in original.

17. Ibid., 259, quoting Papadopoulos, Stephenson, and Tsianos, *Escape Routes*, xii.

18. Leo Ou-fan Lee, "In Search of Modernity," 111.

19. Ibid., 125.

20. See Mittag, "Time Concepts in China," 59.

21. See David Der-wei Wang, *Fin-de-Siècle Splendor*, 15–21.

22. See Daruvala, *Zhou Zuoren*.

23. Xiaobing Tang, "Lu Xun's 'Diary of a Madman' and a Chinese Modernism; Jones, *Developmental Fairy Tales*, 12, 200.

24. Hockx, "Is there a May Fourth Literature?," 49.

25. Hockx, *Questions of Style*, 5.

26. Duara sets a compelling agenda when he writes that "the task remains to explore how, and with what effects, conceptions of time become tied to structures of power" (*Sovereignty and Authenticity*, 26).

27. On the anticipatory aspects of realism in early twentieth-century Chinese literary debates, see Huters, "Ideologies of Realism in Modern China," 159.

28. Pollock, introduction to *Literary Cultures in History*, 18.

29. Hockx, *Questions of Style*, 6. Hockx is referring to several works in modern Chinese literary studies, including Laughlin, *Chinese Reportage*, and McDougall, *Love-Letters and Privacy in Modern China*.

30. Culler, *The Literary in Theory*, 31.

31. Ibid., 39–40.

32. Ibid., 42.

33. Felski, *Uses of Literature*, 4.

34. Ibid.

35. Ibid., 5.

36. Ibid., 5.

37. Ibid., 14 (italics in original).

38. For a genealogy of the concept of "sinophone literature," see Kim Tong Tee, "(Re)mapping Sinophone Literature."

39. If I seem to downplay the coercive aspects of the socialist state, it is because they have already been documented. See especially Goldman's *Literary Dissent in Communist China* and *China's Intellectuals*.

40. Jing Wang, *High Culture Fever*, 242. Wang focuses on Ge Fei's works from the 1980s to the early 1990s.

Chapter 1

1. "Xiayi shiji renlei jiang zenyang shenghuo? Sulian kexuejia yuyan kexue chuangzao gezhong qiji" (How will humanity live in the next century? Soviet scientists predict that science will create all kinds of wonders), *Renmin ribao*, June 12, 1957.

2. See Donald, *Public Secrets, Public Spaces*, 62; McGrath, "Cultural Revolution Model Opera Films and the Realist Tradition in Chinese Cinema," 347–348.

3. See Cai Tiliang, "Tian Han yu tade qingyi 'shiyan tian,'" 9.

4. Ouyang Yuqian, "Wei 'Shisan ling shuiku changxiangqu' dasheng hecai" (Cheers

for *Rhapsody of the Ming Tombs Reservoir*), *Renmin ribao*, July 16, 1958, quoted in ibid., 10. Most post-1980s Chinese assessments of the play are quite negative. See, for instance, Guo Yuqiong, "Zhishifenzi ziwo lixiang de gaoyang yu shiluo." Michael Schoenhals briefly refers to the film version as a "remarkable art film, . . . a unique record of the utopia of Mao's Great Leap Forward." ("Consuming Fragments of Mao Zedong," 110). Krista Van Fleit Hang offers an illuminating discussion of the film in *Literature the People Love*, 153–155.

    5. Tian Han, "Shisan ling shuiku changxiangqu," 56–57.

    6. Ibid., 62.

    7. The drama version describes an explosion propelling the audience twenty years ahead, which is not represented in the film.

    8. See Cai Tiliang, "Tian Han yu tade qingyi 'shiyan tian,'" 10.

    9. The first version of Little Smarty's adventure in 1961 was denied publication. See Ye Yonglie, "Xiao Lingtong shi zenyang yansheng de." Ye Yonglie (b. 1940) graduated in chemistry at Beijing University in 1963. Editor of the series "One Hundred Thousand Whys," scriptwriter at the Shanghai Science Education Film Studio, and author of about 180 works of popular science, science fiction, reportage and biography, he ranks among the most prolific Chinese writers of popular genres and was perhaps the most influential author of science fantasies in the late 1970s and early 1980s. After 1984, apart from the two sequels, *Xiao Lingtong zaiyou weilai* (Xiao Lingtong returns to the future, 1986) and *Xiao Lingtong sanyou weilai* (Xiao Lingtong's third trip to the future, 2000), Ye has mostly written biographies of historical figures and literary reportage.

    10. Yin Chuanhong, "Renshi liangge 'Ye Yonglie.'" According to Perry Link, "decisions on size of print runs were essentially political. Market considerations weighed more or less heavily depending on the political climate, but were always subordinate to political factors" (*The Uses of Literature*, 130).

    11. Guo Moruo, *Zhongguo gudai shehui yanjiu*, 4–5.

    12. See Farquhar, *Children's Literature in China*, 273–274.

    13. Li Siguang, "Kan kan womende diqiu" (Look at our earth), in Li Siguang et al., *Kexuejia tan 21 shiji*, 1–6. Similar books include Xu Jiashi's *Sanshinian houde shijie*.

    14. Gao Sha, "Jieshao *Kexuejia tan 21 shiji*," 122.

    15. Shapiro, *Mao's War against Nature*.

    16. Yang Mou, "Zai weilai de chengshi li" (In the future city), in Li Siguang et al., *Kexuejia tan 21 shiji*, 117–119. Several essays are dedicated to the "cinema of tomorrow" and new means of transportation.

    17. Fang Borong, "Huaxue xianwei de yuanjing" (The future of synthetic fibers), in ibid., 49–52.

    18. Gao Sha, "Jieshao *Kexuejia tan 21 shiji*," 122.

    19. Böhm and Dörge, *Unsere Welt von Morgen*, 220, as quoted in Rubin, *Synthetic Socialism*, 107.

    20. Ibid., 106–107.

    21. "Scar literature" took its name from the famous 1978 short story by Lu Xinhua, which denounced how the Cultural Revolution had torn families apart. Thirty-three

years after the publication of Lu Xinhua's story, the TV series *Xuehua nage piao* (Snow in the wind, 2011) depicts college students in 1978 learning about it from media reports and frantically looking for a copy. They borrow the magazine from an editor, cry many tears while reading it, and spend an entire night hand-copying the text. This is, of course, a fictional reconstruction, but it may well reflect the strong impact the story had at the time.

22. Zhu Qing, "Puji kexue wenyi de sanzhong guandian," 155, 157.

23. Ye Yonglie emphasizes that *kexue wenyi* is primarily addressed to children and young people, and that its task is to depict technologies that are not yet available. He also stresses that it is an imported genre, inspired by Jules Verne's works and other classics of Western science fiction. See Ye Yonglie, *Lun kexue wenyi*, 23, 47. Zheng Wenguang situates *kexue wenyi* "in the vast region between popular science and literature." ("Kexue wenyi zatan" [Random talk on science literature and arts], quoted in Bai Ye, ed., *Xin shiqi wenxue liu nian*, 447).

24. Kinkley, *Chinese Justice, the Fiction*, 271.

25. The Four Modernizations, launched by Deng Xiaoping in 1978, aimed at strengthening agriculture, industry, national defense, and science and technology.

26. See Wang, *Fin-de-Siècle Splendor*, 252–312.

27. Jones, *Developmental Fairy Tales*, 30. On *New Story of the Stone*, see also Ming, "Baoyu in Wonderland," and Huters, *Bringing the World Home*, 151–172.

28. See Liu Weimin, *Kexue yu xiandai Zhongguo wenxue*, 159–178.

29. See Schmalzer, *The People's Peking Man*, 40–63.

30. Zheng Wenguang, "Rang women de shenghuo geng kexue xie," 43.

31. Usually translated as "crosstalk" or "comic dialogue," *xiangsheng* performances consist of humorous stories, witty jokes, and puns generally told by two comedians and often broadcast on television and on the radio. See Link, "The Genie and the Lamp," 83–84.

32. Such overlapping calls to mind Eric Rabkin's suggestion that "science fiction is a system, something much larger than a genre" ("Science Fiction and the Future of Criticism," 461).

33. Many science fiction writers had university degrees in the hard sciences, but only few of them were professional scientists or academics. Zheng Wenguang had studied astronomy but worked as an editor and writer of popular science for most of his life. The archaeologist Tong Enzheng wrote *kehuan xiaoshuo* as a hobby. The writer Guo Moruo often spoke and wrote about the relationship of literature and science in his function of president of the Academy of Sciences. At the first National Science and Technology Convention in Beijing in March 1978, for instance, Guo Moruo delivered the famous speech "The Spring of Science" in which he asked scientists to have the imagination of poets. Reported in Wu Xiaojiang, "Kehuan li xianshi you duoyuan?," 32.

34. Wagner, "Lobby Literature," 22. In this illuminating chapter, Wagner shows that many foreign works, ranging from Russian and Soviet science fiction to Isaac Asimov's robot stories, inspired Chinese writers.

35. See Chi Shuchang, "Gediao bizi de daxiang" in Ye Yonglie, ed., *Zhongguo kexue huanxiang xiaoshuo xuan*, 42–55; Yu Zhi, "Shizong de gege," in ibid., 13–40.

36. Handwritten fiction notebooks started to circulate around 1974. People copied stories to kill time, to practice writing, or simply to further circulate them among family and friends. The stories were mostly drafted by secondary school students sent to the countryside or to construction corps. Such detective stories as "Lüse de shiti" (The Green Corpse) were composed of many episodes, each concluding with a new strange murder that would find resolution in the following section. Several of their characterizing elements—unexpected twists and turns, an emphasis on chance and coincidence, and scarce concern for verisimilitude—also characterize *kehuan* stories. See Bai Shihong, ed., *Anliu*. See also Perry Link, *Uses of Literature*, 222–225.

37. My search is limited to the *People's Daily*.

38. This is a reversal of Peter Brooks's notion of "anticipation of retrospection." For Brooks, we read by making provisional sense of what we read "in anticipation of its larger hermeneutic structuring by conclusions" (*Reading for the Plot*, 23).

39. Rudolf Wagner and Jeffrey Kinkley have lamented the puerile quality and limited imagination of post-Mao Chinese science fiction. See Wagner, "Lobby Literature," and Kinkley, *Chinese Justice, the Fiction*. Lesser known works, such as Yang Beixing and Sun Chuansong's novel *Mei nüshe qi an* (The strange case of the snake beauty), may be better reads than works by such influential authors as Ye Yonglie, on which their assessment is mostly based. The novel had a print run of 180,000 copies.

40. Exotic settings were common in hand-copied stories. See Link, *Uses of Literature*, 235.

41. Tong Enzheng, "Shanhudao shang de siguang," 23.

42. The coral island setting also evokes postcolonial legacies, particularly the international disputes over natural resources in the South China Sea. See Nolan, "Imperial Archipelagos."

43. Tong Enzheng, "Shanhudao shang de siguang," 16.

44. Ibid., 26.

45. Rao Zhonghua, "Huanxiang, Chuangxin, Kexue," 9. In Ye Yonglie's *Little Smarty Travels to the Future*, the family that hosts Little Smarty is aided by Iron Egg Zhuo Hao, a robot who can cook simple dishes, does daily chores, and plays chess with grandpa. This representation was criticized because it portrayed robots as butlers rather than as doing things impossible for humans and thus extending human capabilities. See Cai Zizheng, "Youxie buzu zhi chu."

46. "Wenrou zhi xiang de meng" was awarded the "Beijing Literature" prize in 1981. The story was originally published in *Beijing wenxue*, no. 1 (1981); it is reprinted in *Wei Yahua jiazuo xuan*, 182–212, followed by "Wo jueding yu jiqiren qizi lihun," 213–264. "Wenrou zhi xiang de meng" is translated in English as "Conjugal Happiness in the Arms of Morpheus" in Wu and Murphy, eds., *Science Fiction from China*, 9–52. All translations are mine.

47. Wei Yahua, "Wenrou zhi xiang de meng," 183.

48. Ibid., 185–186.

49. Asimov's three laws of robotics are (1) a robot may not injure a human being or, through inaction, allow a human being to come to harm; (2) a robot must obey any

orders given to it by human beings, except where such orders would conflict with the first law; (3) a robot must protect its own existence as long as such protection does not conflict with the first or second law. They were first introduced in "Runaround," *Astounding Science Fiction* (March 1942), which is reprinted in Asimov, *I, Robot*, 30–47.

50. Wei Yahua, "Wenrou zhi xiang de meng," 194–195.

51. The biochemist defines the "primitive" stage in which Lili finds herself as "theist" (Ibid., 224). According to this notion, robots are stuck in an earlier stage of human development.

52. Ibid., 226.

53. I borrow the notion of "chaotic enumeration" from Spitzer, "Interpretation of an Ode by Paul Claudel," 300.

54. Wei Yahua, "Mengyouzhe," in *Wei Yahua jiazuo xuan*, 24.

55. Named after the date of an earlier Mao directive, the May 7th cadre schools were set up in 1968 and were gradually closed down after 1971. In these schools, cadres participated in manual labor and intense study of Mao's works; their aim was to prevent the formation of a separate, privileged ruling class.

56. Wei Yahua, "Mengyouzhe," 66–67.

57. Engels, *The Part Played by Labor in the Transition from Ape to Man*, 3. The earliest Chinese version of this text was published in 1948. The notion of labor itself underwent major revision in the early 1980s and was expanded to include various forms of skilled, delicate work as well as mental work. See Schmalzer, *The People's Peking Man*, 60–61.

58. "I could feel his happiness, his excitement, his joy—a kind of joy that he mostly attained through sensory stimulation, similar to the excitement and greediness of a dog who has just obtained a fat piece of meat" (Wei Yahua, "Mengyouzhi," 67).

59. Ibid., 68–69.

60. The story "Zhide qingxing de cuowu" (A mistake worthy of celebration), which depicted a doctor who had elaborated a cure for cancer based on bitter almonds, apparently persuaded many readers that such a cure truly existed, and for months after its publication, the editorial board kept receiving letters and phone calls from readers who inquired about it. See Wei Yahua, "Wo yu kehuan xiaoshuo" (Science fiction and I) in *Wei Yahua jiazuo xuan*, 5–6.

61. "Shenqi de tongkong" was first published in *Mangzhong*, no. 4 (1983), and is reprinted in *Wei Yahua jiazuo xuan*, 147–181.

62. Images of corrosion and physical deformation are recurrent in the science fantasies of the early 1980s.

63. Shi Tong, "Kehuan zuopin zhong de jingshen wuran ye ying qingli" (The spiritual pollution in science fiction works also needs to be cleaned up), *Renmin ribao*, November 5, 1983. See also Tao Shilong, "Guanyu kehuan xiaoshuo wenti de taolun," esp. 23.

64. Quoted in Tao Shilong, "Guanyu kehuan xiaoshuo wenti de taolun," 17. Interestingly, Qian's research interests in the early 1980s included *qigong* and other "extraordinary somatic powers" (*renti teyi gongneng*). See Palmer, *Qigong Fever*, 67–85.

65. See Xiao Rong, "*Wenyi bao* bianjibu, Zhongguo wenlian lilun yanjiushi zhaokai kehuan xiaoshuo chuangzuo taolunhui" (*Literary Gazette* editorial board and the Theo-

retical Research section of the China Federation of Literary and Art Circles hold a symposium on science fiction), *Renmin ribao*, November 23, 1983.

66. See Yi Jiayan, "Shuru le shenme yishi—Du mouxie kehuan xiaoshuo suigan" (What was planted in their mind—Jottings on reading some science fiction), *Renmin ribao*, April 21, 1984.

67. One of the earliest critiques against science fiction was raised by Lu Bing, "Bu shi kexue ye bu shi wenxue" (It's neither science nor literature), *Zhongguo qingnian bao*, April 24, 1982. Lu's article was followed by a response signed by twelve science fiction writers who contested its aggressive tone ("Guanyu kehuan xiaoshuo pinglun de yifeng xin").

68. Tong Enzheng, "Tan tan wo dui kexue wenyi de renshi." For some critics, scientific knowledge was to serve as a source of literary inspiration: "If our science fantasy writers pay sustained attention to the new developments in contemporary science and technology, they will be inspired by them and will write amazing plots" (Rao Zhonghua, "Huanxiang, Chuangxin, Kexue," 11).

69. Ma Shunjia, "Guanyu kehuan xiaoshuo de liangge wenti."

70. Wei Yahua, "Kehuan xiaoshuo de weiji," 78–80.

71. The Galaxy Award for science fiction was also established in Chengdu in 1986.

Chapter 2

1. Feng Xuefeng, "Xuexi dangxing yuanze, xuexi Sulian wenxue xianjin jingyan" (Study the party principles and the Soviet advanced literary experience), *Wenyi bao*, no. 21 (1952), quoted in Li Xiu and Qin Linfang, *Ershi shiji zhongwai wenxue jiaoliu shi* 2:563.

2. For a recent assessment of Chinese literary translation in the 1950s, see Volland, "A Linguistic Enclave." On the translation and reception of Russian literature in China throughout the twentieth century, see Gamsa, *The Chinese Translation of Russian Literature*, and his *The Reading of Russian Literature in China*.

3. Some translators were well-known writers with their own spheres of influence in universities or other state institutions. The initiatives of these writers were important factors in the selection and translation of works that fell beyond the scope of leftist literature. Overall, readership of foreign texts in translation was limited to a small group of people with senior high school education. Thanks to Bonnie McDougall for these suggestions.

4. From October 1949 to December 1959, Russian and Soviet works amounted to 65 percent of all translated texts. See Bian Zhilin, "Shinian lai de waiguo wenxue fanyi he yanjiu gongzuo" (Translation and research of foreign literature in the last ten years), *Wenyi pinglun*, no. 5 (1959), quoted in Li Xiu and Qin Linfang, *Ershi shiji zhongwai wenxue jiaoliu shi* 2:572.

5. The terms *yiyi* and *zhiyi* date back to discussions on the early translation of Buddhist texts into Chinese. Lu Xun, Liang Shiqiu, and Mao Dun were the main protagonists of the debates in the 1920s and 1930s. See Leo Tak-hung Chan, *Twentieth-Century Chinese Translation Theory*.

6. Volland, "A Linguistic Enclave," 472.

7. Mao Dun at this time was the Minister of Culture, President of the Writers' Association and editor-in-chief of the journal *Yiwen* (Translations). Guo Moruo was vice-premier of the State Administration Council, chairman of the Chinese Academy of Sciences, chairman of the Chinese Peace Committee, vice-chairman of the Peace Liaison Committee for the Asian and Pacific Regions, and member of the board of directors of the Chinese People's Association for Cultural Relations with Foreign Countries.

8. The term *yingyi* (stiff translation) refers to a debate between Lu Xun and Liang Shiqiu in the late 1920s in which the Liang had criticized Lu's style of translation as "stiff." Guo is in this instance adopting Liang's position against Lu Xun.

9. Collective translation in the Soviet Union had started soon after the Bolshevik Revolution. See Friedberg, *Literary Translation in Russia*, 137–138.

10. Guo Moruo, "Tan wenxue fanyi gongzuo," *Renmin ribao*, August 29, 1954; reprinted in Luo Xinzhang, ed., *Fanyi lunji*, 498–499.

11. Mao Dun, "Wei fazhan wenxue fanyi shiye he tigao fanyi zhiliang er fendou," *Yiwen*, no. 10 (1954); reprinted in Luo Xinzhang, ed., *Fanyi lunji*, 511.

12. Ibid.

13. This point was also addressed by Lao She, who claimed that readers did not like recently translated works because they randomly mixed European and Chinese grammar, classical and vernacular language, which made them unreadable. The Chinese language at that time was, of course, already the result of multiple influences, but this is an issue that neither Mao Dun nor Lao She addressed.

14. Mao Dun, "Wei fazhan wenxue fanyi shiye," 515–516.

15. Ibid., 506–508. Because Mao Dun does not substantiate his claims with any examples, it is difficult to assess their accuracy or to know which texts were being repeatedly translated. The *Quanguo zong shumu* (National book catalogue) of 1956 shows that several Russian texts were issued in two Chinese editions in the early 1950s. They include Alexander N. Ostrovski's *An Ardent Heart* (1952 and 1953), Maxim Gorky's *The Lower Depths* (1950 and 1953), Leo Tolstoy's *Hadji Murat* (1953 and 1954), Fyodor Dostoyevsky's *Poor Folk* (1951 and 1954), Nikolai Ostrovsky's *Born of the Storm* (two editions, both issued in 1953), Tikhon Z. Semushkin's *Alitet Goes to the Hills* (1951 and 1954), Georgii Gulia's *Spring Time in Saken* (1950 and 1951), Ilya Ehrenburg's *The Storm* (1952 and 1953), Pavel T. Zhurba's *Aleksandr Matrosov* (two editions, both issued in 1952), Sergei Dikovskii's *The Commandant of Bird Island* (two editions, both issued in 1953), and Vadim Sobko's *Guarantee of Peace* (also both in 1953). Jack London's *The Call of the Wild* was also published twice in 1953. For full bibliographical references of foreign works translated into Chinese from 1949 to 1954, see *Quanguo zong shumu*, 398–448.

16. Mao Dun, "Wei fazhan wenxue fanyi shiye," 508–509. On the mix of private and public publishers in early 1950s China, see Nunn, *Publishing in Mainland China*.

17. See McDougall, *The Introduction of Western Literary Theories into Modern China, 1919–1925*, 24–31.

18. Ru Long, "Fanyi yu chuban" (Translating and publishing), *Renmin ribao*, June 1, 1957. Chief editor at Shanghai Pingming Publishing House in 1952–1953 and a translator of Russian literature, Ru Long is mostly remembered for his translation of Chekhov's works.

19. See "Jiaqiang bianjibu tong zuojia de tuanjie" (Strengthening the unity between editors and writers), *Renmin ribao*, May 9, 1957.

20. *Yiwen* (Translations) was renamed *Shijie wenxue* (World literature) in 1959. I will address this change of name later in the chapter. Publication was interrupted in 1965, after the editorial board had been sent to rural Anhui province to take part in the Four Cleanups campaign. Publication resumed shortly in 1966 and then ceased again until 1977. *Yiwen / Shijie wenxue* was initially issued by the Chinese Writers' Association and was transferred to the Chinese Academy of Sciences in 1964. Four research groups in the Literature Institute at the Chinese Academy of Sciences (Eastern, Western, Russian, and East European) were merged with the editorial board of *World Literature* to form the Institute of Foreign Literature in 1964. See Gu Fan [Li Huifan], "Huangpi shu ji qita," 118.

21. Some of the translations published by *Yiwen* were executed by the translators who worked at the journal full time, but many others were commissioned to other translators. Chen Bingyi had worked for the journals *Shidai* (The epoch) and *Sulian wenyi* (Soviet literature and arts) in the 1940s, while Dong Qiusi was the translator of *War and Peace* (from English) and the author of influential theoretical articles on translation. They became targets of attack during the Cultural Revolution; Dong Qiusi was denied medical treatment and died in 1969. See Gao Mang, "Baihua shengkai de jijie," 58–59.

22. Thomas Mann, Halldór Kiljan Laxness, and Erskine Caldwell emerged as favorites among the (mostly left-leaning) writers who participated in the survey. *Yiwen*, no. 8 (1956): 188–189. The various sections in which *Yiwen* was divided were remarkably similar to those in the *Short Story Magazine*, which under Mao Dun's editorship from 1920 to 1922 also devoted much space to translations of foreign works and literary news from abroad. See McDougall, *The Introduction of Western Literary Theories*, 24–31.

23. See Jian Chen, *Mao's China and the Cold War*, 53–82.

24. Ibid., 79–82.

25. Wagner, *Inside a Service Trade*, 80. On the translation of Soviet literature in *Yiwen*, see also Fokkema, *Literary Doctrine in China and Soviet Influence, 1956–1960*.

26. Walter Lowenfels is one of the several writers translated or mentioned in *Yiwen* who were imprisoned and persecuted in their countries for their leftist political ideas. Political persecution in the West is one of the selection criteria adopted by *Yiwen*.

27. *Virgin Soil Upturned* won Sholokhov the Lenin Literary Prize. Sholokhov remained one of the most translated Soviet authors in the following years. He received the Nobel Prize for literature in 1965.

28. *Yiwen*, no. 2 (1957): 192–194. The emphasis on pan-Asianism was also an effect of the Bandung Conference in 1955. On the great impact of the conference and how it led to the concept of "Eastern styles," see Qian Liqun, "The Way Our Generation Imagined the World," 526–527.

29. A romantic story of heroism, rebellion, and personal sacrifice set in nineteenth-century Italy, *The Gadfly* had a big impact on the Red Guard generation. See Hinton's documentary *The Morning Sun* (2003).

30. On the "Literary Heritage" sections, see Eber, "Western Literature in Chinese Translation, 1949–1979."

31. Some issues of *Yiwen* included a list of recently published books in the last page. The January 1957 issue, for instance, listed an anthology of poetry by Louis Aragon, novels by Balzac, Anatole France, Georges Duhamel, Sarat Chandra Chatterjee, Noma Hirashi, Kobayashi Takiji, and Shiga Naoya. Other authors translated in 1957–1958 and listed in *Yiwen* were Moliere, Romain Rolland, Rabelais, and Shakespeare (*Hamlet*).

32. On the inclusion of paintings by nineteenth-century and contemporary foreign masters in the *Short Story Magazine*, see Tang, *Origins of the Chinese Avant-Garde*, 50–51.

33. "Brother nations" is used when referring to countries from the Eastern bloc; "sister nations," when referring to Asian and African countries.

34. The English version of this essay also mentions that "Churchill . . . has made derogatory comments on Picasso's work" (Ehrenburg, *Chekhov, Stendhal and Other Essays*, 211), but this sentence does not appear in the Chinese text. Ehrenburg's essay "Sitangda de jiaoxun" (The Lessons of Stendhal) was published in *Yiwen*, no. 7 (1958): 132–154, but it was preceded by a critical article that singled out his ideological mistakes. See Fokkema, *Literary Doctrine in China and Soviet Influence*, 228–229.

35. Ehrenburg, "Lun Bijiasuo," 189.

36. Ibid., 188.

37. Nejedlý, "Lun zhenshi yu bu zhenshi de xianshizhuyi," 169.

38. Ibid.

39. Qin Zhaoyang, for instance, in his famous essay "The Broad Road of Realism" (1956) claimed that socialist realism did not prescribe literary style and therefore did not exclude a plurality of styles of writing. But, in contrast to Nejedlý, he suggested that writers should "seek the truth of life" (142) under socialism, including its negative aspects, rather than indulge in fantasies of a perfect future.

40. "Zuojiamen, nuli manzu renmin de qiwang!" (Writers, work hard to satisfy the people's expectations!), *Renmin ribao*, March 25, 1956, quoted in Shen Zhihua, *Zhonghua renmin gongheguo shi* 3:245.

41. Editors, "A Summary of Readers' Opinions," *Yiwen*, no. 5 (1957): 196–200.

42. McDougall, *Fictional Authors, Imaginary Audiences*, 5.

43. Poems were introduced by two essays, one by Louis Aragon and one by a Soviet critic. The surrealist/communist writer Louis Aragon had an important role in introducing French writers both to the Soviet Union and to China. See *Yiwen*, no. 7 (1957). See also Fang Chang'an, "'Shiqinian' wentan dui Oumei xiandaipai wenxue de jieshao yu yanshuo," 68. On Xu Zhimo's and Lu Xun's translation of Baudelaire, see Lee, *Shanghai Modern*, 235–241.

44. Quoted in Fang Chang'an, *Duihua yu 20 shiji Zhongguo wenxue*, 149.

45. *Shijie wenxue*, no. 1 (1959): 2.

46. Critical essays in previous issues had mainly been translated from the Russian.

47. Yan Wenjing was a prominent writer famous especially for his children's stories.

48. Xu Chi, "Guba de leisheng he Guba de gesheng" (Cuban thunders and Cuban songs), *Shijie wenxue*, no. 2 (1959): 17. Xu Chi became one of the main supporters of *menglong* ("misty") poetry in the early 1980s.

49. *Shijie wenxue*, no. 6 (1959): 170.

50. Cao Yong, "Yingguo de 'fennu de qingnian'"; Bing Xin, "'Fennu de huigu' du hou gan."

51. Cao, "Yingguo de 'Fennu de qingnian,'" 128.

52. A variety of writers continued to be published well into 1963, such as Ishikawa Tatsuzo, Federico García Lorca, Antonio Machado, W. E. B. Du Bois, and Elizabeth Gaskell. The August–September 1961 issue is particularly varied, featuring Mikhailo Stelmakh, an episode from Italo Calvino's *Marcovaldo* (translated from Russian), Gottfried Keller, Stendhal, Katherine Brush, and writings on aesthetic theory of the Italian Renaissance, starting with Dante and ending with Giovanni Battista Guarini (1538–1612).

53. See Eber, "Western Literature in Chinese Translation, 1949–1979."

54. Darnton, "Censorship, a Comparative View," esp. 44.

55. Liu Mingjiu and Zhu Hong, "Faguo 'xin xiaoshuo pai' poushi." Other French writers and related essays in the late 1950s and early 1960s issues of *Shijie wenxue* include Elsa Triolet (Aragon's Russian-born wife) and Pierre Gamarra (July 1959), an overview of French "progressive" writers including Gustave Flaubert and Molière (February 1961), Victor Hugo (March 1961), Guy de Maupassant (April 1961) Stendhal (August and September 1961), and Prosper Mérimée (December 1961).

56. Liu and Zhu, "Faguo 'xin xiaoshuo pai' poushi," 111.

57. Liu Mingjiu graduated from the department of foreign languages at Beijing University and was then appointed at the Chinese Academy of Sciences. He translated and edited studies on Victor Hugo, Jean Paul Sartre, Robbe-Grillet, and the *nouveau roman* from the 1980s onward. His wife Zhu Hong is a specialist of Anglo-American literature and was also affiliated with CAS.

58. See Kong, "For Reference Only," 82.

59. "Revisionism" was defined as "a bourgeois attempt to revise Marxism by removing its revolutionary essence" (Fokkema, *Literary Doctrine in China*, 233). For a list of these publications, see Appendix 1.

60. Shen Zhanyun, *Huipi shu, Huang pishu*. Literary works were issued by People's Literature Publishing House, while those on politics and social sciences were issued by People's Publishing House and Commercial Press.

61. See *1949–1986 Quanguo neibu faxing tushu zongmu.*

62. See Wang Qiaoling, "Naxie Huangse de jingshen zhi liang," 132. The China Drama Publishing House and Writers Publishing House published some literary translations as volumes, but in the 1960s these were in fact part of People's Literature Publishing House. Zhang Fusheng, "Wo liaojie de 'huangpishu' chuban shimo" (The whole story of the publication of the "yellow cover books" as I understand it), *Zhonghua dushu bao*, August 23, 2006, http://www.gmw.cn/01ds/2006–08/23/content_469775.htm.

63. In the 1970s, most of the literature books were published with white or light grey covers but were still called yellow books.

64. See Su Yongtong, "'Neibu' de shu, 'neibu' de dian" ("Internal" books, "internal" stores), *Nanfang zhoumo*, November 20, 2008, http://www.infzm.com/content/20226/0. On the system of internal publications and bookstores, see also Link, *The Uses of Literature*, 172–173.

65. See Zhou Hualei, "Dixia dushu shalong de mimi," 37.

66. Zhang Fusheng, "Wo liaojie de 'huangpishu' chuban shimo"; Wang Qiaoling, "Naxie Huangse de jingshen zhi liang," 131–132. According to Shuyu Kong, the meeting was held in late 1960 (see "For Reference Only," 79).

67. The literature team included included Zhang Guangnian, Chen Mo, Li Zhi, and literary critic and translator Ye Shuifu. See Gu Fan [Li Huifan], "Huangpi shu ji qita," 118.

68. Qin Shunxin, the translator of Ehrenburg's memoirs *People, Years, Life*, and a few other translators also contributed to the selection of material. Li Shuguang, a journalist, writer, cadre at the Central Propaganda Department, and editor at People's Literature Publishing House was in charge of coordinating various units of the editorial and literary world. See Zhang Fusheng, "Wo liaojie de 'huangpishu' chuban shimo," and Wang Qiaoling, "Naxie Huangse de jingshen zhi liang," 132.

69. *On the Road* (1957), for instance, was translated into Chinese in 1962, later than into German (1959) and Russian (excerpts appeared in a Soviet literary journal in 1960), but earlier than into French (1976). *Catcher in the Rye* (1951) was translated into French in 1953, into Russian in 1960, and into Chinese in 1963.

70. "Siren" (this person) is homophone with *siren* (four persons) and indicated the four translators, Cao Suling, Chen Xiaoman, Wang Jiaxiang, and Cheng Daixi. "Wutong" (five tung trees), homophone with the name of the tung tree itself (*wutong*), probably referred to five (unknown) persons. See Zhang Fusheng, "Wo liaojie de 'huangpishu' chuban shimo." Zhang claims that the translations for internal circulation are of excellent quality, and especially praises Wang Shixie's rendition of Aksyonov's *A Ticket to the Stars* (1961; Chinese translation 1963), and Lan Yingnian's translation of Iurii Trifonov's *House on the Embankment* (1976; Chinese translation 1978).

71. Shi Liang, "Guanyu huangpi shu," 89. Shi Xianrong also translated Salinger's *The Catcher in the Rye* and supervised the Chinese translation of Shakespeare's works.

72. Ibid.

73. Ibid.

74. See Wang Qiaoling, "Naxie Huangse de jingshen zhi liang," 131.

75. Important translation journals in the 1970s included *Zhaiyi* (Selected translations), published from 1973 to 1976 and restricted to internal distribution; the widely read *Waiguo wenyi* (Foreign art and literature), begun in 1978 and mostly devoted to contemporary literature; and *Yilin* (Forest of translations), begun in 1979 and mostly devoted to popular foreign literature.

76. Moretti, "Conjectures on World Literature." See also Damrosch, *What Is World Literature?*; Prendergast, ed., *Debating World Literature*; and Casanova, *The World Republic of Letters*. For an insightful critique of the notion of world literature, see Tanoukhi, "The Scale of World Literature."

77. Casanova, *World Republic of Letters*, 87–88.

78. Ibid., 89.

79. See, for instance, Hanneken, "Going *Mundial*."

80. Casanova, *World Republic of Letters*, 352.

81. Jones, "Chinese Literature in the 'World' Literary Economy," 173.

Chapter 3

1. See especially Xiaobin Yang, *The Chinese Postmodern*. Xudong Zhang considers avant-garde fiction as an expression of modernist metafiction and links this genre to the social and ideological changes and increasing urbanization of the 1980s (*Chinese Modernism in the Era of Reforms*, chapter 6). Jing Wang terms the "dramatic entry" of "the experimentalists" a "shocking" event, "a raging esthetic modernity that unfolded itself apart from the sociopolitical configuration of elite culture" (*High Culture Fever*, 234). The works discussed in this chapter were initially variously defined as modern (*xiandai*), experimental (*shiyan*), and exploratory (*tansuo*). The term avant-garde (*xianfeng*) only gained currency in 1988 and was also used in the fields of drama, poetry, and visual arts.

2. See Kaikkonen, "Stories and Legends," 134.

3. The terms "serious" and "pure" are used interchangeably in 1980s debates.

4. See McLaren, "Constructing New Reading Publics in Late Ming China," 174.

5. See Xueqing Xu, "The Mandarin Duck and Butterfly School," 71.

6. "Tantan su wenxue" (On popular literature), *Dushu*, no. 5 (1985): 35–39.

7. The socialist novels of the 1950s and 1960s included many elements of popular vernacular fiction and enjoyed a broad readership; 1980s critical discourse, however, generally emphasizes the abrupt reemergence of popular culture after 1978, as if the notion of *su* or *tongsu* were by definition incompatible with socialist culture.

8. "Tantan su wenxue," 37.

9. Ibid., 38–39.

10. Ibid., 39.

11. Wu offers a compelling discussion of his readings in the 1970s and early 1980s in *Wode Luotuosi*.

12. Wu Liang, "Wenxue yu xiaofei," 71.

13. Ibid., 72.

14. The nominal chief editor of both *Shanghai Literature* and *Harvest* was Ba Jin.

15. See Wang Yao, "1985 nian 'xiaoshuo geming' qianhou de shikong," 110. Cai Xiang's "oral account" is one of ten in the collection, which includes three others by Cai Xiang, three by Han Shaogong, two by Yu Hua, and one each by Li Tuo, Ma Yuan, Mo Yan, and editor Cheng Yongxin. Wang Yao, the proponent of an "oral history method" in literary studies, writes that he was inspired by oral history practices in Taiwan, Hong Kong, and Western scholarship (in ibid., 102).

16. Ibid., 110.

17. The campaign against "spiritual pollution" that had targeted, among others, writers and critics involved in the promotion of modernism had just receded in summer 1984. Roots-seeking fiction represented the possibility of undertaking formal experimentation under the guise of national culture rejuvenation.

18. See Wang Yao, "1985 nian 'xiaoshuo geming' qianhou de shikong," 111. Li Tuo also recalls having met Ma Yuan in early October 1984 to discuss the story with him. See Zha Jianying, ed., *Bashi niandai fangtanlu*, 255.

19. Wang Yao, "1985 nian 'xiaoshuo geming' qianhou de shikong," 102–103.

20. When Li Tuo was appointed deputy editor of *Beijing Literature* in May 1986, he was already an influential critic.

21. According to Mo Yan, this symposium was aimed at criticizing his work, but the fact that it was widely advertised in journals and newspapers had the effect of promoting it. See Wang Yao, "1985 nian 'xiaoshuo geming' qianhou de shikong," 109.

22. Ibid., 109. Li Tuo also helped Liu Suola to publish "Ni bie wu xuanze" (You have no other choice) in *Renmin wenxue*.

23. Ma Yuan was particularly vocal in expressing his opinion on such writers as Sun Ganlu and Can Xue. See Ma Yuan's letters to Cheng Yongxin in Cheng Yongxin, *Yige ren de wenxueshi* 13–14, 34–39.

24. Yu Hua, *Shuohua*, 40.

25. Yu Hua, "Wode 'yidian dian.'"

26. The appeal of late Tang aesthetics in 1980s and 1990s China will be discussed in Chapter 4.

27. "Going to See the Sea" was published anyway in *Beijing Literature* in May 1986.

28. Yu Hua, *Shuohua*, 54–55.

29. Wang Yao, "1985 nian 'xiaoshuo geming' qianhou de shikong," 111.

30. Yu Hua, *Shuohua*, 90.

31. Ibid., 54.

32. See Larson, "Literary Modernism and Nationalism in Post-Mao China"; Wedell-Wedellsborg, "One Kind of Chinese Reality: Reading Yu Hua"; Xiaobin Yang, *The Chinese Postmodern*.

33. I adapt this term from Carpentier, "The Latin American Novel."

34. See Hockx, *Questions of Style*; Link, *The Uses of Literature*.

35. Sun Ganlu, interview by Paola Iovene, Shanghai, December 2003.

36. "Zuoxie Shanghai fenhui qingchuanghui shoujie xueyuan xiaoshuo zhuanji" (Special section: Fiction from the participants in the first meeting of creative writing for the youth by the Shanghai branch of the Writers' Association); Sun Ganlu, "Fangwen mengjing," *Shanghai wenxue*, no. 9, 1986, reprinted in *Fangwen mengjing*. Sun Ganlu's "Xinshi zhi han" was published under the heading "experimental text" (*shiyan wenti*) in *Shouhuo* no. 5, 1987.

37. Sun Ganlu, "Fangwen mengjing," 46.

38. Although Sun's prose appears diametrically opposed to Wang Shuo's far more earthy writing, there are strong parallels in their parodies of political jargon.

39. Sun Ganlu, "Fangwen mengjing," 35.

40. Chen Xiaoming, "Bo—Sun Ganlu, 305.

41. Ibid., 306.

42. Sun Ganlu, "Xiezuo yu chenmo," *Wenxue jiao*, no. 4 (1989); reprinted in Lin Jianfa and Wang Jingtao, eds., *Zhongguo dangdai zuojia mianmian guan*, 228–229.

43. Cf. Northrop Frye's definition of the lyric: "The lyric is the genre in which the poet, like the ironic writer, turns his back on his audience. . . . Poetic creation . . . is an associative rhetorical process, most of it below the threshold of consciousness, a chaos of paronomasia, sound-links, ambiguous sense-links, and memory-links very like

that of the dream" (Frye, *Anatomy of Criticism*, 271–272). Sun also defines reading as a form of "resistance to daily life" ("Xiezuo yu chenmo," 229).

44. As noted by Chen Sihe, "instead of considering Sun Ganlu's writing in connection with the tradition of narrative literature, it would be more appropriate to relate it to postsurrealist poetry. What his experimentation with narrative language leads to is a dreamy lyricism, a state of reverie and contemplation" (*Zhongguo dangdai wenxueshi jiaocheng*, 297).

45. Sun Ganlu, "Fangwen mengjing," 63.

46. See undated letter by Ma Yuan in Cheng Yongxin, *Yige ren de wenxueshi*, 13.

47. Ma Yuan to Cheng Yongxin, October 26, 1987, in ibid., 37–38.

48. In a letter dated April 2, 1988, Yu Hua wrote to Cheng Yongxin that he was concerned for the sales of *Harvest* and committed himself to writing a story that would not alienate its readership (in ibid., 44–45).

49. Ge Fei and Wang met thanks to the poet Xu Fang, who was Ge Fei's colleague at Huadong Normal University. In summer 1986, Ge Fei was invited by Wang Zhongchen to a writing workshop in Qingdao, organized by their journal and by the Chinese Writers' Association, where he met Bei Dao, Bei Cun, and other writers (Ge Fei, interview by Paola Iovene, Beijing, September 2004). In a 2005 interview, Ge Fei recalls: "*China* was a great journal. In our eyes it was one of the best. At that time there were quite a few good journals published by the Chinese Writers' Association, and the two big ones were *China* and *Chinese Writers* [*Zhongguo zuojia*]. There was also *People's Literature*: to be published there in fact was our highest hope; and in Shanghai there was *Harvest*. At that time these were the top Chinese journals for us. But *China* was the only one that published young authors" (Ge Fei and Ren Yun, "Ge Fei zhuanlüe," 113).

50. See Sun Xiaoya, "Fang Niu Han xiansheng tan *Zhongguo*," 164.

51. Ibid., 168–169.

52. In Niu Han's words, "the staffing and salary of the personnel as well as publishing and printing expenses were all provided by the Ministry of Finance, as was the case for all formal publications under the auspices of the Writers' Association. But of course, in comparison with journals having all sorts of favorable circumstances, such as *Chinese Writers*, *China* was of a different sort. Those above looked at it with particular suspicion, while many readers and writers were extremely concerned over its fate. When the editors of *China* applied for official approval, it was included in the system of the Writers' Association, but in fact we edited it ourselves" (ibid., 161).

53. The January 1985 issue, for instance, included poetry by Gu Cheng, Zhang Zhimin, Shu Ting, and Bei Dao. Beginning in January 1986, the second page always carried poetry by young authors. Among works of foreign fiction, the Chinese translation of *La Route des Flandres* by 1985 Nobel Prize winner Claude Simon was serialized from June to September 1986. See ibid., 169.

54. *Zhongguo* wenxue bianjibu, "*Zhongguo* beiwanglu," 2. Can Xue's story had been turned down by *Zhongshan* and *Shouhuo* (see Sun Xiaoya, "Fang Niu Han xiansheng tan *Zhongguo*," 164). Can Xue complained that critics and editors were generally slow in reacting to her works because "they did not understand them and were afraid to lose face"

but acknowledged the help of Hunanese writer He Liwei, and also Li Tuo and Wang Meng. Can Xue, interview by Paola Iovene, Beijing, October 2004.

55. Niu Han and Feng Xiaxiong, "Bianzhe de hua."

56. Cai Xiang also noted the close links between avant-garde fiction and poetry, pointing out a personal and intellectual relationship between the writer Sun Ganlu and the poet Han Dong (Cai Xiang, interview by Paola Iovene, Shanghai, December 2004).

57. *China* was issued by Wenhua yishu chubanshe (Culture and Art Publishing House) in Beijing in the first year; in the second year, the editorial office remained in Beijing but the printing moved to Hunan wenyi chubanshe (Hunan Art and Literature Publishing House) in Changsha. News concerning the memorandum reached the Chinese Writers' Association in Beijing well before it was published. The Writers' Association sent people to block its publication, but before inspectors arrived, editors sent the paper matrix to Xi'an to have copies that included the memorandum printed there. Some copies of the journal were also printed in Changsha, without the memorandum but with a note by the Writers' Association announcing the closing of the journal. Sun Xiaoya, "Fang Niu Han xiansheng tan *Zhongguo*," 170–171.

58. In the memorandum, the editors also mentioned that Wang Meng and Liu Zaifu publicly supported them and that the poet Bei Dao had announced that he would resign from the poetry committee of the Writers' Association, stating that "considering your unfairness toward *China*, I think that all the leaders in charge at the Writers' Association are untrustworthy" (*Zhongguo* wenxue bianjibu, "*Zhongguo* beiwanglu," 3).

59. Ibid. Ah Long was considered a member of the "Hu Feng clique," a group of writers associated with the poet and literary theorist Hu Feng who were arrested and sent to labor camps in the 1950s because of their views on the relation between literature and politics. See Berry, *A History of Pain*, 143–144.

60. Zhongguo zuojia xiehui shujichu, "Zhi duzhe."

61. *People's Literature* itself, for example, got into trouble in 1987 because of the story "Liangchu nide shetai huo kongkong dangdang" (Stick out your furry tongue, or fuck-all) by Ma Jian, who was then based in Hong Kong. See Sylvia Chan, "Two Steps Forward, One Step Back," 118.

62. Cheng Yongxin, interview by Paola Iovene, Shanghai, December 2004. By the mid-1980s, each province had at least one literary journal.

63. In the early 1980s Chinese readers had mostly turned to fiction because it offered reflections on the recent past, as well as information on current economic and political developments. Ibid.

64. Ibid.

65. Wang Yao, "1985 nian 'xiaoshuo geming' qianhou de shikong," 112.

66. Cheng Yongxin interview.

67. Cheng Yongxin, *Yige ren de wenxueshi*, 19.

68. Ibid., 72.

69. Cheng Yongxin interview.

70. The call for Chinese literature to join the ranks of world literature repeatedly resurfaced in 1980s debates, but most editors emphasized the need to redefine mod-

els forged elsewhere in terms of local (Chinese or regional) difference. The ubiquitous phrase "going to the world" entailed finding writing styles that made Chinese literature comparable to other world-class literature and translatable outside China, but that also exhibited local traits. It involved promoting writing modes that could appear simultaneously cosmopolitan and local—an appropriation of specific results and trajectories as universal and hence as also Chinese.

71. Tashi Dawa to Cheng Yongxin, August 8, 1986, in Cheng Yongxin, *Yige ren de wenxueshi*, 3–4.

72. The sixth issue of 1987 also included a story by Yu Hua, which had been "passed on" to Cheng by Li Tuo. Around this time Wang Shuo also submitted his stories to *Harvest*. In this case, Cheng emphasized that it was Wang Shuo who contacted him. In fact, the editor claimed that he did not like Wang Shuo's early works, but when he read "Wanzhu" (The troubleshooters), he liked it and included it in the 1988 special issue. Some editors and critics in Beijing did not agree with his decision to publish Wang Shuo because they thought that he was not "serious" enough.

73. Ge Fei, interview by Paola Iovene, Beijing, September 2004.

74. The sixth issue for 1987 is the only one that had something special in the layout, because it celebrated the thirtieth anniversary of the journal. It included Yu Hua, Wang Shuo, Ge Fei, Sha Hei, Wang Meng, Pi Pi, and others. The sixth issue of 1988 included Shi Tiesheng, Su Tong, Sun Ganlu, Ma Yuan, Yu Hua, Zhao Botao, Pan Jun, Ge Fei, Zhaxi Dawa, and Pi Pi.

75. Yu Hua to Cheng Yongxin, April 2, 1988, in Cheng Yongxin, *Yige ren de wenxueshi*, 44–45.

76. Wang Yao, "1985 nian 'xiaoshuo geming' qianhou de shikong," 111.

77. Cheng Yongxin, *Yige ren de wenxueshi*, 45.

78. From the early 1990s onward, the Guangzhou-based journal *Huacheng* (Flower city) took on a much more prominent role in publishing formally innovative stories.

79. Cheng Yongxin, ed., *Zhongguo xinchao xiaoshuo xuan*. The volume included Ma Yuan, Shi Tiesheng, Ge Fei, Su Tong, Liu Suola, Mo Yan, Yu Hua, Zhaxi Dawa, Sun Ganlu, Hong Feng, Can Xue, Pi Pi, and Zhang Xian.

80. Zhu Wei, ed., *Zhongguo xianfeng xiaoshuo*. The volume was actually issued by a commercial publisher (*shushang*) that bought the publication number from Huacheng. Chen Xiaoming, interview by Paola Iovene, Beijing, October 2003.

81. See Adkins, "Practice as Temporalization," 352 (italics in original).

82. Casanova, *The World Republic of Letters*, 91. A rhetoric of novelty was pervasive and expectations of imminent literary developments were high, as one can see from Li Tuo's influential open letter to the writer Feng Jicai, dated 1982: "We live in a great epoch of transformation. This determines that our literature will surely have a great development, and will lead to a new literary period. The splendor of this literary period will perhaps be comparable to the most glorious periods of Chinese literary history, such as Tang and Song poetry" (Li Tuo, "'Xiandai xiaoshuo' bu dengyu 'xiandaipai,'" 93–94).

83. According to Anita Chan, this widespread frustration among large sections of the urban population was at the root of the Tiananmen protests in 1989. There were, of

course, dramatic inequalities within the group defined as "intellectuals." Chan claims that "academics were actually doing somewhat better financially, not worse, than the average worker. Among the eight occupational groups in the civil service pay scale, academics were ranked second highest, after state-organ officials" (Chan, "The Social Origins and Consequences of the Tiananmen Crisis," 109).

84. Published in *Beijing Literature*, no. 5 (1985): 80. *Harvest* is not among the journals that subscribed the agreement.

85. See, for instance, Xu Jilin, "Shangpin jingji yu zhishifenzi de shengcun weiji." In the late 1980s Wang Shuo was the first writer to be paid royalties and thus to leave behind the system of "manuscript fee," in which writers were paid only once on the basis of the number of characters and without regard to sales. See Kong, *Consuming Literature*, 25–26.

Chapter 4

An earlier version of this chapter appeared as an article in the fall 2007 issue of *Modern Chinese Literature and Culture*.

1. The title of the story refers to Li Shangyin's famous poem "Jinse." The *se* is an instrument with twenty-five strings, although according to a legend it originally had fifty strings; *se* is commonly translated as "zither," while *jin* is generally translated as "brocade." The combination of *jin* and *se* is unusual also in Chinese. James Liu explains that *jinse* refers to a zither "painted with ornamental designs" and translates it as "The Ornamented Zither" (Liu, *The Poetry of Li Shang-yin*, 44). A. C. Graham renders it as "The Patterned Lute," which is less accurate but aptly captures the parallels between the "patterns" on the instrument and those in the poet's life, as suggested by the second verse. Graham translates: "Mere chance that the patterned lute has fifty strings. / String and fret, one by one, recall the blossoming years. / Zhuangzi dreams at sunrise that a butterfly lost its way, / Wangdi bequeathed his spring passion to the nightjar. / The moon is full on the vast sea, a tear on the pearl. / On Blue Mountain the sun warms, a smoke issues from the jade. / Did it wait, this mood, to mature with hindsight? / In a trance from the beginning, then as now." *Poems of the Late T'ang*, 171 (transliteration modified). See Appendix 2 for Chinese original.

2. Ge Fei, "Jinse," 259.

3. Ibid., 263.

4. Ibid.

5. See Li Xiuwen, "Loushang de guanrenmen dou zuile." On Fei Ming's affinities with Li Shangyin, see Liu Haoming, "Fei Ming's Poetics of Representation," and Dong Naibin, "Fei Ming zuopin de wenxue yuanyuan."

6. Qian Zhongshu's study *Tan yi lu* (On the art of poetry, 1948), which includes a discussion of Li Shangyin's use of the techniques of parallel prose (*pianwen*) was republished in 1984. For an overview of Li Shangyin scholarship, see Liu Xuekai, "Zongjie yu chuangxin bingzhong," and Zhang Mingfei, "Li Shangyin wuti shi yanjiu zongshu." "Brocade Zither" is often grouped and discussed with the untitled poems.

7. See Liu Xu, *Jiu Tang shu*, 5077–5078.

8. See Owen, *The Late Tang*, 335–338. Qing editions include: Zhu Heling, *Li Yishan shi jianzhu*; Lu Kunzeng, *Li Yishan shi jie*; and Feng Hao, *Yuxisheng shiji jianzhu*.

9. For an overview of interpretations of Li Shangyin's poetry, see James Liu, *The Poetry of Li Shang-yin*, and Fusheng Wu, *The Poetics of Decadence*.

10. Průšek, *The Lyrical and the Epic*, 9.

11. Ibid., 47.

12. Owen, *The Late Tang*, 5.

13. Su Xuelin, *Yuxi shi mi*.

14. For an elaboration of the similarities between the two approaches, see Dong Naibin, *Li Shangyin de xinling shijie*, 56.

15. Owen, *The Late Tang*, 353, 395–396.

16. Not much was published on Li Shangyin in China between 1965 and 1977. For an overview of publications on Li Shangyin since 1956, see Wang, Liu, and Chen, eds., *Li Shangyin yanjiu lunji 1949–1997*, 783–809. *Yuxisheng shiji jianzhu*, the edition annotated by Feng Hao, Li Shangyin's most accomplished Qing commentator, was reprinted in 1979.

17. Li Shangyin, *Li Shangyin shixuan*, 10, 174–175.

18. Ibid., 16–17.

19. Liu Xuekai and Yu Shucheng, *Li Shangyin*, 88.

20. Ibid., 99.

21. Ibid., 102.

22. The allegorical interpretation of Li Shangyin's erotic poetry, initially proposed by Zhang Jie (*jinshi* 1124), was expanded and systemized in the mid-seventeenth century. See Owen, *The Late Tang*, 338–339.

23. Hao Shifeng, "Qianyan," 14. Hao's argument parallels the May Fourth retrieval of the "literal" meaning of the *Odes* from the allegorical readings imposed on them by traditional exegesis. See Haun Saussy, *The Problem of a Chinese Aesthetic*, 58.

24. Hao Shifeng, "Qianyan," 15.

25. Ibid., 20–21.

26. Ibid., 26–28.

27. Ibid., 33.

28. Huang Shang, "Jinse," 91.

29. On the tensions between the aesthetic, ethico-political, and the cultural subject in 1980s literature and criticism, see Jing Wang, *High Culture Fever*, 195–232.

30. Ibid., 156–159. According to Wang, however, Liu Zaifu's theory of subjectivity did not effectively disconnect the aesthetic from the sociopolitical.

31. Dong Naibin, *Li Shangyin de xinling de shijie*, 3–5, 56–57.

32. Dong Naibin defines the "linguistic image" as "a cultural symbol in which the national collective consciousness (or unconscious) is sedimented over time" (ibid., 45). On the introduction of "system theory" in 1980s literary studies, see Jing Wang, *High Culture Fever*, 148–156.

33. See Dong Naibin, *Li Shangyin de xinling de shijie*, 13–30.

34. "Reading, interpreting, and studying are all creative activities. They are a re-creation on the basis of the texts of the past. While respecting the text and the interpre-

tations of our predecessors, we need to fully mobilize and give free rein to the subjective initiative of the reader, we need to consciously implement and foster contemporary ideas" (ibid., 58–59).

35. Dong Naibin, "Jingshen ziyou de qianglie huhuan," 540.

36. Even though Dong Naibin does not use the word *menglong*, his emphasis on subjectivity and ambiguity is akin to the critical discourse supporting menglong poetry. The first anthology of menglong poetry was published in 1985. See Yan Yuejun, *Menglong shixuan*.

37. According to Xiaomei Chen, "from the very beginning, *menglong* poets also invoked the classical Chinese tradition as a source of artistic innovation" (*Occidentalism*, 63). Jing Wang also notes that "some critics dissipated the alien aura of modernism by emphasizing that techniques such as stream of consciousness could be traced to the Tang dynasty in Li Shangyin's poetry" (*High Culture Fever*, 147).

38. Xie Mian, "Shiqu le pingjing yihou," 51.

39. Zhang Ming, "Ling ren qimen de 'menglong,'" 33. Zhang Ming's essay was published two months before Xie Mian's and was the first that used the term *menglong* in a pejorative sense.

40. I will discuss this poem more in detail later in this chapter.

41. Tao Wenpeng, "Bu neng paoqi minzu shige de yishu chuantong." See also Xu Jingya, "Jueqi de shiqun."

42. "The Strain of Meeting" is the title of the published English translation of the novella in Wang Meng, *Selected Works of Wang Meng* 1: 82–248. A. C. Graham translates "Xiangjian shi nan" as "For ever hard to meet." His translation of the poem reads as follows: "For ever hard to meet, and as hard to part. / Each flower spoils in the failing East wind. / Spring's silkworms wind till death their heart's threads: / The wick of the candle turns to ash before its tears dry. / Morning mirror's only care, a change at her cloudy temples: / saying over a poem in the night, does she sense the chill in the moonbeams? / Not far, from here to Fairy Hill. / Bluebird, be quick now, spy me out the road" (*Poems of the Late T'ang*, 150). See Appendix 2 for Chinese original.

43. Wang Meng, "Dui Li Shangyin jiqi shizuo de yixie lijie," 61–62.

44. Wang Meng, *Xianjian shi nan*, 115; *The Strain of Meeting*, 204. Lan's meditations are conveyed through "associative interior monologues." On this device in Wang Meng's fiction, see Gunn, *Rewriting Chinese*, 169.

45. Wang Meng, *Xianjian shi nan*, 15; *The Strain of Meeting*, 98. Such questioning was quite common in the prose of the time; the countryside was experienced, or at least represented, by city intellectuals as a completely different world.

46. "Never a rope long enough to tie the sun, / How I hate to see streams flow and clouds return! / I wanted to go to Magu and buy the ocean, / All I got was a cup of spring dew cold as ice" (my translation). Ibid., 145; 236. See Appendix 2 for Chinese text.

47. Ibid., 34; 116. *Am Vorabend*, a drama by Leopold Kampf (1881–?), was published in New York in 1907 in Yiddish and English and translated into Chinese first by Li Shizheng in 1908 and then by Ba Jin in 1937. On the impact of this play on Ba Jin, see Ng, "Ba Jin and Russian Literature," 71–72.

48. This popular novel was first published in 1940.

49. William H. Sewell Jr. has proposed a distinction between culture as "a theoretically defined category or aspect of social life that must be abstracted out from the complex reality of human existence" and culture as "a concrete and bounded world of beliefs and practices. Culture in this sense is commonly assumed to belong to or to be isomorphic with a 'society' or with some clearly identifiable subsocietal group" ("The Concept(s) of Culture," 39).

50. Wang Meng, *Xianjian shi nan*, 156; *The Strain of Meeting*, 248.

51. Wang Meng, "Zai tan 'Jinse,'" 15. For a similar point concerning the poem "Xiangjian shi nan," see Wang Meng, "Dui Li Shangyin jiqi shizuo de yixie lijie," 61.

52. Wang Meng, "Zai tan 'Jinse,'" 16.

53. Wang Meng, "'Jinse' de ye hu chan," 24; Wang Meng, "Zai tan 'Jinse,'" 19–20.

54. Wang Meng, "'Jinse' de ye hu chan," 25. Wang borrows the notion of *chao yuyan* from Lu Shuyuan, *Chaoyue yuyan*.

55. Wang Meng, "Dui Li Shangyin jiqi shizuo de yixie lijie," 71.

56. Wang Meng, "Zai tan 'Jinse,'" 22.

57. Ibid. In Chinese overviews of Western experimental fiction, *pukepai xiaoshuo* refers to narrative works that do not follow a linear development and can therefore be read in random order; the genre is associated with the French writer Marc Saporta, author of *Composition numéro 1* (1962), a work written on fifty-two cards contained in a box.

58. Wang Meng, "Zai tan 'Jinse,'" 20–21.

59. *Poems of the Late T'ang*, 24.

60. Kern, *Orientalism, Modernism, and the American Poem*, 216. On Pound's relation with China, see Hayot, *Chinese Dreams*, 1–53.

61. Yu-Kung Kao and Tsu-lin Mei have argued that Tang poetry is characterized by syntactic discontinuity and that this, in turn, allows for "the making of simple images." This view, however, derives from a comparison to "counterparts in English poetry"; the questions the authors address are informed by T. E. Hulme's and Fenollosa's writings on syntax. See Yu-Kung Kao and Tsu-lin Mei, "Syntax Diction and Imagery in T'ang Poetry," 65.

62. James Liu, *The Poetry of Li Shang-yin*, 35–38.

63. Wang Meng, "Guanyu 'yishiliu' de tongxin," 72. For a discussion on the various techniques of "stream of consciousness" in Wang Meng's fiction, see Hagenaar, *Stream of Consciousness and Free Indirect Discourse in Modern Chinese Literature*, 129–145. See also Leo Ou-fan Lee, "The Politics of Technique"; Tay, "Wang Meng, Stream of Consciousness, and the Controversy over Modernism"; and Williams, "Stylistic Variety in a PRC Writer."

64. Wang Meng, "Guanyu 'yishiliu' de tongxin," 71.

65. *Bi* and *xing* are primarily discussed in *Wenxin diaolong* by Liu Xie (ca. 465–522). According to Owen, "for Liu Hsieh [Xie] affective image is 'concealed' from rational understanding, and it is this that radically separates it from comparison. Because the mechanism by which affective image functions is latent (*yin*), its operations are interior

(*nei*) and thus it works on the affections (*ch'ing* [*qing*]) directly, unmediated by the understanding" (*Readings in Chinese Literary Thought*, 256).

66. See, for instance, Tay, "Wang Meng, Stream-of-consciousness, and the Controversy over Modernism," 10.

67. Wang Meng, "Ye de yan," 240.

68. Wang Meng, "Laijin," 142, 144.

69. Wang Meng, "Li Shangyin de tiaozhan," 4.

70. "Wode Zhongguo xin," a popular patriotic song by Zhang Mingmin.

71. Wang Meng, "Li Shangyin de tiaozhan," 4–5.

72. *Poems of the Late T'ang*, 159, transliteration modified.

73. Ge Fei, "Fei Ming de yiyi," 281.

74. Ibid.

75. *Poems of the Late T'ang*, 171. These difficult verses have been translated in various ways. James Liu renders the lines as "This feeling might have become a thing to be remembered, / Only, at the time you were already bewildered and lost" (*The Poetry of Li Shang-yin*, 51). Owen translates them as "One should wait until these feelings become remembrance, it's just that at the moment I was already in a daze" (*The Late Tang*, 394).

76. On "anticipation of retrospection," see Currie, *About Time*, 27–29, which offers an insightful reelaboration of Peter Brook's understanding of this concept.

77. Ge Fei, "Fei Ming de yiyi," 279.

78. Ge Fei, preface to the Italian translation of *Jinse* (*La cetra intarsiata*), 6.

79. In the second story, it is Feng Zicun's sister who tells a story she heard from a tea merchant. The name of the protagonist, Feng Zicun, is homophone with *fengzi cun* ("madman's village").

80. Borges, *Collected Fictions*, 125. Ge Fei mentions Borges (though not this particular story) in his preface to *La cetra intarsiata*, 6.

81. The only mention of a historical date occurs in the second story, the fourteenth era of the Wanli era, or 1586. This period is generally considered as one of slow decline for the Ming, and this particular date could be related to Ray Huang's *1587, A Year of No Significance: The Ming Dynasty in Decline*, translated into Chinese in the early 1980s.

82. Genette, *Narrative Discourse Revisited*, 88.

83. On the "strange loop" in cinema, see Hu Mei and Li Xiaojun, "*Nü'er Lou* daoyan chuangzuo suixiang," and McGrath, "Black Cannon Incident," 30–31.

84. Na Tianlong, "Gedeer dingli de qishi," 22.

85. Zheng Yuxin, "Bu wanbeixing dingli," 13.

86. Wang Bangxiong, "Zuo wei wenhua de meishu."

87. Wei Chongxin, "Xingge, mingyun." Qiu Dali, "Jianlun guanggao de tuxing tonggou."

88. Xiaobin Yang, *The Chinese Postmodern*, 184–185.

89. See Zeitlin, *Historian of the Strange*, 138–164.

90. Ge Fei, "Jinse," 252–253.

91. Ibid., 251.

92. Ibid., 252.

93. Ibid., 255.

94. Ibid., 256.

95. Ibid., 271.

96. As we shall see in Chapter 5, mist is a recurrent trope in Ge Fei's fiction.

Chapter 5

1. Ingold, "The Eye of the Storm" and "Footprints through the Weather-World."

2. Ge Fei's *Jiangnan sanbuqu* (Jiangnan trilogy) includes *Renmian Taohua* (Peach blossom beauty, 2004), *Shanhe rumeng* (Landscapes in dream, 2007), and *Chunjin Jiangnan* (End of spring in Jiangnan, 2011). The three volumes were first published separately and then reissued together as trilogy by Shanghai wenyi in 2012. Page numbers in this chapter refer to the first editions and all translations are mine.

3. In an article discussing Ge Fei's novel *Bianyuan* (On the Margins, 1992), Shuyu Kong writes, "Memory is not merely the subject of Ge Fei's works, but also a guide to his unique structuring and characterization" ("Ge Fei On the Margins," 71). For Jing Wang, "Ge Fei's fictional world can be characterized as a slow process of laboriously and self-consciously extending the present back into the past. It is the past, specifically at the moment when the narrator remembers and registers the fragmentary flashes of his personal past, that anchors the subject-position of Ge Fei's literary persona" (*High Culture Fever*, 246). Xudong Zhang too considers "memory—often memory of a most personal kind (for example, of erotic love or self-identity)—as the central testing ground for [Ge Fei's] philosophy of writing" but argues that the "self-consciousness" that emerges from his stories is not a result of the reconstruction of memory per se but rather of the discernment of "a distance between narration and the referent world." Hence, Zhang characterizes Ge Fei's stories as "meta-fiction," or fiction about fiction (*Chinese Modernism in the Era of Reforms*, 166–167).

4. As we shall see, Luzhu is a friend of the main protagonist Duanwu.

5. Ge Fei, *Chunjin Jiangnan*, 190.

6. Said, *Culture and Imperialism*, 336.

7. Examples are the trilogies by Ah Cheng, Mo Yan, Jia Pingwa, as well as Jin Yong's *Condor Trilogy* in the martial arts genre and Liu Cixin's *Three Body* science-fiction trilogy.

8. On the pervasiveness of trilogies and tetralogies in the different contexts of postcolonial fiction, see Hitchcock, *The Long Space*.

9. Ge Fei, *Chunjin Jiangnan*, 5.

10. The novel Duanwu sets out to write actually overlaps with the first volume of the trilogy. As often happens in Ge Fei's embedded stories, the protagonist turns out to be the author of the narrative in which he is featured.

11. Ge Fei, *Chunjin Jiangnan*, 3.

12. Ibid., 296.

13. Said, "Reflections on Exile," 183–184.

14. "For an exile, habits of life, expression, activity in the new environment inevitably occur against the memory of these things in another environment. Thus both the

new and the old environments are vivid, actually, occurring together contrapuntally" (ibid., 186). In *Culture and Imperialism* Said describes contrapuntal reading as "a simultaneous awareness both of the metropolitan history that is narrated and of those other histories against which (and together with which) the dominating discourse acts. In the counterpoint of Western classical music, various themes play off one another, with only a provisional privilege being given to any particular one; yet in the resulting polyphony there is concert and order, an organized interplay that derives from the themes, not from a rigorous melodic or formal principle outside the work" (51).

15. Ge Fei, *Chunjin Jiangnan*, 30.

16. Ibid., 31.

17. See Solà-Morales, "Terrain Vague."

18. Ge Fei, *Chunjin Jiangnan*, 36.

19. Ibid., 37.

20. Ibid., 39.

21. Ibid., 38.

22. Xijindu is a historical district in Zhenjiang city, on which the fictional Meicheng is modeled.

23. The term *wumai* was newly coined in 1997 official documents to describe Beijing's pollution. See Pasternack, "Beijing's Olympics Weather," 189.

24. Ge Fei, *Chunjin Jiangnan*, 347–349.

25. According to Sandy Flitterman-Lewis, Resnais's documentary infuses the title *Night and Fog* with new meanings:

The darkness of "night" suggests despair, hopelessness, and demoralized inaction; "fog," by contrast, suggests the subjective uncertainty of multiple meanings, a blurring of sense that threatens to turn into either a confusion of meanings or no meaning at all. It is only when the terms are combined in the transforming catalyst of the film that the *salutary* meaning emerges, just as in the seeming paradox of Resnais's "constructive forgetting." Memory of the past is positively combined with responsibility for the future (that is, human agency, the sense of self that makes us capable of compassion and understanding). With *Night and Fog* one survives the desperation of the night, sees through the confusion of the fog, and emerges as a social being with a commitment to that human connection fundamental to life—a sense of shared responsibility to (and for) oneself and others (Flitterman-Lewis, "Documenting the Ineffable," 208).

26. "A classic is a work which constantly generates a pulviscular cloud of critical discourse around it, but which always shakes the particles off" (Calvino, *Why Read the Classics?*, 6).

27. Ge Fei, *Chunjin Jiangnan*, 349.

28. *Xiuchi* occurs quite often throughout the novel, alternating with the related term *chiru*, which is closer to "humiliation" than shame proper.

29. Sedgwick, *Touching Feeling*, 36.

30. Ibid.

31. Ibid.

32. Ibid., 37 (italics in original).

33. Sedgwick discusses how Tomkins considers shame as part of the shame-interest affect polarity, noting that turning one's gaze to someone strange, or to someone assumed to be familiar but suddenly appearing unfamiliar, can generate shame. She also stresses its highly "mercurial" quality, and that not only people but also places can generate this emotion. Ibid., 97.

34. Ge Fei, *Chunjin Jiangnan*, 90.

35. Ibid., 98.

36. Ibid., 4. The six lines will appear twice later in the narrative: the first time when the encounter is recounted again with additional details; the second at the very end of the novel, in the first stanza of a long poem completed many years later and serving as the epilogue for the book.

37. Ge Fei, *Chunjin Jiangnan*, 133.

38. Several Chinese intellectuals considered Haizi's suicide as a symbol of the end of the idealistic 1980s, connecting it to the deaths in Tian'anmen Square in June 1989. On Haizi's suicide and the ensuing mythification of the poet, see van Crevel, *Chinese Poetry in Times of Mind, Mayhem and Money*, 91–136.

39. Ge Fei, *Chunjin Jiangnan*, 105–106.

40. Bataille, *The Accursed Share* 1:59 (italics in original). *The Accursed Share* revolves around the thesis that "*it is not necessity but its contrary, 'luxury,' that presents living matter and mankind with their fundamental problems*" (12, italics in original). For Bataille, any system receives more energy than is necessary to maintain life. The energy in excess (wealth) can be used for the growth of a system, but if the system can no longer grow, or if the excess cannot be completely absorbed, it must be dissipated without profit. Different societies are defined by different modes in which this expenditure takes place, ranging from sacrifice to war (21–24). Sacrifice is emphasized in Bataille's writing as a human practice, affording an experience of the constitutive excess of humanity: "Sacrifice restores to the sacred world that which servile use has degraded, rendered profane. Servile use has made a *thing* (an *object*) of that which, in a deep sense, is of the same nature as the *subject*, is in a relation of intimate participation with the subject. It is not necessary that the sacrifice actually destroy the animal or plant of which man had to make a *thing* for his use. They must at least be destroyed as things, that is, *insofar as they have become things*. Destruction is the best means of negating a utilitarian relationship between man and the animal or plant. . . . What the ritual has the virtue of rediscovering is the intimate participation of the sacrificer and the victim, to which a servile use had put an end" (55–56, italics in original).

41. Ibid., 10.

42. Bataille, "De l'âge de pierre à Jacques Prévert" (review of Jacque Prévert's *Paroles*), *Critique* 3–4 (August–September 1946), quoted in ffrench, *After Bataille*, 90 (italics in original).

43. The conference takes place in a luxury hotel in Huajiashe, which in the first volume of the trilogy (*Peach blossom beauty*) is a village run by bandits who aspire to build a utopian society. The description of the poetry conference itself is a satire of intellectuals and poets who pose as social outsiders.

44. Ge Fei, *Chunjin Jiangnan*, 296. Ge Fei's use of *jufeng* (hurricane) calls to mind the synonym *baofeng* in the title of Zhou Libo's novel *Baofeng zhouyu* (Hurricane, 1948), which in turn drew the weather metaphor from Mao Zedong, who compared land reform to a tempest.

45. Ibid., 186. In the novel Stevens's verses are quoted in Chinese translation.

46. Ibid., 186–187.

47. Ibid., 148.

48. Ibid., 149.

BIBLIOGRAPHY

Adams, Vincanne, Michelle Murphy, and Adele Clarke. "Anticipation: Technoscience, Life, Affect, Temporality." *Subjectivity* 28:1 (2009): 246–265.

Adkins, Lisa. "Practice as Temporalization: Bourdieu and Economic Crisis." In *The Legacy of Pierre Bourdieu: Critical Essays*, edited by Simon Susen and Bryan S. Turner, 347–365. London: Anthem Press, 2011.

Asimov, Isaac. *I, Robot*. New York: Ballantine Books, 1983.

Bai Shihong, ed. *Anliu: "Wenge" shouchao wencun* (Undercurrents: Extant hand-copied texts from the Cultural Revolution). Beijing: Wenhua yishu chubanshe, 2001.

Bai Ye, ed. *Xin shiqi wenxue liunian, 1976.10–1982.9* (Six years of literature of the new period, October 1976–September 1982). Beijing: Zhongguo shehui kexue chubanshe, 1985.

Bataille, Georges. *The Accursed Share: An Essay on General Economy*. Vol. 1, *Consumption*. Translated by Robert Hurley. New York: Zone, 1991.

Bauman, Zygmunt. *Legislators and Interpreters: On Modernity, Post-Modernity, and Intellectuals*. Ithaca, NY: Cornell University Press, 1987.

Berlant, Lauren Gail. *Cruel Optimism*. Durham, NC: Duke University Press, 2011.

Berry, Michael. *A History of Pain: Trauma in Modern Chinese Literature and Film*. New York: Columbia University Press, 2008.

Bing Xin, "'Fennu de huigu' du hou gan" (Reactions to *Look Back in Anger*), *Shijie wenxue*, no. 11 (1959): 129–132.

Böhm, Karl, and Rolf Dörge. *Unsere Welt von Morgen*. Berlin: Verlag Neues Leben, 1960.

Borges, Jorge Luis. *Collected Fictions*. Translated by Andrew Hurley. New York: Viking, 1998.

Bourdieu, Pierre. *The Field of Cultural Production: Essays on Art and Literature*. Edited and introduced by Randal Johnson. New York: Columbia University Press, 1993.

Brooks, Peter. *Reading for the Plot: Design and Intention in Narrative*. New York: Knopf, 1984.

Cai Tiliang. "Tian Han yu tade qingyi 'shiyan tian'" (Tian Han and his "experimental field" at Youth Art Theater). *Zhongguo xiju*, no. 8 (1998): 9–12.

Cai Zizheng. "Youxie buzu zhi chu" (Some insufficiencies). *Kepu chuangzuo*, no. 1 (1980): 90.

Calvino, Italo. *Why Read the Classics?* Translated by Martin McLaughlin. New York: Pantheon Books, 1999.

Cao Yong, "Yingguo de 'fennu de qingnian'" (England's "angry youth"), *Shijie wenxue*, no. 11 (1959): 121–128.

Carpentier, Alejo. "The Latin American Novel." Translated by Ann Wright. *New Left Review* 154:1 (1985): 99–111.

Casanova, Pascale. *The World Republic of Letters*. Translated by M. B. DeBevoise. Cambridge, MA: Harvard University Press, 2004.

Chan, Anita. "The Social Origins and Consequences of the Tiananmen Crisis." In *China in the Nineties: Crisis Management and Beyond*, edited by David Goodman and Gerald Segal, 105–130. Oxford: Clarendon Press, 1991.

Chan, Tak-hung Leo. *Twentieth-Century Chinese Translation Theory: Modes, Issues and Debates*. Amsterdam: Benjamins, 2004.

Chan, Sylvia. "Two Steps Forward, One Step Back: Towards a 'Free' Literature." *The Australian Journal of Chinese Affairs* 19/20 (1988): 81–126.

Chen, Jian. *Mao's China and the Cold War*. Chapel Hill: University of North Carolina Press, 2001.

Chen Sihe. *Zhongguo dangdai wenxueshi jiaocheng* (Lectures on Chinese contemporary literary history). Shanghai: Fudan daxue chubanshe, 1999.

Chen, Xiaomei. *Occidentalism: A Theory of Counter-Discourse in Post-Mao China*. New York: Oxford University Press, 1995.

Chen Xiaoming. "Bo—Sun Ganlu: juedui de xiezuo" (Postscript—Sun Ganlu: Absolute writing). In *Fangwen mengjing* (Visit to dreamland), by Sun Ganlu, 305–312. Wuhan: Changjiang wenyi chubanshe, 1993.

Cheng Yongxin. *Yige ren de wenxueshi* (One person's literary history). Tianjin: Tianjin renmin chubanshe, 2007.

———, ed. *Zhongguo xinchao xiaoshuo xuan* (Selected Chinese new wave fiction). Shanghai: Shanghai Shehui kexueyuan chubanshe, 1989.

Clark, T. J. "Origins of the Present Crisis." *New Left Review* 2 (March–April 2000): 85–96.

Crevel, Maghiel van. *Chinese Poetry in Times of Mind, Mayhem and Money*. Boston: Brill, 2008.

Culler, Jonathan. *The Literary in Theory*. Stanford, CA: Stanford University Press, 2007.

Currie, Mark. *About Time: Narrative, Fiction and the Philosophy of Time*. Edinburgh: Edinburgh University Press, 2007.

Damrosch, David. *What Is World Literature?* Princeton, NJ: Princeton University Press, 2003.

Darnton, Robert. "Censorship, a Comparative View: France, 1789–East Germany, 1989." *Representations* 49 (1995): 40–60.

Daruvala, Susan. *Zhou Zuoren and an Alternative Chinese Response to Modernity*. Cambridge, MA: Harvard University Asia Center, 2000.

Donald, Stephanie Hemelryk. *Public Secrets, Public Spaces: Cinema and Civility in China*. Lanham, MD: Rowman & Littlefield, 2000.

Dong Naibin. "Fei Ming zuopin de wenxue yuanyuan" (Literary sources of Fei Ming's works). *Wenyi yanjiu*, no. 4 (2004): 39–47.

———. "Jingshen ziyou de qianglie huhuan" (A strong call for spiritual freedom). In *Li Shangyin yanjiu lunji, 1949–1997* (Collected studies of Li Shangyin, 1949–1997), edited by Wang Meng and Liu Xuekai, 540–547. Guilin: Guangxi Shifan daxue, 1998.

———. *Li Shangyin de xinling shijie* (The spiritual world of Li Shangyin). Shanghai: Shanghai guji, 1992.

Duara, Prasenjit. *Sovereignty and Authenticity: Manchukuo and the East Asian Modern.* Lanham, MD: Rowman & Littlefield, 2003.

Eber, Irene. "Western Literature in Chinese Translation, 1949–1979." *Asian and African Studies* 3:1 (1994): 34–54.

Edelman, Lee. *No Future: Queer Theory and the Death Drive.* Durham, NC: Duke University Press, 2004.

Ehrenburg, Ilya. *Chekhov, Stendhal and Other Essays.* Translated by Anna Bostock in collaboration with Yvonne Kapp. London: MacGibbon & Kee, 1962.

———. "Lun Bijiasuo" (On Picasso). *Yiwen*, no. 2 (1957): 186–191.

Engels, Frederick. *The Part Played by Labor in the Transition from Ape to Man.* New York: International Publishers, 1950.

Fang Chang'an. *Duihua yu 20 shiji Zhongguo wenxue* (Dialogue and twentieth century Chinese literature). Wuhan: Hubei renmin chubanshe, 2005.

———. "'Shiqinian' wentan dui Oumei xiandaipai wenxue de jieshao yu yanshuo" (Introduction and discussions of Euro-American modernism in the literary field of the 'Seventeen Years'). *Wenxue pinglun*, no. 2 (2008): 67–73.

Farquhar, Mary Ann. *Children's Literature in China: From Lu Xun to Mao Zedong.* Armonk, NY: M. E. Sharpe, 1999.

Felski, Rita. *Uses of Literature.* Malden, MA: Blackwell Publishing, 2008.

Feng Hao. *Yuxisheng shiji jianzhu* (Collected poems of Yuxisheng [Li Shangyin] with annotations). Shanghai: Shanghai guji chubanshe, 1979.

ffrench, Patrick. *After Bataille: Sacrifice, Exposure, Community.* London: Legenda, 2007.

Fitzpatrick, Sheila. *Everyday Stalinism: Ordinary Life in Extraordinary Times: Soviet Russia in the 1930s.* New York: Oxford University Press, 1999.

Flitterman-Lewis, Sandy. "Documenting the Ineffable: Terror and Memory in Alain Resnais's *Night and Fog.*" In *Documenting the Documentary: Close Readings of Documentary Film and Video*, edited by Barry Keith Grant and Jeanette Sloniowski, 204–222. Detroit: Wayne State University Press, 1998.

Fokkema, Douwe Wessel. *Literary Doctrine in China and Soviet Influence, 1956–1960.* The Hague: Mouton, 1965.

Friedberg, Maurice. *Literary Translation in Russia: A Cultural History.* University Park: Pennsylvania State University Press, 1997.

Frye, Northrop. *Anatomy of Criticism: Four Essays.* Princeton, N.J.: Princeton University Press, 1957.

Gamsa, Mark. *The Chinese Translation of Russian Literature: Three Studies.* Boston: Brill, 2008.

————. *The Reading of Russian Literature in China: A Moral Example and Manual of Practice*. New York: Palgrave Macmillan, 2010.

Gao Mang. "Baihua shengkai de jijie: xin shiqi *Shijie wenxue* zazhi sanji" (Season of hundred flowers in full bloom: Notes on *World literature* in the New Era). In *Shengji: xin shiqi zhuming renwen qikan sumiao* (Vitality: A sketch of the famous cultural periodicals of the New Era), edited by Jin Dacheng, 57–95. Beijing: Zhongguo Wenlian chubanshe, 2003.

Gao Sha. "Jieshao *Kexuejia tan 21 shiji*" (Introducing *Scientists talk about the twenty-first century*). *Renmin wenxue*, no. 6 (1960): 121–123.

Ge Fei. *La cetra intarsiata*. Translated into Italian by Paola Iovene. Rome: Fahrenheit 451, 2000.

————. *Chunjin Jiangnan* (End of spring in Jiangnan). Shanghai: Shanghai wenyi chubanshe, 2011.

————. "Fei Ming de yiyi" (Fei Ming's significance). In *Sairen de gesheng* (Siren songs), 226–337. Shanghai: Shanghai wenyi chubanshe, 2001.

————. "Jinse" (Brocade zither). In *Xianghui zai zui hou de daoyu* (Meetings on the last island), 251–281. Beijing: Beijing daxue chubanshe, 1994. Originally published in *Huacheng*, no. 1, 1993.

————. *Renmian taohua* (Peach blossom beauty). Shenyang: Chunfeng wenyi chubanshe, 2004.

————. *Shanhe rumeng* (Landscapes in dream). Beijing: Zuojia chubanshe, 2007.

Ge Fei and Ren Yun. "Ge Fei zhuanlüe" (Ge Fei's biographical sketch). *Dangdai zuojia pinglun*, no. 4 (2005): 105–116.

Genette, Gérard. *Narrative Discourse Revisited*. Translated by Jane E. Lewin. Ithaca, NY: Cornell University Press, 1988.

Goldman, Merle. *China's Intellectuals: Advise and Dissent*. Cambridge, MA: Harvard University Press, 1981.

————. *Literary Dissent in Communist China*. Cambridge, MA: Harvard University Press, 1967.

Gu Fan [Li Huifan]. "Huangpi shu ji qita: Zhong-Su lunzheng shiqi de jizhong waiguo wenxue neibu kanwu" (Yellow books and other things: Some internal publications at the time of the Sino-Soviet dispute), *Wenyi lilun yu piping*, no. 6 (December 2001): 117–124.

"Guanyu kehuan xiaoshuo pinglun de yifeng xin" (A letter on the critique of science fiction). *Dangdai wentan*, no. 8 (1982): 18–21.

Gunn, Edward M. *Rewriting Chinese: Style and Innovation in Twentieth-Century Chinese Prose*. Stanford, CA: Stanford University Press, 1991.

Guo Moruo. *Zhongguo gudai shehui yanjiu* (Research on ancient Chinese society). 1929. Reprint Shanghai: Qunyi chubanshe, 1947.

————. "Tan wenxue fanyi gongzuo" (On the work of literary translation). In Luo Xinzhang, ed., *Fanyi lunji* (Collected talks on translation), 498–499. Beijing: Shangwu yinshuguan, 1984.

Guo Yuqiong. "Zhishifenzi ziwo lixiang de gaoyang yu shiluo: Tian Han 1958 nian chuangzuo zhong zhishifenzi xingxiang bijiao" (Achievements and loss in the intellectuals' ideal of self: Comparing the images of the intellectual in Tian Han's 1958 works). *Xiju wenxue*, no. 11 (2002): 57–62.

Hagenaar, Elly. *Stream of Consciousness and Free Indirect Discourse in Modern Chinese Literature*. Leiden: Centre of Non-Western Studies, Leiden University, 1992.

Hanneken, Jaime. "Going *Mundial*: What It Really Means to Desire Paris." *Modern Language Quarterly* 71:2 (2010): 129–152.

Hao Shifeng. "Qianyan" (Preface). In Jiang Bingzhang, *Xuan Yuxisheng shi bushuo* (Selected Yuxisheng [Li Shangyin]'s poetry with annotations), edited by Hao Shifeng, 1–35. Tianjin: Nankai daxue chubanshe, 1985.

Hayot, Eric. *Chinese Dreams: Pound, Brecht, Tel Quel*. Ann Arbor: University of Michigan Press, 2004.

Hinton, Carma. *Morning Sun: Ba jiu dianzhong de taiyang*. Long Bow Group, 2005, DVD.

Hitchcock, Peter. *The Long Space: Transnationalism and Postcolonial Form*. Stanford, CA: Stanford University Press, 2010.

Hockx, Michel. "Is There a May Fourth Literature? A Reply to Wang Xiaoming." *Modern Chinese Literature and Culture* 11:2 (Fall 1999): 40–52.

———. *Questions of Style: Literary Societies and Literary Journals in Modern China, 1911–1937*. Boston: Brill, 2003.

Hu Mei and Li Xiaojun. "*Nü'er Lou* daoyan chuangzuo suixiang" (Directors' thoughts on the making of *Army Nurse*). *Dangdai dianying*, no. 3 (1986): 43–46.

Huang, Ray. *1587, A Year of No Significance: The Ming Dynasty in Decline*. New Haven, CT.: Yale University Press, 1981.

Huang Shang. "Jinse" (Brocade zither). *Dushu*, no. 6 (1988): 88–92.

Huters, Theodore. *Bringing the World Home: Appropriating the West in Late Qing and Early Republican China*. Honolulu: University of Hawai'i Press, 2005.

———. "Ideologies of Realism in Modern China: The Hard Imperatives of Imported Theory." In *Politics, Ideology, and Literary Discourse in Modern China*, edited by Liu Kang and Xiaobing Tang, 147–173. Durham, NC: Duke University Press, 1993.

Ingold, Tim. "The Eye of the Storm: Visual Perception and the Weather." *Visual Studies* 20:2 (October 2005): 97–104.

———. "Footprints through the Weather-World: Walking, Breathing, Knowing." *Journal of the Royal Anthropological Institute*, n.s. 16, Supplement s1 (2010): S121–S139.

Iovene, Paola. "Why Is There a Poem in This Story? Li Shangyin's Poetry, Contemporary Chinese Literature, and the Futures of the Past." *Modern Chinese Literature and Culture* 19:2 (Fall 2007): 71–116.

Jameson, Fredric. *Postmodernism, or, The Cultural Logic of Late Capitalism*. Durham, NC: Duke University Press, 1991.

Jones, Andrew F. "Chinese Literature in the 'World' Literary Economy." *Modern Chinese Literature* 8:1–2 (Spring/Fall 1994): 171–190.

———. *Developmental Fairy Tales: Evolutionary Thinking and Modern Chinese Culture*. Cambridge, MA: Harvard University Press, 2011.

Kaempffert, Waldemar. "Miracles You'll See in the Next Fifty Years." *Popular Mechanics* (February 1950): 112–118, 264–272.

Kaikkonen, Marja. "Stories and Legends: China's Largest Contemporary Popular Literature Journals." In *The Literary Field of Twentieth Century China*, edited by Michel Hockx, 134–160. Honolulu, University of of Hawai'i Press, 1999.

Kao, Yu-kung, and Tsu-lin Mei. "Syntax, Diction, and Imagery in T'ang Poetry." *Harvard Journal of Asiatic Studies* 31 (1971): 49–136.

Kern, Robert. *Orientalism, Modernism, and the American Poem*. New York: Cambridge University Press, 1996.

Kinkley, Jeffrey C. *Chinese Justice, the Fiction: Law and Literature in Modern China*. Stanford, CA: Stanford University Press, 2000.

Kong, Shuyu. *Consuming Literature: Best Sellers and the Commercialization of Literary Production in Contemporary China*. Stanford, CA: Stanford University Press, 2005.

———. "For Reference Only: Restricted Publication and Distribution of Foreign Literature During the Cultural Revolution." *Yishu: Journal of Contemporary Chinese Art* 1:2 (Summer/August 2002): 76–85.

———. "Ge Fei on the Margins." *B.C. Asian Review* 10 (Winter 1996/97): 70–120.

Koselleck, Reinhart. *Futures Past: On the Semantics of Historical Time*. Cambridge, MA: MIT Press, 1985.

Larson, Wendy. "Literary Modernism and Nationalism in Post-Mao China." In *Inside Out: Modernism and Postmodernism in Chinese Literary Culture*, edited by Wendy Larson and Anne Wedell-Wedellsborg, 172–197. Aarhus, Denmark: Aarhus University Press, 1993.

Laughlin, Charles. *Chinese Reportage: The Aesthetics of Historical Experience*. Durham, NC: Duke University Press, 2002.

Lee, Leo Ou-fan. "In Search of Modernity: Some Reflections on a New Mode of Consciousness in Twentieth-Century Chinese History and Literature." In *Ideas Across Cultures: Essays on Chinese Thought in Honor of Benjamin I. Schwartz*, edited by Paul A. Cohen and Merle Goldman, 109–126. Cambridge, MA: Council on East Asian Studies, Harvard University: Distributed by Harvard University Press, 1990.

———. "The Politics of Technique: Perspectives of Literary Dissidence in Contemporary Chinese Fiction." In *After Mao: Chinese Literature and Society, 1978–1981*, edited by Jeffrey C. Kinkley, 159–190. Cambridge, MA: Council on East Asian Studies, Harvard University: Distributed by Harvard University Press, 1985.

———. *Shanghai Modern: The Flowering of a New Urban Culture in China, 1930–1945*. Cambridge, MA: Harvard University Press, 1999.

Levin, Kim. "Farewell to Modernism." *Arts Magazine* (October 1979): 90–92.

Li Shangyin. *Li Shangyin shixuan* (Selected poems of Li Shangyin). Selected and annotated by Anhui Shifan daxue zhongwenxi gudai wenxue jiaoyanzu (Classical literature teaching and research group of the Chinese Department of Anhui Normal University). Beijing: Renmin wenxue chubanshe, 1978.

Li Siguang et al. *Kexuejia tan 21 shiji* (Scientists talk about the twenty-first century). Shanghai: Shaonian ertong chubanshe, 1959.

Li Tuo. "'Xiandai xiaoshuo' bu dengyu 'xiandaipai': Li Tuo gei Liu Xinwu de xin" (Modern fiction is not equivalent to modernism: Li Tuo's letter to Liu Xinwu). *Shanghai wenxue*, no. 8 (1982): 91–94.

Li Xiu and Qin Linfang. *Ershi shiji zhongwai wenxue jiaoliu shi* (History of Chinese-foreign literary exchanges). 2 vols. Shijiazhuang: Hebei jiaoyu chubanshe, 2001.

Li Xiuwen. "Loushang de guanrenmen dou zuile" (The officials upstairs are all drunk). In *Zhongguo dangdai zuojia mianmian guan: xunzhao wenxue de linghun* (Perspectives on contemporary Chinese writers: Searching for the soul of literature), edited by Lin Jianfa and Xu Lianyuan, 504–511. Shenyang: Chunfeng wenyi chubanshe, 2003.

Link, E. Perry. "The Genie and the Lamp: Revolutionary *Xiangsheng*." In *Popular Chinese Literature and Performing Arts in the People's Republic of China, 1949–1979*, edited by Bonnie S. McDougall, 83–111. Berkeley: University of California Press, 1984.

———. *The Uses of Literature: Life in the Socialist Chinese Literary System*. Princeton, NJ: Princeton University Press, 2000.

Liu, Haoming. "Fei Ming's Poetics of Representation: Dream, Fantasy, Illusion, and Ālayavijñāna." *Modern Chinese Literature and Culture*, 13:2 (Fall 2001): 30–71.

Liu, James J. Y. *The Poetry of Li Shang-yin: Ninth-Century Baroque Chinese Poet*. Chicago: University of Chicago Press, 1969.

Liu Mingjiu and Zhu Hong. "Faguo 'xin xiaoshuo pai' poushi" (A dissection of the French 'nouveau roman'). *Shijie wenxue*, no. 6 (1963): 87–111.

Liu Weimin. *Kexue yu xiandai Zhongguo wenxue* (Science and modern Chinese literature). Hefei: Anhui jiaoyu chubanshe, 2000.

Liu Xu. *Jiu Tang shu* (Old history of the Tang). Beijing: Zhonghua shuju, 1975.

Liu Xuekai. "Zongjie yu chuangxin bingzhong: jianguo yilai Li Shangyin yanjiu zongshu" (Paying equal attention to continuity and innovation: A summary of Li Shangyin studies from 1949 on). In *Li Shangyin yanjiu lunji, 1949–1997* (Collected studies of Li Shangyin, 1949–1997), edited by Wang Meng and Liu Xuekai, 760–770. Guilin: Guangxi Shifan daxue chubanshe, 1998.

Liu Xuekai and Yu Shucheng. *Li Shangyin*. Beijing: Zhonghua shuju, 1980.

———, eds. *Li Shangyin shige jijie* (Li Shangyin's poems with collected annotations). Beijing: Zhonghua shuju, 1988.

Liu Yisheng, ed. *Li Shangyin shixuan* (Selected poems of Li Shangyin). Hong Kong: Sanlian shudian, 1980.

Lu Kunzeng. *Li Yishan shi jie* (Annotated poems by Li Shangyin). 1726. Taipei: Xuehai chubanshe, 1986.

Lu Shuyuan. *Chaoyue yuyan: wenxue yanyuxue chuyi* (Metalanguage: My humble opinion on the study of literary discourse). Beijing: Zhongguo shehui kexue chubanshe, 1990.

Luo Xinzhang, ed., *Fanyi lunji* (Collected talks on translation). Beijing: Shangwu yinshuguan, 1984.

Ma Shunjia. "Guanyu kehuan xiaoshuo de liangge wenti" (Two problems on science fiction). *Yunnan minzu daxue xuebao*, no. 4 (1987): 84–86.

Mao Dun, "Wei fazhan wenxue fanyi shiye he tigao fanyi zhiliang er fendou" (Striving to develop the profession of literary translation and elevate the quality of translation). In Luo Xinzhang, ed., *Fanyi lunji*, 501–517.

McDougall, Bonnie S. *Fictional Authors, Imaginary Audiences: Modern Chinese Literature in the Twentieth Century*. Hong Kong: The Chinese University Press, 2003.

——. *The Introduction of Western Literary Theories into Modern China, 1919–1925*. Tokyo: Centre for East Asian Cultural Studies, 1971.

——. *Love-Letters and Privacy in Modern China: The Intimate Lives of Lu Xun and Xu Guangping*. Oxford: Oxford University Press, 2002.

McGrath, Jason. "Black Cannon Incident: Countering the Counter-espionage Fantasy." In *Chinese Films in Focus II*, edited by Chris Berry, 25–31. New York: Palgrave Macmillian, 2008.

——. "Cultural Revolution Model Opera Films and the Realist Tradition in Chinese Cinema." *Opera Quarterly*, 26:2 (2010): 343–376.

——. *Postsocialist Modernity: Chinese Cinema, Literature, and Criticism in the Market Age*. Stanford, CA: Stanford University Press, 2008.

McLaren, Anne. "Constructing New Reading Publics in Late Ming China." In *Printing and Book Culture in Late Imperial China*, edited by Cynthia Joanne Brokaw and Kai-Wing Chow, 152–183. Berkeley: University of California Press, 2005.

Ming, Feng-ying. "Baoyu in Wonderland: Technological Utopia in the Early Modern Chinese Science Fiction Novel." In *China in a Polycentric World: Essays in Chinese Comparative Literature*, edited by Yingjin Zhang, 152–172. Stanford, CA: Stanford University Press, 1998.

Mittag, Achim. "Time Concepts in China." In *Time and History: The Variety of Cultures*, edited by Jörn Rüsen, 44–64. New York: Berghahn Books, 2007.

Moretti, Franco. "Conjectures on World Literature." *New Left Review* 1 (2000): 54–68.

Muñoz, José Esteban. *Cruising Utopia: The Then and There of Queer Futurity*. New York: New York University Press, 2009.

Na Tianlong. "Gedeer dingli de qishi" (What Gödel's theorems teach us). *Zhongguo yiyuan guanli*, no. 1 (1987): 22.

Nejedlý, Zdeněk. "Lun zhenshi yu bu zhenshi de xianshizhuyi" (On true and false realism). *Yiwen*, no. 3 (1957): 167–175.

Ng, Mau Sang. "Ba Jin and Russian Literature." *Chinese Literature: Essays, Articles, Reviews* 3:1 (January 1981): 67–92.

1949–1986 Quanguo neibu faxing tushu zongmu (Catalogue of 1949–1986 nationwide internal publications). Beijing: Zhonghua shuju chubanshe, 1988.

Niu Han and Feng Xiaxiong. "Bianzhe de hua" (Editors' words). *Zhongguo*, no. 2 (1986): 1.

Nolan, Peter. "Imperial Archipelagos: China, Western Colonialism and the Law of the Sea." *New Left Review* 80 (March–April 2013): 77–95.

Nunn, Raymond G. *Publishing in Mainland China*. Cambridge, MA: MIT Press, 1966.

Osborne, Peter. "Modernity Is a Qualitative, Not a Chronological, Category." *New Left Review*, I/192 (March–April 1992): 65–84.

Owen, Steven. *The Late Tang: Chinese Poetry of the Mid-Ninth Century (827–860)*. Cambridge, MA: Council on East Asian Studies, Harvard University, 2006.

——, ed. *Readings in Chinese Literary Thought*. Cambridge, MA: Council on East Asian Studies, Harvard University: Distributed by Harvard University Press, 1992.

Palmer, David A. *Qigong Fever: Body, Science, and Utopia in China*. New York: Columbia University Press, 2007.

Panchasi, Roxanne. *Future Tense: The Culture of Anticipation in France between the Wars*. Ithaca, NY: Cornell University Press, 2009.

Papadopoulos, Dimitris, Niamh Stephenson, and Vassilis Tsianos. *Escape Routes: Control and Subversion in the 21st Century*. London: Pluto Press, 2008.

Pasternack, Alex. "Beijing Olympic Weather: 'Haze,' Blue Skies, and Hot Air." In *China in 2008: A Year of Great Significance*, edited by Kate Merkel-Hess, Kenneth L. Pomeranz, and Jeffrey N. Wasserstrom, 187–191. Lanham, MD: Rowman & Littlefield, 2009.

Poems of the Late T'ang. Translated by A. C. Graham. New York: Penguin, 1977.

Pollock, Sheldon, ed. *Literary Cultures in History: Reconstructions from South Asia*. Berkeley: University of California Press, 2003.

Prendergast, Christopher, ed. *Debating World Literature*. London: Verso, 2004.

Průšek, Jaroslav. *The Lyrical and the Epic: Studies of Modern Chinese Literature*. Bloomington: Indiana University Press, 1980.

Qian Liqun. "The Way Our Generation Imagined the World." Translated by Jingyuan Zhang. *Inter-Asia Cultural Studies* 6:4 (2005): 523–534.

Qian Zhongshu. *Tan yi lu* (On the art of poetry), 1948. Rev. ed. Beijing: Zhonghua Shuju, 1984.

Qin Zhaoyang. "The Broad Road of Realism—A Reassessment of Realism." In *Literature of the Hundred Flowers*, edited by Hualing Nieh, 1:121–144. New York: Columbia University Press, 1981.

Qiu Dali. "Jianlun guanggao de tuxing tonggou" (A brief discussion on graphic isomorphism in advertisement). *Zhuangshi*, no. 1 (1986): 16–18.

Quanguo zong shumu (National book catalogue). Beijing: Xinhua shudian zongdian, 1956.

Rabkin, Eric S. "Science Fiction and the Future of Criticism." *PMLA* 119:3 (May 2004): 457–473.

Rao Zhonghua. "Huanxiang, chuangxin, kexue: 1979–1980 nian quanguo kehuan xiaoshuo du hougan" (Fantasy, innovation, science: My feelings after reading 1979–1980 science fantasy fiction from all over the country). *Kepu chuangzuo*, no. 2 (1981): 9–11.

Reynolds, Jack. *Chronopathologies: Time and Politics in Deleuze, Derrida, Analytic Philosophy, and Phenomenology*. Lanham, MD: Lexington Books, 2012.

Ricoeur, Paul. *Time and Narrative*, vol. 3. Translated by Kathleen McLaughlin and David Pellauer. Chicago: University of Chicago Press, 1988.

Rubin, Eli. *Synthetic Socialism: Plastics and Dictatorship in the German Democratic Republic*. Chapel Hill: University of North Carolina Press, 2008.

Said, Edward W. *Culture and Imperialism*. New York: Vintage Books, 1994.

——. *Reflections on Exile and Other Essays*. Cambridge, MA: Harvard University Press, 2000.

Saporta, Marc. *Composition numéro 1*. Paris: Éditions du Seuil, 1962.

Saussy, Haun. *The Problem of a Chinese Aesthetic*. Stanford, CA: Stanford University Press, 1993.

Schmalzer, Sigrid. *The People's Peking Man: Popular Science and Human Identity in Twentieth-Century China*. Chicago: University of Chicago Press, 2008.

Schoenhals, Michael. "Consuming Fragments of Mao Zedong: The Chairman's Final Two Decades at the Helm." In *A Critical Introduction to Mao*, edited by Timothy Cheek, 110–128. New York: Cambridge University Press, 2010.

Scott, David. *Conscripts of Modernity: The Tragedy of Colonial Enlightenment*. Durham, NC: Duke University Press, 2004.

Sedgwick, Eve Kosofsky. *Touching Feeling: Affect, Pedagogy, Performativity*. Durham: Duke University Press, 2003.

Sewell, William H., Jr. "The Concept(s) of Culture." In *Beyond the Cultural Turn: New Directions in the Study of Society and Culture*, edited by Victoria E. Bonnell and Lynn Hunt, 35–61. Berkeley: University of California Press, 1999.

Shapiro, Judith. *Mao's War against Nature: Politics and the Environment in Revolutionary China*. New York: Cambridge University Press, 2001.

Shen Zhanyun. *Huipi shu, huang pishu* (Grey books, yellow books). Guangzhou: Huacheng chubanshe, 2007.

Shen Zhihua. *Zhonghua renmin gongheguo shi*. Vol. 3, *Sikao yu xuanze: Cong zhishifenzi huiyi dao fanyoupai yundong (1956-1957)* (History of the People's Republic of China. Vol. 3, Reflections and choices: The consciousness of the Chinese intellectuals and the Anti-Rightist Campaign, 1956–1957). Hong Kong: The Chinese University of Hong Kong, 2008.

Shi Liang. "Guanyu huangpi shu" (On yellow books). *Bolan qunshu*, no. 4 (April 2006): 89–90.

Sholokhov, Mikhail Aleksandrovich. *Virgin Soil Upturned*. Translated by Stephen Gerry. New York: Knopf, 1959.

Solà-Morales, Ignasi de. "Terrain Vague." In *Anyplace*, edited by Cynthia Davidson, 118–123. Cambridge, MA: MIT Press, 1995.

Spitzer, Leo. "Interpretation of an Ode by Paul Claudel." In *Leo Spitzer: Representative Essays*, edited by Alban K. Forcione, Herbert Lindenberger, and Madeline Sutherland, 275–326. Stanford, CA: Stanford University Press, 1988.

Su Xuelin. *Yuxi shi mi* (The enigma of Yuxi [Li Shangyin]'s poetry). Taipei: Taiwan shangwu yinshuguan, 1969.

Sun Ganlu. "Fangwen mengjing" (Visit to dreamland). In *Fangwen mengjing* (Visit to dreamland), 33–70. Wuhan: Changjiang wenyi chubanshe, 1993.

———. "Xiezuo yu chenmo" (Writing and silence). In *Zhongguo dangdai zuojia mianmian guan: sisui, sisui, sisuile shi pinjie* (Perspectives on contemporary Chinese writers: Tearing up, tearing up, tearing up to put it back together), edited by Lin Jianfa and Wang Jingtao, 228–232. Changchun: Shidai wenyi chubanshe, 1991.

———. "Xinshi zhi han" (The messenger's letter). *Shouhuo*, no. 5 (1987): 75–88.

Sun Xiaoya. "Fang Niu Han xiansheng tan *Zhongguo*" (An interview with Niu Han on

China). In *Shengji: xin shiqi zhuming renwen qikan sumiao* (Vitality: A sketch of the famous cultural periodicals of the New Era), edited by Jin Dacheng, 159–172. Beijing: Zhongguo Wenlian chubanshe, 2003.

Tang, Xiaobing. *Chinese Modern: The Heroic and the Quotidian*. Durham, NC: Duke University Press, 2000.

———. "Lu Xun's 'Diary of a Madman' and a Chinese Modernism." *PMLA* 107:5 (Oct. 1992): 1222–1234.

———. *Origins of the Chinese Avant-Garde: The Modern Woodcut Movement*. Berkeley: University of California Press, 2008.

Tanoukhi, Nirvana. "The Scale of World Literature." *New Literary History* 39:3 (Summer 2008): 599–617.

"Tantan su wenxue" (On popular literature). *Dushu*, no. 5 (1985): 35–39.

Tao Shilong. "Guanyu kehuan xiaoshuo wenti de taolun" (Debates on the problems of science fiction). *Wenyi jie tongxun*, no. 10 (1983): 16–20.

Tao Wenpeng. "Bu neng paoqi minzu shige de yishu chuantong" (The artistic tradition of national poetry should not be discarded). *Wenxue pinglun*, no. 6 (1983): 17–19.

Tay, William. "Wang Meng, Stream-of-consciousness, and the Controversy over Modernism." *Modern Chinese Literature* 1:1 (1984): 7–24.

Tee, Kim Tong, "(Re)mapping Sinophone Literature." In *Global Chinese Literature: Critical Essays*, edited by Jing Tsu and David Der-wei Wang, 77–92. Leiden: Brill, 2010.

Tian Han. "Shisan ling shuiku changxiangqu" (Rhapsody of the Ming Tombs Reservoir). *Juben*, no. 8 (1958): 38–85.

Tong Enzheng. "Shanhudao shang de siguang" (Death ray on a coral island). *Renmin wenxue*, no. 8 (1978): 41–58. Reprinted in *Shanhudao shang de siguang*, 1–50. Hefei: Anhui shaonian ertong chubanshe, 1993.

———. "Tan tan wo dui kexue wenyi de renshi" (On my understanding of science literature). *Renmin wenxue*, no. 6 (1979): 110.

Van Fleit Hang, Krista. *Literature the People Love: Reading Chinese Texts from the Early Maoist Period (1949–1966)*. New York: Palgrave Macmillan, 2013.

Volland, Nicolai. "A Linguistic Enclave: Translation and Language Policies in the Early People's Republic of China." *Modern China* 35:5 (September 2009): 467–494.

Wagner, Rudolf. *Inside a Service Trade: Studies in Contemporary Chinese Prose*. Cambridge, MA: Council on East Asian Studies, Harvard University, 1992.

———. "Lobby Literature: The Archaeology and Present Functions of Science Fiction in the People's Republic of China." In *After Mao: Chinese Literature and Society 1978–1981*, edited by Jeffrey C. Kinkley, 17–62. Cambridge, MA: Council on East Asian Studies, Harvard University: Distributed by Harvard University Press, 1985.

Wang Bangxiong. "Zuo wei wenhua de meishu: guanyu meishu wenti de jidian sikao" (Art as culture: Some reflections on the problems of art). *Meishu*, no. 12 (1986): 4–6.

Wang, David Der-wei. *Fin-de-siècle Splendor: Repressed Modernities of Late Qing Fiction, 1849–1911*. Stanford, CA: Stanford University Press, 1997.

Wang, Jing. *High Culture Fever: Politics, Aesthetics, and Ideology in Deng's China*. Berkeley: University of California Press, 1996.

Wang Meng. "Dui Li Shangyin jiqi shizuo de yixie lijie" (A few thoughts on Li Shangyin and his poetry). In Wang Meng, *Shuang fei yi*, 52–76.

———. "Guanyu 'yishiliu' de tongxin" (Communication on the 'stream of consciousness'). In *Wang Meng wenji* (Collected works of Wang Meng), 7:70–75. Beijing: Huayi chubanshe, 1993.

———. "Hudie" (Butterfly). In *Wang Meng wenji* (Collected works of Wang Meng), 3:70–134. Beijing: Huayi chubanshe, 1993.

———. "'Jinse' de ye hu chan" (The heresy of "Brocade zither"). In Wang Meng, *Shuang fei yi*, 23–28.

———. "Laijin" (Thrilling). In *Wang Meng wenji* (Collected works of Wang Meng), 5:139–144. Beijing: Huayi Chubanshe, 1993.

———. "Li Shangyin de tiaozhan" (The challenge of Li Shangyin). In *Li Shangyin yanjiu lunji, 1949–1997* (Collected studies of Li Shangyin, 1949–1997), edited by Wang Meng and Liu Xuekai, 1–9. Guilin: Guangxi Shifan daxue chubanshe, 1998.

———. *Shuang fei yi* (A pair of wings). Beijing: Sanlian shudian, 1996.

———. "The Strain of Meeting." In *Selected Works of Wang Meng* 1:82–248. Translated by Denis C. Mair. Beijing: Foreign Languages Press, 1989.

———. *Xiangjian shi nan* (The strain of meeting). Beijing: Zhongguo qingnian chubanshe, 1982.

———. "Ye de yan" (Eyes of the night). In *Wang Meng wenji* (Collected works of Wang Meng), 4:235–244. Beijing: Huayi chubanshe, 1993.

———. "Zai tan 'Jinse'" (Talking again about "Brocade zither"). In Wang Meng, *Shuang fei yi*, 15–22.

Wang Meng and Liu Xuekai, eds. *Li Shangyin yanjiu lunji, 1949–1997* (Collected studies of Li Shangyin, 1949–1997). Guilin: Guangxi Shifan daxue chubanshe, 1998.

Wang Qiaoling. "Naxie huangse de jingshen zhi liang" (That yellow spiritual nourishment). *Xin shiji zhoukan*, no. 19 (2008): 131–132.

Wang Yao. "1985 nian 'xiaoshuo geming' qianhou de shikong" (Space-time around the 1985 "fiction revolution"). *Dangdai zuojia pinglun*, no. 1 (2004): 102–112.

Wedell-Wedellsborg, Anne. "One Kind of Chinese Reality: Reading Yu Hua." *Chinese Literature: Essays, Articles, Reviews*, 18 (December 1996): 129–143.

Wei Chongxin. "Xingge, mingyun—yige qite de guaiquan: guanyu *Jin Ping Mei* renwu xingge jiqi jiegou xitong dingxiang xingcheng moshi de sikao" (Character, destiny—A strange loop: A reflection on the characters of *Jin Ping Mei* and on how structural systems orient the formation of models). *Xuzhou Shifan xueyuan xuebao*, no. 3 (1987): 20–24.

Wei Yahua. "Kehuan xiaoshuo de weiji" (The crisis of science fiction). *Xiaoshuo pinglun*, no. 4 (1986): 78–80.

———. *Wei Yahua jiazuo xuan* (The best of Wei Yahua), edited by Ye Yonglie. Zhengzhou: Haiyan chubanshe, 1998.

Williams, Philip. "Stylistic Variety in a PRC Writer: Wang Meng's Fiction of the 1979–1980 Cultural Thaw." *The Australian Journal of Chinese Affairs* 11 (1984): 59–80.

Williams, Raymond. *Modern Tragedy*. London: Verso Editions, 1979.

Wu, Dingbo, and Patrick Murphy, eds. *Science Fiction from China.* New York: Praeger, 1989.

Wu, Fusheng. *The Poetics of Decadence: Chinese Poetry of the Southern Dynasties and Late Tang Periods.* Albany, NY: State University of New York Press, 1998.

Wu Jianren. *Xin shitouji* (The new story of the stone). Zhengzhou: Zhongzhou guji chubanshe, 1986.

Wu Liang. "Wenxue yu xiaofei" (Literature and consumption)." *Shanghai wenxue,* no. 2 (1985): 70–75.

———. *Wode Luotuosi: Shanghai qishi niandai* (My own Rhodes: Shanghai's 1970s). Beijing: Renmin wenxue chubanshe, 2011.

Wu Xiaojiang. "Kehuan li xianshi you duoyuan?" (How distant is science fantasy from reality?). *Shijie kexue,* no. 5 (1998): 32–34.

Xie Mian. "Shiqu le pingjing yihou" (After having lost peace). In *Menglong shi lunzheng ji* (Debates on menglong poetry), edited by Yao Jiahua, 44–52. Beijing: Xueyuan chubanshe, 1989. Originally published in *Shikan* 12 (1980).

Xu Chi. "Guba de leisheng he Guba de gesheng" (Cuban thunders and Cuban songs). *Shijie wenxue,* no. 2 (1959): 16–18.

Xu Jiashi. *Sanshinian hou de shijie* (The world thirty years from now). Taipei: Zhonghua ribao she, 1977.

Xu Jilin. "Shangpin jingji yu zhishifenzi de shengcun weiji" (The commodity economy and the intellectuals' existential crisis). *Dushu,* no. 2 (1988): 5–11.

Xu Jingya. "Jueqi de shiqun: ping woguo shige de xiandai qingxiang" (A volant tribe of bards: A critique of the modernist tendencies of Chinese poetry). In *Menglong shi lunzheng ji* (Debates on menglong poetry), edited by Yao Jiahua, 247–285. Beijing: Xueyuan chubanshe, 1989. English translation in *Renditions* 19/20 (1983): 59–68.

Xu Xu. *Jibusai de youhuo* (Lure of the gypsies). Hong Kong: Yechuang shuwu, 1955.

Xu, Xueqing. "The Mandarin Duck and Butterfly School." In *Literary Societies of Republican China,* edited by Kirk Denton and Michel Hockx, 47–78. Lanham, MD: Lexington Books, 2008.

Yang Beixing and Sun Chuansong. *Mei nüshe qi an* (The strange case of the snake beauty). Zhengzhou: Henan renmin chubanshe, 1982.

Yang, Xiaobin. *The Chinese Postmodern: Trauma and Irony in Chinese Avant-garde Fiction.* Ann Arbor: University of Michigan Press, 2002.

Yan Yuejun, ed. *Menglong shixuan* (Selected menglong poems). Shenyang: Chunfeng wenyi chubanshe, 1985.

Ye Yonglie. *Lun kexue wenyi* (On science literature and arts). Beijing: Kexue puji chubanshe, 1980.

———. *Xiao Lingtong manyou weilai* (Xiao Lingtong travels to the future). Illustrated by Du Jianguo. Shanghai: Shaonian ertong chubanshe, 1978.

———. *Xiao Lingtong manyou weilai* (Xiao Lingtong travels to the future). Adapted by Pan Caiying, illustrated by Du Jianguo and Mao Yongkun. Shenyang: Liaoning meishu chubanshe, 1980.

———. *Xiao Lingtong sanyou weilai* (Xiao Lingtong's third trip to the future). Shanghai: Shaonian ertong chubanshe, 2000.

———. "Xiao Lingtong shi zenyang yansheng de" (How Xiao Lingtong was born). *Zhongguo keji yuebao*, no. 1 (2001): n.p.

———. *Xiao Lingtong zaiyou weilai* (Xiao Lingtong returns to the future). Shanghai: Shaonian ertong chubanshe, 1986.

———, ed. *Zhongguo kexue huanxiang xiaoshuo xuan* (Selected Chinese science fantasy fiction). Shenyang: Liaoning renmin chubanshe, 1982.

Yin Chuanhong. "Renshi liangge 'Ye Yonglie'—cong (xinban) *Xiao Lingtong manyou weilai* shuo kaiqu" (I know two 'Ye Yonglie': A few comments inspired by (the new edition of) *Xiao Lingtong travels the future)." Zhongguo keji yuebao*, no. 1 (2001): n.p.

Yu Hua. *Shuohua* (Talks). Shenyang: Chunfeng wenyi chubanshe, 2002.

———. "Wode 'yidian dian.' Guanyu 'Xingxing' ji qita" (My "little bits." On "Xingxing" and other things). *Beijing wenxue*, no. 5 (1985): 79–80.

Zeitlin, Judith T. *Historian of the Strange: Pu Songling and the Chinese Classical Tale.* Stanford, CA: Stanford University Press, 1993.

Zha Jianying, ed. *Bashi niandai fangtanlu* (Interviews on the 1980s). Beijing: Shenghuo, Dushu, Xinzhi sanlian shudian, 2006.

Zhang Ming. "Ling ren qimen de 'menglong'" (The vexing 'menglong'). In *Menglong shi lunzheng ji* (Debates on menglong poetry), edited by Yao Jiahua, 28–34. Beijing: Xueyuan chubanshe, 1989. Originally published in *Shikan* 10 (1980).

Zhang Mingfei. "Li Shangyin wuti shi yanjiu zongshu" (A summary of the studies of Li Shangyin's untitled poems). In *Li Shangyin yanjiu lunji, 1949–1997* (Collected studies of Li Shangyin, 1949–1997), edited by Wang Meng and Liu Xuekai, 771–780. Guilin: Guangxi Shifan daxue chubanshe, 1998.

Zhang, Xudong. *Chinese Modernism in the Era of Reforms: Cultural Fever, Avant-Garde Fiction, and the New Chinese Cinema.* Durham, NC: Duke University Press, 1997.

Zheng Wenguang. "Rang women de shenghuo geng kexue xie" (Let's make our life a bit more scientific). *Kexue yu shenghuo*, no. 2 (1981): 43.

Zheng Yuxin. "Bu wanbeixing dingli: yiqie zhishi de zhongxin. Du *GEB—yitiao yonghengde jindai*" (Incompleteness theorems: The center of all knowledge. Reading *GEB—An Eternal Golden Braid*). *Dushu*, no. 8 (1985): 12–16.

Zhongguo wenxue bianjibu [*China's* literary editorial board]. "*Zhongguo* beiwanglu: zhongkan zhi duzhe" (*China's* memorandum: The last issue speaks to readers). *Zhongguo*, no. 12 (1986): 1–3.

Zhongguo zuojia xiehui shujichu [Secretariat of the Chinese Writers' Association]. "Zhi duzhe" (To readers). *Zhongguo*, no. 12 (1986): 3

Zhou Hualei. "Dixia dushu shalong de mimi" (The secret of underground reading salons). *Zhongguo xinwen zhoukan*, September 21, 2009: 36–40.

Zhu Heling. *Li Yishan shi jianzhu: 8 juan* (Annotated edition of Li Yishan's poetry: Eight juan). 1646. Shanghai: Hui wen tang, 1917.

Zhu Qing. "Puji kexue wenyi de sanzhong guandian" (Three perspectives on the literature of science dissemination). *Shehui kexue*, no. 2 (1981): 155–157.

Zhu Wei, ed. *Zhongguo xianfeng xiaoshuo* (Chinese avant-garde fiction). Guangzhou: Huacheng Chubanshe, 1990.

INDEX

Literary works will be found under the author's name when available. Chinese periodicals will be found under their transliterated Chinese names.